Living with Difference

CALIFORNIA SERIES IN PUBLIC ANTHROPOLOGY

The California Series in Public Anthropology emphasizes the anthropologist's role as an engaged intellectual. It continues anthropology's commitment to being an ethnographic witness, to describing, in human terms, how life is lived beyond the borders of many readers' experiences. But it also adds a commitment, through ethnography, to reframing the terms of public debate—transforming received, accepted understandings of social issues with new insights, new framings.

Series Editor: Robert Borofsky (Hawaii Pacific University)

Contributing Editors: Philippe Bourgois (University of Pennsylvania), Paul Farmer (Partners In Health), Alex Hinton (Rutgers University), Carolyn Nordstrom (University of Notre Dame), and Nancy Scheper-Hughes (UC Berkeley)

University of California Press Editor: Naomi Schneider

1. *Twice Dead: Organ Transplants and the Reinvention of Death*, by Margaret Lock
2. *Birthing the Nation: Strategies of Palestinian Women in Israel*, by Rhoda Ann Kanaaneh (with a foreword by Hanan Ashrawi)
3. *Annihilating Difference: The Anthropology of Genocide*, edited by Alexander Laban Hinton (with a foreword by Kenneth Roth)
4. *Pathologies of Power: Health, Human Rights, and the New War on the Poor*, by Paul Farmer (with a foreword by Amartya Sen)
5. *Buddha Is Hiding: Refugees, Citizenship, the New America*, by Aihwa Ong
6. *Chechnya: Life in a War-Torn Society*, by Valery Tishkov (with a foreword by Mikhail S. Gorbachev)
7. *Total Confinement: Madness and Reason in the Maximum Security Prison*, by Lorna A. Rhodes
8. *Paradise in Ashes: A Guatemalan Journey of Courage, Terror, and Hope*, by Beatriz Manz (with a foreword by Aryeh Neier)
9. *Laughter Out of Place: Race, Class, Violence, and Sexuality in a Rio Shantytown*, by Donna M. Goldstein
10. *Shadows of War: Violence, Power, and International Profiteering in the Twenty-First Century*, by Carolyn Nordstrom
11. *Why Did They Kill? Cambodia in the Shadow of Genocide*, by Alexander Laban Hinton (with a foreword by Robert Jay Lifton)
12. *Yanomami: The Fierce Controversy and What We Can Learn from It*, by Robert Borofsky
13. *Why America's Top Pundits Are Wrong: Anthropologists Talk Back*, edited by Catherine Besteman and Hugh Gusterson

Living with Difference

How to Build Community in a Divided World

ADAM B. SELIGMAN,
RAHEL R. WASSERFALL,
AND DAVID W. MONTGOMERY

UNIVERSITY OF CALIFORNIA PRESS

University of California Press, one of the most distinguished university presses in the United States, enriches lives around the world by advancing scholarship in the humanities, social sciences, and natural sciences. Its activities are supported by the UC Press Foundation and by philanthropic contributions from individuals and institutions. For more information, visit www.ucpress.edu.

University of California Press
Oakland, California

© 2015 by The Regents of the University of California

Library of Congress Cataloging-in-Publication Data

Seligman, Adam B., author.
   Living with difference : how to build community in a divided world / Adam B. Seligman, Rahel R. Wasserfall, and David W. Montgomery.
        p.   cm. — California series in public anthropology ; 37)
   Includes bibliographical references and index.
   ISBN 978-0-520-28411-1 (cloth, alk. paper) —
   ISBN 978-0-520-28412-8 (pbk., alk. paper) —
   ISBN 978-0-520-95977-4 (electronic)
   1. Cultural pluralism.   2. Community develop-
ment.   3. Ethnic relations.   4. Difference
(Philosophy)   I. Wasserfall, Rahel R., author.   II.
Montgomery, David W., author.   III. Title.   IV.
Title: How to build community in a divided
world.   V. Series: California series in public
anthropology ; 37.
HM1271.S434   2015
305.8—dc23   2015022635

Manufactured in the United States of America

24   23   22   21   20   19   18   17   16   15
10   9   8   7   6   5   4   3   2   1

In keeping with a commitment to support environmentally responsible and sustainable printing practices, UC Press has printed this book on Natures Natural, a fiber that contains 30% post-consumer waste and meets the minimum requirements of ANSI/NISO Z39.48-1992 (R 1997) (*Permanence of Paper*).

CONTENTS

All books are collective enterprises. This one, however, is more. It is a communal enterprise. For fourteen years now, we have been running schools devoted to learning to live with difference. These schools have taken place all over the world: from Birmingham, England, to Plovdiv, Bulgaria; from Jogjakarta, Indonesia, to Nicosia, Cyprus; from Mostar, Bosnia, to Boston, United States; from Istanbul, Turkey, to Tel Aviv, Israel; and from Kampala, Uganda, to Toronto, Canada, and many more places in between.

During those years and across these many countries, hundreds have been involved in CEDAR programs, participating as fellows, local hosts, visiting lecturers, local staff, and board members. It would be impossible to thank them all. It would also be impossible to thank all those who contributed to the funding of the schools—the many institutions (such as the Henry Luce Foundation), organizations (such as the U.S. Agency for International Development in Albania, Bosnia, Central Asia, Uganda, and West Bank/Gaza), and most especially individuals. Checks from eighteen dollars to ten thousand, grants of hundreds of thousands and in-kind support, have all been necessary to make CEDAR schools a reality. More important, the willingness to develop the pedagogy and principles of the school in different countries and in the face of different challenges has been the mainstay of our programs and the commitment of all involved.

Learning to live with difference is a never-ending project. Each of us—staff and hosts, as well as fellows—has had to confront our own taken-for-granted assumptions about the world, about ourselves, and about our other.

This has not always been comfortable. Nevertheless, we have all learned to face up to that discomfort and have come out, we hope, wiser and richer.

We are grateful for the opportunity to have developed some of the ideas presented here in talks given at the University of Utrecht; Yamaguchi Prefecture University; Smith College; the Anglican Diocese in Harare; the final RELIGARE conference on Secularism and Diversity in Europe; the American Corner in Sofia, Bulgaria; the University of Lethbridge; the Bringing Theory to Practice Conference; the Canadian Institute for Advanced Research; the Methodology Narrative Study Group at the Women Studies Research Center at Brandeis University; and the Living with Difference in a Global Society Workshop at the University of Pittsburgh. All presented important opportunities to formulate the experience of the CEDAR schools in terms accessible to those who had not participated in them, provided a crucial testing ground for some of our ideas, and gave us the benefit of many helpful comments. Our thanks are also due to the Boston Iyengar Yoga community, especially to Peentz Dubble and Patricia Walden for their yoga wisdom that has slipped into this project.

Our very special thanks go to the teams of CEDAR affiliates in Bulgaria and Uganda. Both the Balkan Summer School on Religion and Public Life, located with the Paissi Hilendarksi University of Plovdiv, and the Equator Peace Academy, located within the Uganda Martyrs University, have taken up the challenge of establishing permanent schools devoted to the pedagogy and practice of the CEDAR approach. The current growth and development of these schools in the wider context of the Balkans and East Africa is the best vindication of the CEDAR approach that we can imagine.

We also owe a note of thanks to the many people who have volunteered their time and labor and ideas at various stages in the history of CEDAR, not least in its first iteration as the International Summer School on Religion and Public Life. Among these we would like to single out Rusmir Mahmutćehajić, Shlomo Fischer, Saul Schapiro, and Nélia Ponte. A special thanks goes to Deborah Fogel, who has helped so much in all matters of communication, including her crucial work on this text.

Without the spirit of voluntarism and sharing equally in the burdens and responsibilities of the school, it could never have become a reality. We are grateful to all who stepped forward to bear this burden and who continue to carry the burden of living with difference in their lives and work.

Introduction

Living with difference. The challenge, the difficulty, the point of contention, is inherent in the notion of living permanently with, as opposed to simply temporarily experiencing, difference. Most of us like to encounter difference, are attracted to it, and go to some considerable trouble and expense—at least occasionally—to expose ourselves to it. We may spend thousands of dollars on a trip to Nepal or Machu Picchu. We may engross ourselves in novels of faraway times and places. As students, we may take advantage of a liberal arts curriculum to learn about peoples or places we would otherwise never come across; or perhaps we may major in anthropology or in hitherto unknown languages. We may choose to frequent ethnic restaurants, to visit or live in big cities specifically for the variety of strange and different cuisines they offer. All of us seek to touch, see, smell, taste, and experience difference in many ways, depending on our individual preferences and comfort levels.

But here is the rub. In all the cases listed, we remain in control of the encounter and can calibrate, within certain boundaries, the degree of difference to which we wish to expose ourselves. When vacationing in Seoul, we can decide to stay in a local hostel catering to visiting Koreans or stay in the Ritz-Carlton—in food, smells, service, comfort, and so on, each will provide divergent experiences of difference. We may study anthropology, but it does not provide (nor is it meant to) the comfort of the Easter ham we are used to eating with our family ever since we can remember. Studying Latin may be exhilarating, but curling up with a good Dashiell Hammett whodunit on a rainy day is one sure way to find contentment. Eating out is great, but some nights we just prefer to cook up some steak and fries and have a beer with friends. We control all of these experiences, and if we do not wish to go to foreign climes this year, but visit Grandma in Connecticut or Kansas instead, that is fine. No one will fault us for that decision.

Living with difference, however, means that we no longer control the experience. Specifically, it means being open, by choice or circumstance, to the other in what is by definition an unbounded and uncontrolled situation. Experiencing difference is leaving your neighborhood to have a meal in Chinatown; living with difference is having a Chinese neighbor downstairs whose Chinese cooking smells are constantly wafting into your home. It is no longer being able to choose among a dozen pubs when you go to the Sparkhill neighborhood in Birmingham, England, for a few drinks with your new date, because all the pubs have been boarded up now that the neighborhood, once working-class Irish, is now predominantly South Indian Muslim. Forget learning a foreign language of your choosing. If you grew up in, and now are aging in, Brooklyn's Brighton Beach, you can no longer go shopping for groceries without knowing Russian—and even that does not really help, because the norms of conduct in shops and in lines (if there are lines) are not what you have been accustomed to for the past seventy years.

Attracted as we are to difference, its presence also makes us somewhat—and sometimes a good deal more than somewhat—nervous, anxious, and occasionally downright afraid. In fact, the danger may actually be part of the attraction. Much of what we are drawn to, what we find desirable and exciting, is, or appears to be, dangerous. This is true of romantic and sexual desire, sports and many other forms of play (whether participating or spectating), careers (though in the end we may well settle for the less attractive and less dangerous), spouses, and even fashion choices. The attraction and the danger go together—*within limits*. The critical caveat is that what is beyond those limits is no longer exciting and attractive; it is just plain frightening. Navigating class 5 rapids is exciting and attractive; contemplating class 6, however, is just plain frightening.

As long as we control the limits, define them, and stay within them, danger is attractive. What is true for shooting the rapids is also true for our relations with the other. Indeed, in this sense, we can think of flirting as a playful attempt to define certain shared limits in an interaction that is otherwise emotionally fraught and perhaps also dangerous. Living with difference, however, means that the limit is constantly being negotiated and renegotiated at the level of family, neighborhood, city, and nation-state. Yet the global world we inhabit these days is one of massive demographic shifts, ever-changing neighborhoods and cities, easy and relatively cheap intercontinental travel, and diaspora communities of every possible religion and ethno-religious group. Consequently, it is also one in which we can no longer control or define the limit on what is dangerous, or perceived by us to be dangerous. We must continually engage an other—one with different sights, smells, commandments and obligations, ideas of home and belonging, different moral visions and virtues, and different ideas of self and community.

This has always been a great challenge. The development of the modern nation-state was accompanied, to a greater or lesser extent, by attempts to homogenize the population so that citizens would all share one language, one cuisine, one idea of home and belonging, and one moral vision and definition of community. In fact, under Sukharno's Swasembada pangan policy in the 1960s, rice was promoted as the staple of Indonesia's national cuisine to homogenize the food choices and so create a sense of shared community across the archipelago's different religious and ethnic groups (people in the east of Indonesia, for example, do not eat rice). The need to create a unified culture within the modern nation-state was, in fact, well expressed in the title of Eugene Weber's famous book on nineteenth-century France, *From Peasants to Frenchmen*.[1] France is an interesting case, especially in terms of its Jews, the "other" par excellence in nineteenth-century Europe. A contemporary ideology, *fusion sociale*, attempted to transform Jews into Frenchmen by divesting them of their particular covenantal obligations. Napoleon even proposed that every third Jewish marriage be with a non-Jew in order to force assimilation.[2] Perhaps the most illustrative example here is in the writings of Arthur Beugnot, the lawyer, senator, and National Assembly delegate whose essay "Les Juifs d'Occident" expressed the deepest belief in both the Jews' capacity for "regeneration" and their need to reject such backward practices as Jewish dietary prohibitions, observance of the Sabbath on Saturday, holiday observances, and so on.

The paradigmatic case for this approach was famously stated by the French national assemblyman Stanislas Marie Adélaïde, comte de Clermont-Tonnerre in 1789:

The Jews must be denied everything as a nation, but granted everything as individuals; they must disown their judges, they must have only ours; they must be refused legal protection for the maintenance of the supposed laws of their Jewish corporation; they must constitute neither a state, nor a political corps, nor an order, they must individually become citizens; if they do not want this, they must inform us, and we shall then be compelled to expel them. The existence of a nation within a nation is unacceptable to our country.[3]

Today, of course, there are, or are perceived to be, "nations within nations" everywhere; from Canada to Coventry, Bulgaria to Birmingham, Malaysia to Montgomery. This is the challenge that we are all facing, admittedly with little success. Even a cursory glance at the newspapers will make this point. Whether we look at attitudes in Bulgaria toward Jehovah's Witnesses, in Malaysia toward Indians and Chinese, in Israel toward Palestinians, in Turkey toward Kurds and Alevis, in much of western Europe toward Muslims, or in western Canada toward members of the Blood Tribe, the seeming impossibility of living with difference (as opposed to merely visiting it briefly) is continually at the forefront of a never-ending series of crises and confrontations.

In Denmark, halal and kosher slaughter of animals has been prohibited, because, in the words of the minister of agriculture and food, "animal rights come before religion."[4] At the same time, Muslims in major English cities are reporting that they stay more and more within their own familiar ethnic and religious neighborhoods and feel unsafe and threatened when they venture beyond these enclaves. This sentiment is not surprising; it has been reported that

in London, anti-Muslim episodes rose from 318 in 2011 and 336 in 2012 to 500 by mid-November in 2013. . . . The Greater Manchester Police recorded 130 offenses in 2013 compared with 75 in 2012. The West Midlands Police force, which covers Birmingham, reported in response to a freedom of information act request that there were 26 anti-Islamic hate crimes in 2011, 21 in 2012 and 29 through October 2013.[5]

In America, the Arizona legislature approved legislation (later vetoed by Governor Jan Brewer) that allowed business owners (bakers, florists, event planners, and so on) to refuse services to gay couples, citing religious beliefs.

Similar bills have been proposed in New Mexico, Colorado, and Washington State as well.[6] In Lodi, Italy, some years ago, pig urine was poured on a site designated for a mosque; and as we write this, ethnic Russians are engaged in a rapidly escalating series of conflicts with ethnic Ukrainians in eastern Ukraine, while the sixty-four different ethnicities of South Sudan—including the Dinka, Moru, Bari, Nuer, Lotuko, and Shilluk—are failing disastrously in their efforts to build a united state.

We could fill a whole chapter with such examples, but what interests us far more is why they occur. Why this need for difference, and why the equally strong impulse to repress it? Why do the Jews need to eat kosher food and the Muslims halal? Why cannot they eat and dress and behave "like everyone else"? Why cannot the Bulgarians stay in the Orthodox Church into which they were born? Why do they need a different religion? Why do the First Nations persevere in pursuing their native culture? Why cannot the Alevis become normative Sunni Muslims? Why do they maintain their strange practices, "impure" food, and prayer on Thursday nights, and still claim to be Muslim?

Such complaints, as well as the behavior and claims that provoke them, bring us to the other core issue related to difference and why we cannot do without it, perhaps best expressed in the words of the eclectic anthropologist Gregory Bateson: "Difference is information."[7] The more we know about something, the more we differentiate it from its surroundings and can understand its uniqueness and its distinction from other, similar things. This is true of seashells, rocks, bears, paintings, and people. It is in fact true of everything, though this book is of course concerned with people and groups of people. Conversely, the more we recognize a thing's uniqueness, its distinction, its difference from similar things, the more information we have about it. We separate, we divide, we distinguish, and in so doing we build our world and the basic cognitive mechanisms through which we make sense of our world. Some sense of this tendency can be found at the beginning of the biblical Book of Genesis, in which the world is created by differentiation and distinction: dividing land from water, heavenly from earthly waters, light of day from that of night, and so on. Similar stories of differentiation and distinction can be found in the creation myths of many civilizations and peoples. They all point to how important difference is to the very existence of the world, at least as people understand it.

This is one of the problems with all the attempts to search for "common ground" or a "humanity beyond our differences," the endless efforts to claim that we are all the "children of Abraham," to play down differences and emphasize that, at the core, we are all the same.[8] That claim may be true, but it is not helpful. After all, we share over 90 percent of our DNA with baboons, but the insights and understanding—that is, the information this fact gives us about human societies and civilizations—is surprisingly minimal. Indeed, when I want you to recognize me, to see and address me, to be present in our interaction, it is not in general terms that I demand recognition but in very particular terms. We want our lovers to love us for who we are, not what we are. We do not wish to be interchangeable with the rest of humanity, let alone with baboons, in the eyes of those whose love and respect we desire. When I wish you to recognize me, I wish you to recognize me in my difference, in my distinct and unique being, not as someone else who has brown eyes like you and is going somewhat bald, and so on. It is my uniqueness, my difference, that I want recognized. And you want the same for yourself.

Our mothers all told us that we were special. It is that specialness, the irreducible quality of who we are, that we want recognized, respected, and in certain circumstances even loved. We never imagine ourselves existing in the abstract, but always only in the particular—as particular people, with particular identities, histories, future trajectories, senses of home, friendship, obligations, cares, and concerns. These particularities are the distinctions that make a difference, to borrow another aphorism from Bateson. They encode the necessary information about us, and often about our ethnic or religious group or sexual preference, to distinguish us from them.

Thus, not only are we attracted to difference but also, quite simply, we need it to exist. Our whole conceptual framework, as well as the workings of our cognition, are predicated on differences. The very construction of categories through which cognition progresses is dependent on a process of differentiation and the existence of difference. This is, moreover, the real reason why all attempts to belittle, negate, trivialize, ignore, or privatize difference are doomed to failure. We could not live in such a world. Imagine a map like the one mentioned in Lewis Carroll's *Hunting of the Snark*, a map without any "conventional signs." While other maps had "Mercator's North Poles and Equators, Tropics, Zones and Meridian Lines" and were covered with "shapes, with their islands and capes," what Carroll's Bellman presented to his crew was "a perfect and absolute blank."[9] All of which makes for one of the great nonsense poems in the English language but is totally useless in real life. A map with no distinctions conveys no information.

Similarly, the statement that we are all mammals or all primates or all humans contains much less information than we need in order to build a world together. Every attempt to reduce our social and human complexities—that is, our differences—to such general categories is thus doomed to failure. It may make for great rhetoric, but it is bad civics; for denying difference removes the robustness necessary to deal with the differences that must arise as people strive to make sense of themselves and their place in the world.

How, then, do we live with difference? Given that it cannot be denied, controlled, or even delineated, we must accept that in today's world we are increasingly forced to confront difference. Our now almost reflexive attempts at denial can at best be only temporary and illusory responses. So the question remains: how do we live with difference, or in our preferred locution, how can we learn to live together differently?

One common tactic most liberal democracies employ to deal with difference is not outright denial but something close to it. This approach has many forms, most commonly what may be termed the aestheticization of difference: Differences are a matter of tastes, not morals, and because there is no accounting for tastes, there is no real need for us to tolerate difference, but only to recognize each individual's "right" to his or her own opinion. This process of aestheticization often also involves trivializing difference. Here the argument is that arenas of difference are not important enough to merit a principled acceptance or tolerance of them. Your rather poor taste in neckties is not something to which we need to develop a tolerant attitude, even though we may find them offensive. Precisely because they are a matter of taste (aesthetics) and of no great significance (trivial), we are not called upon to engage with your difference in any substantive manner.

These tendencies toward aestheticizing or trivializing difference do, of course, enable us to avoid having to engage with difference, or what has so fashionably come to be called *alterity*. By trivializing what is different, we claim the essential similarity or sameness of the nontrivial aspects of selfhood and shared meaning. What makes us the same as Jews, Presbyterians, Americans, or radical feminists thus becomes much more critical to our definitions of who we are than what divides us (your horrendous taste in bathroom fixtures). And in this way we continually deny difference rather than engaging with it, so much so that nonengagement is the very stuff of our social life.

In a certain sense, denying difference by relegating it to the aesthetic or trivial is itself a form of indifference toward what is other and different. By framing our difference from the other's position, or action, in terms of tastes or triviality, we exempt ourselves from engaging with it and can maintain an attitude of indifference. I may find your religious beliefs foolish and your sexual appetites objectionable, but neither are illegal or hurtful to others. They do not affect me in my relations with you as, say, a member of the same university department and so, in the long run, are a matter of indifference to me.

Of course, as we push this argument one step further, we come to realize that indifference, at least in liberal individualist societies, is not simply a psychological state or a form of social etiquette. It is in fact ensconced as a fundamental aspect of the social order, in the form of our legal and principled separation of public and private spheres. What is deemed private is removed from public scrutiny and no longer subject to tolerant or intolerant attitudes on the part of other members of society. Defining a realm of privacy is tantamount to defining a realm of principled indifference in which substantive differences—classically, matters of belief, but by extension many other realms as well, including sexual preference—are not to be broached and are indeed rendered irrelevant. Not surprisingly, freedom of conscience—which in fact amounts to freedom of religion—goes hand in hand with its privatization. One has no right to intervene in private matters or even to judge them. In this reading then, all conflicting views are reduced to an almost aesthetic realm of different matters of taste (or, in the popular imagery of lifestyles, as they say so tellingly in the United States, "different strokes for different folks").

We should note as well that the privatization of religion, and a politics based on rights rather than a politics of the good, together with a secularized public sphere, are all in some sense the hallmarks of a liberal vision of the public sphere. However, if we are neutral toward different conceptions of the good, we have essentially taken them off the drawing board as forms of difference that we must come to terms with. But here is the problem: accepting these principles essentially means accepting a certain liberal, post-Protestant vision of selfhood and society that many human civilizations across the globe simply do not share.

More to the point, these different liberal attitudes, accepting and even embracing difference—which to the uncritical eye seem to be of a tolerant nature—are in fact less than tolerant, because they actually disengage from difference rather than attempt to come to terms with it. They are perhaps nothing more than a way to elide the whole problem of difference in modern society rather than realize it. Principled indifference is not the same as acceptance and is hardly a spirited form of "living with."

This book argues for a very different approach to the problem of difference and how to live with it. It categorically rejects denial, trivialization, privatization, and the endless search for common ground, advocating instead shared experience and reflection on that experience as a primary way to create new approaches and develop new capacities to live with difference rather than just explore its edges. In this, we authors feel ourselves to be part of a much-needed initiative, taking off from the academy but engaging the world beyond to deal with one of the most challenging conundrums of our time.

Whether looking at divided cities like Nicosia and Tel Aviv–Jaffa, or marginal populations such as Roma in Plovdiv, Alevi communities in Istanbul, or LGBT in Birmingham, England, there is a felt need for academics to engage beyond the university with communities around the world and, together, to address the practical problems of living with difference. This book builds on the work of one group of academics who do just that. CEDAR—Communities Engaging with Religion and Difference is composed of academics who have worked with community leaders, activists, and other partners in many different countries to take the insights of anthropology and social science out of the classroom and into the world.[10]

While the work of CEDAR is the lens through which we discuss the issues of living with difference, the theoretical insights and pedagogy of practice we advocate represent an approach that will be valuable to anyone interested in what it means to live in community with others. Rather than attempting to mitigate conflict by emphasizing what is shared, we argue for recognizing the centrality of difference in creating community and provide a blueprint for how to do so. Our vision acknowledges the occasionally uncomfortable nature of sociability yet finds promise in the doing of things together. In the presence of the other we see ourselves; and in living with the other without negating differences, we come to understand the prejudices we have when imagining community with the other. From this self-reflective space there emerges the possibility of living together differently.

In this sense the book is an ethnography of a problem rather than of a place. For the past fourteen years, CEDAR has used fundamental tools of anthropology to help people from Indonesia to Israel, England to Turkey, Bosnia to Cyprus, learn to live together with difference. For more than a decade its school has brought together hundreds of people from over fifty countries for two intensive weeks to explore just what it means to live in community and still be members of different communities.

A nongovernmental organization dedicated to learning to live with difference, the school uses anthropological knowledge as a road map for living in our world of diverse communities—all with their own particular histories, jokes, tastes, and smells, but also with their own commitments, moral claims, obligations, boundaries, and definitions of home and of the other.

These communities of belonging—with their own beliefs, myths, codes of conduct, and taken-for-granted worlds—present the baseline of knowledge through which we learn to know the world and our place in it. Knowledge, as anthropologists from Marcel Mauss and Bronislaw Malinowski to Franz Boas and Claude Lévi-Strauss have taught us, is fundamentally collective. Our categories, ways of knowing, and very image of the world are elements that we share with others, and very particular others at that. Because those with whom we share this knowledge are part of our community of belonging, we differentiate them, both in our minds and our actions, from those with whom we do not share such knowledge.

Through a very particular pedagogy of practice, the school and its organizers in over a dozen different countries have committed to sharing this simple truth. Each year, together with some thirty fellows from all over the world, we share the implications of this knowledge in terms of the boundaries of our own moral communities and our attitudes toward those beyond those boundaries—whether they are defined in terms of religion, ethnicity, sexual preference, class, or nation.

This book is the story of CEDAR and its organizers' quest to find a new way to live with difference. It is a story of a lived anthropological practice that takes knowledge out of the classroom and into the streets of cities such as Jerusalem, Sarajevo, Yogyakarta, Birmingham, Nicosia, Istanbul, and Kampala. It brings to the study of difference the mass of ethnographic data we have accumulated in over a decade of running the school in many different countries. It is thus a case study of how academic knowledge as a way of understanding the world can also be used as a way to live in it.

Ultimately, CEDAR programs create a laboratory that facilitates the serendipitous opening of possibilities. Individually, participants attest to a deep personal transformation of their taken-for-granted ways of thinking; collectively, they achieve a new awareness of what can be done, evidenced by the emergence of what are effectively new spaces and modes of interaction.

Characteristic of these new spaces and modes of interaction is a change in our claims about the other as we come to understand that knowledge must be understood as *knowledge for* (action), rather than *knowledge of* (content). We can never know the other in his or her essence, but we can know what we need in order to work together for a specific goal. This reframing of our meeting with the other in terms of a new epistemology is critical to any attempt to live together differently and to abide by the ambiguity, uncertainty, and inherent risk of such a life with others.

The following chapters explore these themes in greater detail. Chapter 1 tells the story of CEDAR's practice. It reviews the formal and informal structures of learning that constitute the school experience and the rules that govern the interaction of all participants. Beginning with three vignettes taken from the history of the school, this chapter examines the processes through which learning takes place and how responses to the challenge of being "together apart" begin to crystallize. It explores how the commitment to maintaining (rather than denying) difference in the shared, public realm of the school challenges our taken-for-granted assumptions about the other and forces cognition in new directions to allow new categories and ways of understanding to develop and encompass the challenge of shared experience. Finally, it draws on the pragmatic philosophy of John Dewey to develop a tentative and partial "tool kit" of practices to adopt in order to achieve the goal of living together differently, as opposed to just enjoying the frisson of a different experience.

Chapter 2 explores the pedagogy of experience and shared practice in light of the overall problem of tolerance and its accompanying challenges. Explicating the pedagogical principles developed in over a decade of practice, it argues for the collective, or group-based, nature of our social knowledge and the moral claims that go with it. It emphasizes the continuing importance of group-based identities, rooted in people's need for a sense of belonging, and demonstrates how this need contributes to the creation of communities of trust and belonging that by definition also exclude those who are not members of such groups. Using examples from the history of the school, the chapter goes on to show how shared experience can reframe and reconceptualize relations between self and other, as well as between self and community. This process, it explains, is less about removing or denying boundaries between individuals or groups than about reframing them and learning that to live with the other means to live with a certain degree of ambiguity as well.

Chapter 3 explores different stories of reflective practice and unpacks them to get at the core of such practice. Reflective practice has been on the agenda of evaluators and practitioners in the fields of peace building and conflict resolution for some time now. CEDAR brings this practice into play in confronting difference and the challenges and opportunities that building a group around difference entails. Reflective practice, we learn, is not just an individual process but a collective practice of immense power in a diverse group of people. Through such practice we learn to confront our own taken-for-granted assumptions about the other and work out their implications, as both obstacles and resources, for creating new social spaces and arenas for new types of human interaction. This chapter explains how reflective practice provides a critical tool for learning to live with ambiguity despite the feelings of discomfort that ambiguity so often engenders in us. Indeed, it teaches us that discomfort itself is often a necessary stage in learning to appreciate and respond to an alien narrative and sense of understanding.

Chapter 4 presents three stories of fellows confronting their own boundaries: in matters of poverty and social marginalization in Bulgaria, in encounters with traditional folk healing and religion in Uganda, and in meetings with religiously committed transgendered Muslims in Indonesia. In each case certain fellows experienced a profound sense of discomfort and confusion, which was then transformed into a shared, collective narrative. This chapter analyzes the profound insights and transformations that can occur when we are forced to come to terms with our own boundaries and engage in a form of ethnography of the self at those boundaries. As we are forced to recalibrate our understandings of self and other, the experience (as opposed to simply the knowledge of difference) is a deeply decentering one that repositions us with respect to our own communities of belonging. Moments of discovery, we learn, are moments of transformation as well, in which the grid of our experiences is recalibrated in light of new understandings of the other and the constitutive conditions of his or her world.

Chapter 5 moves beyond stories of CEDAR to engage briefly with other realities and look at the dynamics of identity and exclusion in other contexts. Using the example of race in America, the chapter broadens our vision beyond the examples taken from past CEDAR programs and enables us to understand the relevance of the program's pedagogy in relation to a much wider set of cases. While the social mechanisms of dealing with difference are markedly divergent in different environments, the necessity to confront difference, rather than shy away from it, is a critical insight everywhere. At the chapter's end, the importance of this engagement with difference, and the forging of the set of practices necessary to undertake it, becomes the subject for reflection on the part of three community leaders who have brought CEDAR pedagogy into their home communities and established CEDAR programs there.

Chapter 6 reframes the issues dealt with in the book in more abstract terms and returns to the issue of boundaries first raised in chapter 2. It explores what it means to live with boundaries that are fuzzy—that is, permeable, like a cell membrane—as opposed to impassible barriers such as the Great Wall of China. The chapter develops this theme by questioning the sufficiency of a "rights-based" approach to dealing with difference and by postulating that the human need for community, care, and belonging cannot be adequately met by a purely legal and abstract set of mechanisms, however necessary these may be for political democracy. It argues that religious communities are particularly salient examples of communities of trust and shared moral sentiments, in which the bonds between members are very different from those between members of communities defined solely in terms of rights-bearing individuals. The continuing tensions between the divergent communities of truth and trust, reason and empathy, justice and mercy, rights and belonging, are thus critical to understanding contemporary failures to live together in global societies. The chapter ends by asserting that the basis of a shared world will best be reached not through any forced attempt to "share meanings" but rather through a pedagogy of shared practice and usage.

Our conclusion argues for the challenging nature of tolerating difference and living with and among peoples and practices that make one uncomfortable. It reviews some traditions of shared practice that formed bridges between communities in premodern times and discusses the increasing difficulty of continuing such shared practices across communities given the divisions and segmentations of the contemporary world. It ends with a call for empathy across the boundaries of difference, rather than settling for a world defined simply by legal rights and entitlements.

Our appendices present a guide for prospective organizers and evaluators, as well as study questions and a guide for further reading. Appendix 1 provides basic information on what is necessary to organize programs based on CEDAR's model in one's home country and community. This appendix outlines the core of the pedagogy and covers issues such as planning a program, building a schedule, and running the program. Appendix 2 lays out the nuts and bolts of a central component of our reflective practice, which, as we have seen, is critical to the program's proper working and continual evolution. Appendix 3 is made up of questions for discussion, organized around the different chapter themes, that are intended to help interested individuals begin discussions of the issues dealt with in CEDAR programs, the better to familiarize themselves with issues of difference. These issues can then be academically explored in some of the readings in appendix 4, our recommended reading list.

The Story of Practice

A radical Muslim activist from the United Kingdom, organizer of anti-Israel demonstrations and Relief for Gaza convoys, calls home in dismay when she finds herself participating in a program with Zionists— and then sums it up after two weeks saying, "I learned I could be friends with people I hate."

HISTORY AND DEVELOPMENT OF THE PROGRAM

The key to the CEDAR approach is the requirement that participants, known as fellows, confront one another's differences—and then learn how to live with them anyway. In two intensive weeks of combined lectures, site visits, and hands-on learning, these fellows experience unfamiliar religious customs, grapple with beliefs that contradict their own, reexamine lifelong assumptions, and figure out how to share time and space.

CEDAR programs create new social and interpersonal spaces, broadening the range of possibilities to present a new way of "living together differently." They do not seek to build a new community in which everyone agrees and shares the same assumptions, but rather to teach people how to live with their different understandings of home, life, faith, worlds of meaning, and belonging. In short, they model the reality of how to live in our existing communities with people who are not like us—whether these differences are religious, national, tribal, linguistic, or sexual.

CEDAR was conceived of during a multireligious discussion around a restaurant table in the central market of Sarajevo in December 2001. There, against a background of wartime destruction, a conversation among a group of Jews, Muslims, and Christians sparked the idea for an experimental program using religion as a tool for understanding, not as a weapon for intolerance. In 2003 CEDAR launched its first two-week program in Bosnia and Herzegovina and Croatia as the International Summer School on Religion and Public Life, creating a unique model for people with divergent religious identities to live with, recognize, and learn about "the other" together. Since then, the school has been held in a different country or countries each year, meeting in over a dozen locations on four continents. During its first decade of operation, it attracted more than four hundred fellows from fifty countries and a variety of backgrounds.

In 2013 the school changed its name to CEDAR and transformed itself as an organization. Instead of running one school a year, under the direction of an international team and local hosts, CEDAR is now an international network of programs—in Africa, the Balkans, and North America.[1] The different programs that we have run over the last fourteen years have taught all involved a good deal about difference and how to get people to live with difference—not just with the cognitive dissonance it produces but also with the challenges to building trusting relations across different communities of belonging that result. We learned early that while religion may be a prime marker of difference, it is far from the only one. As we expanded our programs beyond the first schools in Bosnia, Croatia, and Israel, we gradually realized that the issues we were addressing were not limited to differences between religions, or even to those between religious and secular individuals. We came to recognize as well the importance of ethnic and tribal identities, and of sexual orientation, as sites of conflict, intolerance, and distrust among many people. Consequently, we integrated these themes into our programming.

We learned too that shared experience, as opposed to academic learning, is critical to providing a safe space in which people can explore their differences, even in the face of challenges to their own taken-for-granted categories and expectations. Shared experiences provide the frame within which fellows process and make sense of intellectual analysis. In addition, we came to realize just how important the group itself was to the work we wished to accomplish. In the first years of programming, we believed that the "other" whom the fellows would encounter, interact with, and come to understand was someone in the selected environment: Palestinian refugee camps, gay and lesbian churches, Alevi communities in Istanbul, Pomak villages in

Bulgaria, and so on. What we discovered, however, was that these site visits and meetings were really just the backdrop for the real encounter—of the fellows with one another. We realized then how critical it was to bring together fellows from all over the world with as much diversity as possible in race, nation, ethnicity, religion, age, gender, sexual orientation, profession, and so on. The "other," we came to recognize, was not outside the group, but inside—and it was in that internal encounter, and the act of building a group despite these multiple differences, that the key learning took place.

With time, we came to appreciate the importance of "reflective practice" in a program such as ours, and we decided to have an internal evaluator function as a resident anthropologist in every program. In dealing with the myriad problems that arise in a program that necessarily makes the details of so many private lives issues of public concern—matters of halal and kosher food, of prayer time for those so obligated, of restricted travel on holy days, and so on—the "executive" branch has little opportunity on the ground to reflect on its concrete decisions and their implications. To learn what works and what does not—indeed, just to keep one's finger on the pulse of the program as it develops during those intense two weeks—it is critical to have someone present whose only job is to observe, question, and record the significant events of the day. Hard data are much more reliable than anecdotal recollections in answering questions such as the following: Did people of different communities eat together, or did they stay with their own countrymen? How did most of the fellows react to the challenging meeting with the gay and lesbian community in the Birmingham church? Did certain groups feel excluded from one or another activity—or, alternatively, coerced into participating in one? As an evaluating tool, this reflective practice helps us assess the learning outcomes. Every year the internal evaluator produces a long, detailed report that enables staff and organizers to learn from their mistakes, as well as showing the staff how fellows responded to the programming. Each year this process allows staff to create and integrate new aspects into the programming after they reflect on the data collected. We discuss the importance and insights of such a reflective practice much more in chapters 3 and 4.

Finally, we discovered—often the hard way—that the group needed to be by itself at times, to form itself sometimes in opposition to staff and organizers, and to have time and space to construct its own intimate spaces of trust and shared difference. So we encouraged the development of small facilitation groups of five or six fellows, without staff supervision, as a vehicle for trust building and shared experience. The challenge that fellows then immediately faced was mediating between their membership in these small groups and that of the whole group of thirty fellows. It took a good deal of time to comprehend these processes and to recognize their importance.

After over a decade of trial and error—holding daily staff meetings during the schools, debriefing following them, and poring over evaluation reports—we have produced a body of knowledge and a methodology, as well as a comprehensive pedagogy that is universally applicable and which those trained in it can adopt to operate their own programs. It is this pedagogy that we present here.

THE LEARNING PROCESS

On Tuesday, July 12, 2005, the tenth day of the two-week program, we boarded our bus just after breakfast to visit the Palestinian village of Anata. It is only four miles from the center of Jerusalem to Anata, but as the bus slowly moved through traffic toward the West Bank, the transition was palpable. Soon enough the main road became a smaller street, and the architecture changed from apartment buildings to one-story houses. We found ourselves in a small town set on a winding road on an arid-looking hill, trying to find the house of the mother of the Palestinian Authority's deputy chief of security, whom we were scheduled to meet. As our bus driver navigated the narrow street, we looked at the small stores whose merchandise overflowed onto the street. The houses in Anata were large, multifamily structures that opened onto the street through long, glassed-in verandas. Wasserfall took note of the blues and the greens of the verandas interspersed with the white of the stones and the strong light of this dry, Middle Eastern day. As we finally arrived at the house and climbed the few steps to the veranda, we were welcomed by a ten-year-old, who fetched drinks for the group. Nobody else was there, and the house felt eerily empty. We finally learned that the deputy chief had been dragged from his car and beaten senseless by Hamas activists while en route to meet us. The initial response of the Israeli Jews in our group to his nonappearance was, in essence, that once again there was "no one to speak to," that Palestinians "are not inter-

ested in meeting; they are ignoring us; they are refusing us recognition."
Once we had ascertained the reason, however, the Israeli Palestinians began
to air their taken-for-granted assumptions: "Why didn't you find someone
else? Our voice is never heard." (As can be imagined, it had taken months
and months to arrange this meeting, and it was simply not possible to turn
on a dime and find someone else to replace the deputy minister.)

+ + + +

After a long day under the hot July sun in Plovdiv, Bulgaria, we were all happy
to reconvene in the air-conditioned room at the university. The atmosphere
was pleasant, with people joking, when staff introduced a quandary to the
group. Staff had not been able to decide among themselves if the group
should or should not attend an Orthodox ritual that happens once a year in
Plovdiv. Because people had been late boarding our bus the previous Sunday,
we had missed worship at the Bulgarian Orthodox church in Velingrad-
Kamenitza. Staff felt that this situation was not acceptable, since our tardi-
ness had prevented our Orthodox fellows from participating in a mass. The
local host had explained to the staff that there would be a special event happening the following Saturday night, just one day before the end of the program: a special liturgy read only once a year at the end of a long service. Some
staff thought that this would be a wonderful opportunity for our Orthodox
fellows. The caveat was that only baptized Orthodox individuals could attend
this part of the liturgy, and that the church's metropolitan, being a highly
traditional person, would not allow others in the church at this time. Staff
were afraid that the metropolitan would single out people who were obvi-
ously not Orthodox, such as people of color or those wearing the hijab, and
worried that some of our fellows might not be able to attend the whole service, although it would start with a public procession that everyone could
watch. Unable to agree on the importance of the visit for our program, the
staff brought it to the fellows to negotiate among themselves. The atmosphere
in the room changed as we learned about this possibility. One black African
fellow (a priest, actually) said, "And do not tell me that it is not because of my
skin color that I will not be invited in. I will not believe you." He feared that
he and his friends would be singled out because of their race. In the case of
the Muslim women, it was their religion that would bar their entry. In the

discussion that followed, a Bulgarian Orthodox man asked one of the Muslim women why she could not remove her hijab, saying, "For God's sake, you were not born with it!" The room exploded. Some fellows were appalled; others clapped in agreement. The noise actually drowned the second part of what he said: "And if you are asked to leave, even if I do not really understand that hijab thing, I will leave with you, as an act of solidarity."

+ + + +

The Metropolitan Church in Birmingham, England, is in a hardscrabble area of town, close to the railroad overpass and off some deserted streets. Its marginal status reflects that of the gay and lesbian community it serves. It is not surprising, then, that when confronted with close to forty foreign visitors from Israel, Palestine, Belarus, Albania, Bosnia, Bulgaria, France, Germany, Kyrgyzstan, the Netherlands, Pakistan, Russia, South Africa, Uzbekistan, and the United States, the congregants wanted to make the visitors feel welcome and accepted. To that end they invited each member of the group to take a flower from the central table, meditate on it, return it to the table, and then take the flower of another person who had done the same. Somewhere in the middle of the proceedings it was announced that all were partaking in the "Flower Communion," a ritual recognized by the Unitarian Universalist Church. We can still see the faces of the two Muslim women (with heads covered) and one Jewish woman when the word *communion* was uttered. Flowers in hand, they were at a total loss—not knowing what to do or how to retreat from this ritual, which was after all Christian and so not theirs, but also not wanting to offend their hosts. We recall the chagrin of one of our Protestant fellows at the violation of boundaries between communities that sharing a communion implied (for him). The irony was that the English organizing team had feared that fellows from the Balkans, Middle East, and Far East might have trouble with the homosexuality of the church members, which turned out not to be the case at all; rather, the problems revolved around boundaries and the feeling of violation, perhaps even subtle religious coercion, that some experienced that day.[2]

+ + + +

Incidents like these three happen every year, in every school, regardless of the formal topic. They are where the real learning of the school takes place.

The daily lectures, facilitation work in small groups, and site visits (to which all these stories pertain) are the structure, or scaffolding, upon which the real learning of the group, as a group, takes place. The process of sharing an experience, sorting out just what was and was not shared, and then constructing a common story of what happened is one of the school's prime learning tools. Real knowledge begins to emerge on the morning following the church visit in Birmingham, or the visit to the village of Anata, or the ceremony in the church in Plovdiv, when the group dissects the experience, begins to understand what happened, and sees how individuals with different group identities experienced what appeared to be a shared event differently. Christians taking part in the ritual came to see that the Muslims and Jews could not participate in the Flower Communion as they did. Some even came to appreciate the distance that at least one Protestant participant felt from a ritual that included all and, hence, seemed to belie the very purpose of ritual action. White participants could begin to understand the feelings of the Zimbabwean priest on being told he might be asked to leave the Orthodox church, and Israelis and Palestinians began to see how their own previous experiences made it virtually impossible to understand the plain meaning of the day's unfolding events (the deputy chief's absence).

This type of learning can take place only over time, after repeated meetings, as participants build a certain amount of trust in one another. To learn from shared experience, they must not only share the experience but also process it, give it form and language, and turn it into a story that they can tell others and, in so doing, make part of their common memory. The cognitive (academic, lecture-oriented) sessions of the school and the facilitation groups of five or six fellows (who remain a group throughout the program and share thoughts among themselves in response to questions posed by staff and related to school themes)—which are discussed in greater length in chapter 3—are all necessary tools to help formulate and validate what participants go through together.

While the situations described in the three vignettes occur in every school, usually more than once or twice in a program, they are not the stuff of everyday life there but only one aspect of it. For participants, daily routine at the school is, after all, a bustle of getting to class on time, or finding the buses taking them on the daily trips, or figuring out what staff meant in today's facilitation question ("Relate a time when you were uncomfortable in a sacred space, whether sacred to your community of belonging or to that of another group"), or managing not to be last in the lunch line—or, perhaps most important, figuring out just who all these other fellows are and what the program is really about.

The daily lectures are (mostly) very interesting, though some lecturers are clearly more skilled than others. Being in a foreign country with so many unfamiliar people is, of course, fascinating. The daily trips too are both enjoyable and informative. Yet participants develop the sense early on that the trips are not simply that, but are actually connected in some way—not only to the lectures but also to some other aspect of the program that has not yet made itself felt. From the second or third day, fellows begin to feel that something is being asked or expected of them that is not in the advertised program—something other than absorbing information and processing new knowledge of the history or sociology or theology of the places they are living in or visiting.

Usually by the beginning of the second week, this inchoate sense begins slowly to find form: something is going on that has nothing to do with the lectures, or the trips, or even the small facilitation groups. What is going on is, in fact, the gradual restructuring of possibilities, the opening of new ways of thinking and interacting with others, and the emergence of new understandings of self in such interactions. Accepted definitions of self and other are challenged; long-established borders, or the lack thereof, are renegotiated; and a new sense, not only of difference, but also of the possibility of being "together apart," begins to dawn. Participants recognize that it is not necessary to tell themselves a story either of sameness or of converging interests in order to share a world with others. These modes of mutuality and civility, rooted in either a market model of social life (interests) or a more communitarian view of shared or common visions, are not the only options possible. Fellows can, in fact—and they learn this in fits and starts, over the course of the program—"live together differently" without conformity. Slowly—though every year is different in its rhythm, cadences, and the extent to which group processes are articulated openly—a group of difference is formed and a new form of solidarity tested.

Being together with about forty other people from breakfast at 7:30 A.M. until well after dinner, sometimes as late as 10:30 P.M., is an intense experience. The great diversity of each group, and each individual's starting assumptions, begin to be upended somewhere in the middle of the first week. Of course fellows must adhere to the full schedule of daily meals, classes, trips, group work, and films. On top of all that, sorting out what they thought they knew—of Jews, Muslims, Pomaks, Catholics, Russian Orthodox, homosexuals, Zionists, radical Muslims, Turks, or Tutsi—from their experiences of the people they are actually living with and daily experiencing and learning about is an exhausting and challenging task.

Viewing *We Are All Neighbours*, a documentary by Tone Bringa on the war in Bosnia and the breakdown of neighborliness leading to the destruction of the Muslim community, is one thing on a college campus in Boston or Bloomington, and quite another in the Balkans—especially when your fellow viewers there are the cohort you have lived with for the past ten days and include Serbs, Bosniaks, Croats, and Kosovars. In this latter case, the discussion after the film was fraught, loaded, and emotional, yet the Serb and Bosniak who were inseparable before the screening remained inseparable after it as well. Such a point is when fellows realize that there is more at play in human relations than their existing categories and ways of thinking allowed for.

Slowly, then, around the end of the first week, the school's only two rules, which seem so simple when first encountered, at last begin to make sense, however tough they are to obey.

Rule 1: You must come to every event. If you are to learn to live with "the other," you have to be with her and share time, space, the table, and travel; going by yourself to the spa does not count. Fellows are here to be together, and after five days or so that is not an easy thing to do. But the sense of it begins to come through at this point, and commitment to the program is renewed.

Rule 2: You must recognize that no one has a monopoly on suffering. The importance of this second rule is soon even more obvious. After a week or so it becomes apparent that quite a few groups are making precisely the claim that they do have a monopoly on suffering: the Jews in reference to the Holocaust, the Africans in reference to slavery, the gays and lesbians in reference to their continued oppression, the Muslims in reference to their treatment today in Europe, the Palestinians in reference to the *nakba*, and so on. On the one hand, it is not so easy for these group members to divest themselves of such claims; on the other, it becomes clear that only by at least holding such claims in abeyance, even if not fully renouncing them, can there be any room for the other.

And when, inside the Armenian Orthodox Church, one Turkish fellow (a lawyer from Ankara) personally apologizes to the priest for the Armenian genocide and both exchange a few words in Turkish that no one understands except the other Turkish fellow, it is evident that this is a very different type of program than anyone expected.

What is so difficult about being in the school is that fellows cannot retreat to their former, safe, and reassuring assumptions about self and other, us and them, our group and their group. Categories are challenged, assumptions no longer hold, and taken-for-granted views of one's own group and of the other are all thrown into disarray. What seemed a certainty is no longer so. Difference, fellows learn in the school, is neither good nor bad; it is just an unavoidable fact of life. Bringing fellows together for two weeks, where all must live together, share every meal, and participate in all school activities, makes this undeniable.

No concept of an overarching community is put forward to mask differences. Even swimming breaks, for example, in which an observant Muslim woman may not participate owing to modesty requirements, will underscore this reality. Entering one another's sacred space also provides a palpable experience of difference. Everything, from the architecture to the symbols to the rituals, is a reminder that this is not shared. Yet for others in the cohort, the school is taking place in their home environment, their place of belonging. Some are strangers, others are at home, and next week the situation may be reversed.

THE PROGRAM AND ITS PRACTICE

Central to the practice of the school is thus the building of an (albeit temporary) community of difference, where the different school fellows come, not as autonomous, liberal, individual, self-regarding moral agents, though they can be so if they wish, but mostly as members of different religious, ethnic, national, and racial communities—each with its own histories, fears, moral demands, and obligations. These lived worlds of difference are not left at the door of the school, nor are they particularly celebrated or made the subject of some sort of show-and-tell. Rather, their obligations and encumbrances—for example, food restrictions for observant Jews and Muslims; travel restrictions on Sabbath for Jews; attendance at religious services for Christians on Sunday, Muslims on Friday, and Jews on Saturday—become part of the public life of the school. A shared public space is constructed where the differing commitments and obligations of the group members are recognized and accommodated as part of the schedule and shared life of the whole group.

The commitment to allow difference its public face and expression—and the discomfort this may engender among individuals from other communities who are school members—quickly led us to recognize that the usual ways of knowing developed in academia would not fit our agenda. A purely cognitive approach to learning and knowing was one that by definition privileged the private over the public; the individual over the group; the mind over the emotions; and the general, abstract, and formal over the messy, mangled particulars of life as it is really lived. To build a new form of shared, collective knowledge tied to the dynamics of group belonging—and so also the awareness of the role of group boundaries in structuring such knowledge—we needed to seek a different route: the rough ground of practice. What this required was the development of a pedagogy that in two intensive weeks combines cognitive, experiential, and affective ways of learning how to live with difference.

We share experience and what we call "embodied knowledge," both of which are central to any attempt to construct new communities of understanding across different communities of belonging. Shared experience provides the necessary bases for constructing what are by definition new frames of knowledge across our different communities of belonging.

What makes the other *other*, one comes to learn, is not any ethnic or racial marker but the fact that the other tells different stories. Telling themselves different stories, the others inhabit a different moral—that is, normative— universe. The saliency of these differences is not easy to grasp in the abstract. Only when we really experience it can we understand just how serious the differences between disparate communities are and how deeply they are embedded in the stories those communities tell. Even among friends and colleagues, who may share common space and understandings in the workplace or sports club, the experience of stepping into one another's communal narratives is profoundly disturbing. The shared frames of the liberal marketplace, or of individual aspirations such as we pursue in our consumer-driven worlds, all tend to shatter around the collective stories that are, in their essence, particular, exclusionary, and largely opaque to the other.

In fact, the problem of divergent meanings is not restricted to narratives but can often be found in the very meanings we attach to discrete words or images. Often, words come heavily laden with meanings, and while we in our innocence believe these to be shared across cultures and histories, this is far from the case. A particularly salient example of this divergence in meanings occurred in Bosnia and Herzegovina, in the city of Mostar. Many will remember the images of Mostar and its famous bridge (*mostar* means "bridge" in the Serbo-Croatian and Bosnian languages) that was shelled and destroyed by the Croatian forces of Franjo Tudjman in the 1992–1995 war in the former Yugoslavia. The bridge remained destroyed until the spring of 2006; and much of the town, especially the Bosnian side of the Neretva River, remained in ruins. In fact, even after the bridge was restored, much of the town continued to look like Stalingrad after the Germans were defeated there in World War II. As was said at the time, it is easier to reconstruct a bridge than to rebuild human relations, and while the international community invested millions in the historically accurate reconstruction of the sixteenth-century structure, the city remained fundamentally divided to the extent that Bosnian cell phone networks did not work on the Croatian side of the river; nor was it possible in 2006 to purchase a bus ticket to Sarajevo on that side.

The program and its fellows were in Mostar in 2006 after spending a difficult, somewhat dangerous, and extremely tense week in Stolac, fifty kilometers to the east. Stolac was then still the least reconstructed township in Bosnia and Herzegovina. A beautiful oasis of a town inhabited since Paleolithic times, it had a prewar population composed of Orthodox, Catholics, and Muslims. During the war the town's eleven mosques were totally destroyed and their stones scattered in nearby quarries and riverbeds. The Orthodox churches in the area were either destroyed or damaged. The Muslim population was forced to flee, pigs were roasted on the site of the central

Figure 1. Mostar Bridge being rebuilt.

Figure 2. In Mostar, the bridge that had been built by the Ottomans and had survived natural disasters and earlier wars became symbolic of the destruction of the Bosnian War. Figure 1 shows the reconstruction process of the bridge in 2003; this image of the reconstructed bridge is from 2006. Photos by David W. Montgomery.

Figure 3. The Mostar palace of Yugoslav President Josip Tito, which was destroyed during the Bosnian War and has served as one of many physical reminders of the war. Photo by David W. Montgomery, 2006.

mosque, and a torture center was erected on the outskirts of the town in a former orthopedic hospital. After the war, some of the Muslim population began to return, and a project to rebuild the mosques was initiated. The town, however, remained in a state of horrible tension, with de facto segregation in city government and in the schools; Muslim and Catholic children were put on totally different schedules so that they would not have to meet and interact in school. Muslim and Catholic citizens frequented different cafes, ate in different restaurants, and maintained no more than a minimum of contact. According to personnel from the U.S. Agency for International Development, it was the most unreconstructed township in Herzegovina and, in 2006, was still patrolled by members of the UN Stabilization Force. In fact, the reconstruction of the Charshiya (market) Mosque was initiated under the protection of the force's tanks parked outside the construction site.

We had been in Stolac as part of this project to help rebuild and restore mosques and Orthodox churches destroyed in the war. During our week there, many Catholic residents eyed us with great suspicion, some threats were made, and symbolic attacks on some of our (Muslim) hosts were

Figure 4. SFOR armored personnel carrier outside the Charshiya Mosque in Stolac, Bosnia. Photo by David W. Montgomery, 2003.

perpetrated—for example, human urine was voided on the inside of a court-yard. After Stolac, Mostar was a most welcome relief. That first evening, walking in the reconstructed area around the bridge, with klieg lights illu-minating that part of the town (and the destroyed area a good five hundred meters away), one of us (Seligman) was in the company of one of our fellows, a Catholic priest from Brazil, then resident at the Vatican. We had all had a few drinks and were extremely relaxed. Walking at night, Seligman pointed out to the priest the huge cross, over one hundred feet high, that dominated the skyline on the Croatian, Catholic, side of the river. Pointing out that it had not been there before the war and was a clear provocation to the Muslim population on the other side, he slapped the priest on the back and said, "See that cross there, that's a bad one isn't it?" At this, the priest, with whom Seligman was, and would remain, very friendly, got visibly upset, crossed himself, and said, "How can a cross be bad! Say it is poorly placed, say it is here provocative; but a cross cannot be bad." Indeed, for a Catholic priest a cross cannot be bad. For an observant Jew (or for most observant Jews) its associative universe will always carry at least some negative meanings.

Thus the same word, not to mention the actual object, which ostensibly "means" the same for all, actually carries very different resonances, valences, associations, hues, and values depending on who we are and what context of meanings we carry inside. Indeed, how could a cross mean the

Figure 5. A cross on the hillside in Mostar marking the Croatian, Catholic, side of the river. Photo by David W. Montgomery, 2006.

same for an observant Jew as for a Catholic priest? How could it mean the same for even a secular Italian and a nonobservant Muslim (in Bosnia or anywhere else)? How could a cityscape with minarets resonate equally for an Indonesian Chinese and an Egyptian Muslim? We could go on with examples, but the point is clear. People believe that they share meanings, but the meanings they actually share are probably no more than 10 percent or so of those that are invoked.

There is, of course, one area where we do need to share meanings in order to engage in social interaction: when making use of generalized media of exchange—that is, money. But then we are limited to only one meaning on which we must agree: the price. Hence, when a woman sells the house she lived in for close to fifty years, it is not at all necessary to convey to the buyer what each and every crack in the wall or chipped paint on the banister means to her. In truth this agreement on price, together with the 10 percent (we posit somewhat haphazardly) overlap of other meanings, seems enough to allow us to get by and constitute a society—at least under "normal" circumstances. In these times we can easily fool ourselves into believing that we share deeper meanings, are indeed "of one mind" and "in tune" with one

The Story of Practice

another. However, and often enough, in periods of tension—economic crises, wars, revolutions, civic upheavals, and the like—these meanings break down. Or rather they seem to break down. They do not really break down, because they were actually never there to begin with. Only the illusion of shared meaning was there. When we are not pushed by circumstances to go much deeper than the pleasantries exchanged at a cocktail party, there is no reason to think that meanings diverge. When, however, we are forced to acknowledge different meanings, we generally feel a strong sense of betrayal, as the other no longer hews to our sense of meaning and purpose. Though of course that was never the case to begin with—it only appeared that way through the rituals of civic courtesy and the like.

The interesting—and increasingly crucial question—becomes: What do we do when meanings fall apart, or rather, when the curtain that hid the separate meanings we invested in those heavily freighted words (*love, responsibility, civic virtue, religion, cross, Muslim,* etc.) is torn asunder? What, then, is the next step? To a great extent, figuring out this next step is incumbent on all who seek a way to live together differently.

In fact, what is called for in such circumstances is analogous to what Donald Schön and Martin Rein term "reframing."[3] This involves a subtle process of both tweaking and accommodating existing beliefs. It does not require a wholehearted adoption of the other's perspective and the relegation of one's own to the dustbin of history. Rather, it is often evident in a conscious, or partially conscious, bracketing out of one's ultimate truth claims in light of a new appreciation of how complex and multivariate reality actually is. One does not undergo a conversion experience; rather, one learns that to accommodate the other in the pursuit of a common goal—perhaps a goal as mundane as living together in close proximity for two weeks—one must put on hold certain idols of the tribe or the marketplace that had been regarded as ultimate truths for far too long.

A Christian Evangelical fellow provided a good example of this at one school when he was forced to confront certain firm convictions of his and view them through a different frame. Close contact with Muslims—including, especially, Western liberal Muslims finishing doctoral studies at prestigious European universities—brought him to recognize that not everyone viewed the issue of conversion in the same light that he did. By the time the school ended, he had come to see that, while he, as a Christian, could not forgo the idea of conversion to Christianity as an important good to be shared and propagated among all of humankind, he did now understand that Muslims perhaps saw the matter somewhat differently. Hence (and this is the critical point) he came to see that while he continued to believe in the virtues of conversion as a positive good, he could also, in order to share in civic life with non-Christians, imagine these conversions as taking place at the eschaton, when all hidden truths would be known. In this new position we can see the process of reframing at work. He did not eschew his previous position, nor did he reject his Christian past or come to assent to the Muslim position on conversion. Rather, he reframed his deeply held beliefs in a manner that could accommodate both his position and that of his Muslim interlocutors.

This individual was challenged even more deeply by the time he spent in a gay and lesbian church, where participants in the school also viewed *Trembling Before G-d*, a film about gay and lesbian Orthodox Jews. These are individuals who have been rejected by their families and communities—and as Judaism is a set of practices that can be observed only in community and in family, their isolation and pain were especially devastating to see. Indeed, it is a heartbreaking movie. Here, too, the young man did not change his view of homosexuality. But when he saw the reaction of religiously committed and observant individuals—Jews, Muslims, and especially Christians (including a vicar)—who saw primarily the pain and suffering of these individuals rather than their sexual practices, he too came to reframe his understanding of the issue away from morality and sexuality and toward compassion and empathy.

As these experiences shattered the Christian Evangelical fellow's relatively one-dimensional reality, what emerged was his recognition of complexity and the need for a more subtle response. Again, his response was not an abjuration of past positions and, by implication, past visions of self, but a new recognition that there are multiple frames through which reality can be viewed. How did this reframing, or decentering, occur? Through what cognitive processes did the reframing take place, and how can we characterize such processes?

Perhaps the key has to do with explanation. From an aphorism famously attributed to David Hume, we learn that "explanation is where the mind rests." Thus, explanation is not the arrival at some final truth, or the "real" state of affairs, the final causal or prime mover of whatever event or sequence of events we are inquiring into. This task is, in fact, simply beyond our power as human beings. Rather, we deem a particular conundrum explained when we cease, for whatever reason, to ask further questions. There is something pragmatic about this claim. For when does the mind rest? Minds are, after all, very busy things—always moving, restless, questioning, and querying. People spend a lifetime engaging in yoga and meditation to get the mind to rest. If so, when, indeed, does the mind rest? One place it rests is, most often, when the particular purpose of its questioning has been fulfilled. I may have a need to explain why the hammer is not in its proper place (because Joey forgot to return it after he made his workbox for shop) so as to be sure that next time it will be in its place (and I make a mental note to tell Joey in no uncertain terms to return my tools whenever he takes them). I do not need (or think I do not need) to know why Joey forgot to return the hammer (that is, it is irrelevant to me whether he forgot because his friend Pete called him out to play ball before he had finished cleaning up after he made the workbox, or because he came in for a glass of milk and dropped the bottle and slipped on the milk when cleaning it up and had to change his shirt and then his grandmother called, and so on). The endless litany of reasons is irrelevant to my purpose (of making sure the hammer is always returned to its place after use). The mind rests when the purpose for which an explanation has been pursued has been met.

We can observe this dynamic in action when we draw inferences to explain the behavior of others without full knowledge of them (and of course there is essentially no such thing as full knowledge of any person or situation). In such situations the purpose pursued, consciously or not, is a validation of our own existing assumptions or prejudices. The mind thus rests in a place where it is comfortable or habituated to resting, one that does not challenge our existing conceptions and perceptions of the world. In many ways the suspicion of just such a dynamic lies at the core of so much concern over police violence, especially of white police officers against young black males, which led to civil unrest in various cities in the United States in 2014 and 2015 (and to which we will turn in chapter 5).

The American pragmatist philosopher John Dewey offered one way to tackle this problem, by giving us the tools necessary to reframe our ideas and so achieve a certain critical distance from them. Dewey defined an idea as "not some little psychical entity or piece of consciousness-stuff, but . . . the interpretation of the locally present environment in reference to its absent portion, that part to which it is referred as another part so as to give a view of the whole."[4] An idea, then, is a mental construct that frames and so gives meaning to (in Dewey's terms, "interprets") a given and empirically present reality in terms of a set of factors not immediately present. At the same time, by completing the picture of what is before me, it also serves to make it meaningful to me. For example, we may not know what that fellow from Bosnia is doing on the floor every day at about 1:15 P.M., but if we put that image together with ideas we have about Muslim prayer (five times a day, involving the salat, etc.) we can reach the conclusion that he is praying. What we wish to suggest is that the explanation at which the mind rests in fact constitutes Dewey's definition of an idea. When we have an idea of something, it generally means that we have explained it to our satisfaction. Our satisfaction is in turn determined by our ability to frame the given reality facing us (the fellow from Bosnia on his knees) with sufficient supplementary information for us to know what to do (act respectfully toward him; or run to help him, because perhaps he is suffering from internal bleeding; or wait for further help to arrive; or—as was actually enacted in a most macabre fashion in at least one U.S. airport because it was feared to be a prelude to a suicide bombing—call the police).

Framing, then, is all about action. One frames in order *to do*. One's frames are—or, as we maintain, should be understood to be—all about a *to do*. The mind comes to rest, and an explanation is proffered only in relation to some purpose. Explanation rests with an idea that we form of something; this idea is, according to Dewey, an amalgam of the currently available physical reality before us, together with additional, interpretive data that frames this reality in a broader, meaning-giving context defined by our specific purposes. In the case of attitudes toward police violence, the purpose may well be to substantiate our own views of police racism. In the case of the changing perceptions of our young fellow with regard to the Christian Evangelical mission as well as to gays and lesbians, what we saw was a reframing—that is, a recalibration of the specific purposes toward which the explanation (the meaning-giving framework) was oriented. In fact, what took place there was a reframing of meaning through the positing of a new goal, or a new "to do." Here, the new goal was the perceived need for a shared civic space or, at the very least, a two-week period of intensive shared interaction with others.

EMERGENT SPACES

It is this reframing that is so critical to the process of learning to live with difference. It allows us to present a story or narrative frame that the other may not share but can nevertheless negotiate and interact with, so that we can do things together as a result. To achieve this reframing, we must in essence eschew any final explanation and agree to set aside broad, inclusive, and generalized explanations of the other, even those that accord with our existing, taken-for-granted understandings of the world. And while none of us question our own belonging to meaning-giving communities (which could be Jewish, Muslim, Christian, secular-humanist, or something else), our shared environment and time together forces us to bracket out or tentatively suspend the types of explanations and ideas (precisely those interpretive frames around experience) that these communal memberships so often provide. What we must attempt to do, in fact, is to accept willfully and intentionally a new, shared experience and, at the same time, hold in abeyance the usual frames through which experience is interpreted. Doing so leads to a process of reframing or tweaking existing frames in a manner well illustrated by the story of the cosmic delay of conversion as perceived in the thought of our Evangelical friend.

Agreeing to submit ourselves to this hiatus in explanation is no mean feat. It is an extremely difficult and exhausting exercise, for it demands living in suspense and with an appreciation of the fact that our understanding of the situation is incomplete, doubtful, and problematic. We admit a lack of full knowledge, without yet accepting that we live in total ignorance; and by blurring any absolute distinction between the states of knowledge and ignorance, we set up the possibility of "forming conjectures to guide action"—the very process that Dewey described as the foundation of scientific thought.

To quote him at some length:

> Reflective thinking is always more or less troublesome because it involves overcoming the inertia that inclines one to accept suggestions at their face value; it involves the willingness to endure a condition of mental unrest and disturbance. Reflective thinking, in short, means judgment suspended during further inquiry, and suspense is likely to be somewhat painful. . . . To maintain a state of doubt and to carry on a systematic and protracted inquiry—these are the essentials of thinking.[5]

This thinking through experience, suspending judgment even as one forms new conjectures leading us to new forms of action, is the heart of any experience of living with difference. In the particular realm of our interactions with people we understand as different—that is, as sharing different terms of meaning, who participate in different truth communities, and who generalize trust and sense of belonging in very different ways—this is especially challenging. Not surprisingly, it is precisely those differences in religious belonging (between Christians and Muslims, or Orthodox and Reform Jews) that are at the forefront of so much conflict in today's world. Significantly, this suspension of judgment and corresponding ability to live with ambiguity is a key element in John Paul Lederach's strictures on peacemaking and conflict resolution. It is this that allows interlocutors, and for that matter combatants, to break out of a polarized situation and find a resolution this side of violence.[6]

To refer back to the earlier quote by Dewey, what we seek to arrive at through the suspension of judgment is a situation in which the "absent portion" of the "present environment" is no longer defined by the collective representations that each of us brings to the encounter. Or perhaps more properly, when these representations are made public, they are most often challenged and thus shown to have much more to do with the reality of the group making the interpretation (Muslims of Jews, Christians of Muslims, Orthodox Jews of secular Jews, etc.) than to any "objective" or "empirical" reality that is "out there," outside the representations of the group in question. This is the value gained by the suspension of judgment.

What is created at the end of the two-week program is an opening of possibilities and the emergence of new spaces and modes of interaction. Paradoxically, by recognizing differences, we can often make connections that are lost by denying them. An ideology of sameness and relative homogeneity traps us into continually maintaining a false reality. On the other hand, acceptance of difference frees us from investing vast amounts of time and energy in what is essentially a pretense. As noted earlier, the first step in this process is the realization that knowledge must be understood as *knowledge for* (action) rather than *knowledge of* (content). We can never know the other in his or her essence, but we can know what we need to do in order to work with her or him to fulfill this promise or complete that project. This knowledge, based on an orientation toward joint action, or joint "problem-posing," is the opposite of the more common "banking" model of teaching and learning that educators and reformers such as Paulo Freire were so keen to overcome.[7] Like him, we recognize that to truly learn to "be with" is a matter of both the head and the heart, of cognition as well as affect—joined in a shared purpose.[8]

In fact, by the end of the program, fellows have assembled a working tool kit of the following guidelines to further such reflective thinking and openings to shared experience:

+ Hold all claims to absolute truth in abeyance.
+ Recognize the partial nature of any and all understandings.
+ Allow experience to precede judgment.
+ Place *knowledge for* action above *knowledge of* others.
+ In approaching "the other," distance yourself from commitments to your own group.

These are the tools, or building blocks, with which CEDAR equips fellows for use in the new space for interaction and joint action with those who are different.

CHAPTER TWO

A Pedagogy of Community

A conservative Catholic priest from Africa feels deep personal and theological chagrin when he has to confront intensely pious transgendered Muslims in Indonesia—and then returns home to organize just such encounters with difference in his home country.

TOLERATING DIFFERENCE

Tolerance implies living with, abiding—or in the medieval usage, *suffering*—the presence of that which we find objectionable. If something or someone were not distasteful, there would be no need to *tolerate* its presence.

Tolerance thus presents us with a double burden. It demands that we not only accept the presence of that which we find objectionable but also, in so doing, suffer discomfort at this presence. It requires us to live in some form of cognitive dissonance.

Simply stated, the concept is not so simple to practice, for a number of reasons.

First and foremost, tolerance assumes the existence of difference. For tolerance to be evoked as a mechanism of social interaction, we must find ourselves in the presence of something that is both different and objectionable. If it were just different (someone's rather odd taste in kitchen tiles, say), but not objectionable, there would be no need for tolerance. The objectionable is, moreover, almost always seen as the different. One could, as we say, "tolerate" one's own heroin habit or alcohol addiction; but even here, usage of the term implies some split, some reflective differentiation of one's "self" from that part of the self that is addicted to the substance in question.

Relevant here is Freud's notion of the "narcissism of the small difference"—namely, that individuals who are slightly different from me are in some way a continual threat to my identity and sense of self, constantly calling into question the distinguishing characteristics of my own sense of self, precisely because they are so like me in all other ways.[1] Difference is thus almost always seen as containing some objectionable element. We almost always attribute a negative valence to the difference, precisely because that difference brings into question our sense of self-worth.

Consequently, when faced with the "small difference," we tend toward one of two moves. The first is to turn it into a large difference by "othering" the other—that is, pushing the individual or group beyond the boundaries of shared humanity. Such a process to a great extent defined traditional Christian attitudes toward Jews, many current attitudes toward Muslims in the West, the orientation of some Christian Evangelicals in the United States to gays and lesbians, and so on. We discuss this further in chapter 3, in the context of some feminists' response to the Muslims who, during the 2003 CEDAR program, left during a discussion of women's menstruation. When this happens, tolerance is ruled out as unnecessary, because the other is now totally other, dangerous, and beyond the pale. It is no longer a matter of someone or some behavior being objectionable; rather, the boundaries between us and them have become absolutized into boundaries of good and evil, humane and barbaric. Therefore, no tolerance is called for (clearly tolerance has limits, if it is not to fall into total relativism). Tolerance in this case is defined out of existence, the person or persons who are different being seen as not simply objectionable but downright dangerous.

The second, equally common, response is to obviate the need for tolerance in the opposite direction. In this scenario we tend to elide the problem of tolerance with an appeal to some essential, underlying, or overarching similarity to what is different. We trivialize the difference and posit some essential shared characteristic that in effect makes us all one. Here too, then, there is no need to tolerate, for we have done away with what is different and trivialized what we saw as objectionable. Once again, we have done away with difference and thereby absolved ourselves of the need for tolerance.

There are two problems with this second move: First, it usually happens in tandem with the first. Thus, when we define our common bond with one group of people, we usually do so through defining a third group as being beyond that common bond. A unites with B by defining itself in opposition to C. To a great extent this seems to be what is happening now in the relations of Jews and Christians with respect to the Muslim world. We all did this as children, and the behavior is a staple of group psychology. It is also extremely dangerous, if for no other reason than that it demands the continual production of a C group. There must be a continual impulse to redefine some difference in a subgroup of A or B as so egregious that it can no longer be part of the conjoined group and has to be pushed out beyond a common, shared definition of solidarity. To no small extent, this pattern is the history of heresy and sectarianism in the great world religions.[2]

There is, however, yet another reason that this process cannot be stable (leaving aside the normative or ethical aspect). Each and every one of us wants recognition and respect precisely for what makes us unique, singular, and different. By defining others in terms of an overarching similarity or sameness, we define away what is unique and particular to each. It is, however, precisely this uniqueness and particularity that each of us wishes to be recognized in and through. It is in our difference, or "specialness" that we wish to be recognized, not our sameness. In effect, invoking sameness, our shared values or shared humanity, as a basis for tolerance does away with tolerance, leaving us bereft of that sense of unique, personal worth that is so critical to our idea of ourselves in the world.

However simple the idea, practicing tolerance is almost always unworkable in reality. The effort typically either resolves itself into affirmations of sameness, which obviate the need for tolerance by positing the essentially identical nature of all relevant social actors, or posits the absolute and dangerous nature of the other (or others), to whom the proper response is not tolerance but some form of extermination (either physical or symbolic). In both cases we are seemingly running away from the extremely difficult demands of tolerance—that double burden noted earlier.

Ironically, in the course of these many years, those of us engaged in this project have often been confronted by colleagues who advance the very reasonable claim that *tolerance* is too negative a term, weighted down with medieval baggage and pejorative associations. Tolerance was, after all, but a second-best solution, the real and preferential (if often unstated) goal being to rid society of the presence of those who for one reason or another had to be tolerated. Rather than the negative and begrudging accommodation

A Pedagogy of Community

inherent in tolerance, what is really called for, they claim, is pluralism, a rejoicing and celebration of difference in its myriad forms and voices.

Our own approach is that even the burden of tolerance is difficult to bear and needs work and commitment to maintain. And while the construction of a social and public space that is shared by very different and opposing organizations and points of view is a goal—a pluralistic goal, if you will—that we willingly embrace, the question remains: how do we attain such a goal? Merely stating it does not answer that question. In fact, to declare the goal and leave it at that begs the crucial question of how we even begin to realize it, especially in a world of radically divergent agendas, commitments, interests, identities, and orientations.

The usual next step is to invoke different theories of democratic and participatory politics that allow the free movement of ideas and actors in a neutrally constituted public space. At this point the discussion usually shifts to the intricacies of democratic political theory, the sociology of social movements, the history of the transitions to democratic regimes, and so forth. Moreover, we tend to regard the particular individual virtues imputed to the citizenry of such democratic regimes as those of a liberal individualist (often secular) variety—that is, we believe in the moral autonomy of the individual social actor pursuing his or her aspirations in such a public space. What we do not adequately contemplate is the possibility that other virtues and ways of living, which do not necessarily equate to the moral autonomy of the individual, may also enable us to abide by and even protect difference. In fact, these may be more important to the practice of tolerance than the liberal individualist model is.

What we do not actually have so far is a serious inquiry into the types of actors and actions necessary to engage in such a politics of pluralism. We do not yet understand the social virtues and capacities necessary for democratic politics to constitute themselves. We simply assume that they are of the liberal individualist model (a throwback to the old modernization studies, perhaps), but that is not necessarily the case. Indeed, if we take a page from Lederach's *The Moral Imagination*, we can see just how important individual qualities such as imagination, curiosity, courage, and self-awareness are to the construction of a civil polity.[3] None of these necessarily presuppose a liberal political agenda.

Simply put, if we intend to realize our dreams of pluralism, we need more than specific, legally recognized institutional rules of social organization (freedom of organization, conscience, universal franchise, rights, etc.) acting as third-party enforcers; we also need an appreciation of tolerance as a virtue, and this must be inculcated at the most fundamental levels of socialization. What is missing but necessary is the actual practice of tolerance, which can be rooted in very different traditions (and not necessarily secular ones) as a pragmatic mode of living in the world, among people of differing interests, commitments, and even fundamental values.

We, the authors, would stress the aspect of living in and living with—that is, the experiential component of any practice. In today's world, knowledge and experience are often confused. Most believe, or act as if, knowing something is the same as having an experience of it—and of course it is not. The availability of instant information on the Internet has led to a greater than ever confusion of knowledge and experience and the false belief that having knowledge of bits of data or information is tantamount to having had an experience of it. All too often we go one step further and privilege such knowledge over experience. Experience, however, is a mode of assimilating the world wholly different from cognitive knowledge; it is both more practical and more contingent, more powerful and less general, capable of moving us in new directions as it appeals to our emotions as well as our intellect. While knowledge can be falsified, experience cannot, though of course the generalizations we make from it certainly can, and often need be. However, when it comes to the problem of living with difference, cognitive knowledge cannot even begin to approach the importance of experience—precisely, that is, of experiencing the *presence* of the other in all its depth, complexity, ambiguity, discomfort, uncertainty, and uncanniness. So often we claim knowledge, based on the mental assimilation of bits of data, but what we actually have are mere abstractions, bits of idea-like stuff that are but weak foundations for any real life, lived with different people.

As in so many other fields, John Dewey is helpful in clarifying this issue. He makes the important distinction between science, as a statement that gives directions or states meanings, and art, which expresses those directions and meanings. The giving of directions (say, to a city) in no way supplies one with an experience of the object of those directions. Statements of

A Pedagogy of Community

direction may be good or bad, confusing or clear, comprehensive or partial; but in no case can they give us the experience of their object. Art, on the other hand, does not simply lead us to an experience; "it constitutes one."[4] It is expressive of experience. This distinction is helpful in the present context. It clarifies the difference between knowledge (of meanings) and the type of lived experience that we are noting. Tolerance—that is to say, living with difference—can be expressed only in action, as an experience. It is constituted in the doing, and only in the practice of doing and in pragmatic orientations taken when tolerance of what one finds wrong or distasteful is called for. Tolerance as a practice is also an art. It constitutes experience. And experience constituted in and through tolerant orientations is a type of learning experience very different from that provided through textual study, cognitive appreciation, and abstract knowledge.

In the following chapters we present some of the "containers of difference" that we provide in the program to allow this experience of the other, creating an environment in which cognitive meanings and practical experience continually mediate one another. The remainder of this chapter offers only some tentative descriptions of what such experience entails, how to achieve it, what are its constitutive as well as limiting conditions, and how it may operate. We can propose no more than an introduction to such experience.

THE PRINCIPLES OF SHARED PRACTICE

Art, as we learn from Dewey, presupposes practice. And practice is always temporary, contingent, and fallible, since it deals with the concrete, particular, and circumstantial. Unlike theoretical artifices, practical experience can make no enduring claims, nor stake out any final demands. All action (as opposed to theorizing) must recognize that its effects, and for that matter its provenances, are only partial. Action must take account of the ambiguity of the world and of the fact that the effects of action are always limited. Consequently, the claims of action are not truth claims but only claims about what is "good enough" for the purpose at hand. For example, when I hang a shelf in the kitchen, I make no claim to having achieved the perfect straight angle, only one "good enough" for the purpose of mounting a kitchen shelf.

However, when practice is devalued relative to the theoretical work of positing the "true end," totalizing tendencies and unrealistic claims come to dominate, as they do in all cases marked by the division of theory and practice; and it is precisely against these tendencies that thinkers like Dewey and educators like Joseph Schwab railed.[5] Traditions of practice thus become the touchstone of a much broader problem, but they are also particularly relevant to the problem of living with difference in the contemporary world. For we must learn to live by the plumb line of practice rather than the abstract algorithm of "eternal truths" when sharing space with those who are different from us or other than we are. We too must learn to live with "good enough," not final answers: just a set of practices that will, more or less, allow us to live with difference.

The issue of practice and of the experience of doing, however, is also extremely complicated, for it divides as much as it brings together. We do not, after all, do everything with everyone—not in our conjugal relations and not in our "truth communities." We do not, we cannot, do our collective rituals with everyone; partaking in the Eucharist is not the same as a pickup game of stickball. So how can we develop practices—shared experiences—that preserve difference while at the same time engaging with the different? This is the pedagogic challenge of our century. By definition there can be no formulas and no algorithms; the process must always be a creative one, a poetics of action.[6] Nevertheless, there are indications, resources, experiments, and past experiences that may present us with some model, however rough and undeveloped, of how to proceed. Explaining the basic framework and assumptions on which we believe a practice of tolerance must be based takes us back, in some ways, to the origins of the social sciences and the insights of the nineteenth-century sociologists.

We begin with the basic insight of sociology and anthropology that knowledge is collective, not individual. For most of us, who believe that knowledge is little bits of information that we store in our brains, this concept is counterintuitive. Yet Emile Durkheim and the other founders of the social sciences have shown that in fact we know what we know as part of a group.[7] Our categories, our ways of understanding, our moral judgments, the boundaries of what we deem permissible and prohibited, our basic frames of meanings, many of our fears and desires—all are, in a strong sense, social. We hold them together with others and not simply as individual beliefs. These categories and ways of understanding the world, including the

A Pedagogy of Community

worlds of human action, tie us to specific groups of individuals—be they national, tribal, religious, ethnic, or even those with whom we may share a similar sexual orientation. This may be true of us as Baptists, Bulgarians, Shona, or members of the local LGBT alliance.

Because knowledge is collective, an important part of what we know is bound up with whom we trust. We are almost always called upon to grant moral credit to some source in matters that are by their nature morally ambiguous. In setting out to understand any particular event or action, we may not dispute the specific "fact" or "set of facts" under discussion—the building of a mosque in lower Manhattan, the knifing of a participant in a gay pride parade in Jerusalem, the murder of a Jew in Paris, the establishment of hidden cameras in the Muslim neighborhoods of Birmingham, England, and so on. But the frame of the act, the set of relevant external bits of information, and the histories needed to explain them will frequently be decided on the bases of our group-belonging and the moral credit that we, as members of a group, grant to a source of such data.

Those communities within which moral credit is granted, and which thus develop the very structure of our knowledge, tend to be what many call communities of belonging. Secular communities too have their own beliefs, codes, and myths. Communities of belonging, however, are not universal or fully open; they are bounded, just as families are. They have their own histories and their own trajectories, their own languages and jokes, their own obligations, their own taken-for-granted worlds, their own flavors and smells—their own understandings of home. They may be more or less open, more or less ascribed, (that is, based on unalterable factors such as race or age or gender), and their boundaries may be more or less permeable; but they do have boundaries, and they always define some "us" as against some "other." In fact, the notion that such communities (and the trust that they engender) can be totally open and without any constitutive boundary is a dangerous illusion that ultimately denies the reality not only of the "other" and the community in which she is embedded but also that of oneself.

These communities are, moreover, real, live, active entities that human actors are born into and in which they thrive, live, die, and make sense of their worlds and the worlds of others. Despite all the dangers that arise from these communities, we cannot live without them. The dangers are well known, and different moral visions, as well as different historical memories and senses of belonging, can lead to a deep sense of distrust and enmity that can span generations, even millennia. The relations between Jews and Christians in Europe provide a tragic and telling example of how divergent historical narratives and a sense of group membership have divided people who nevertheless carried out economic and civil exchange in a shared public space for centuries. Similar examples of exclusion built on different communities of belonging can be found in the Great Lakes region of East Africa, the nation-states carved out of the remnants of the Ottoman Empire following World War I, and the First Nations of North America.

Given the conflicts communities of belonging historically created with those who are outside them, the purpose of constructing interreligious and interethnic programs must be not to stress what we have in common with the other but to accept and attempt to build on our differences. For our differences are precisely the markers of these different communities of belonging that define who we are and provide the settings and meanings for our lives. Any attempts to deny or negate them, including efforts to privatize and so remove them from the realm of shared public space, end up denying precisely what makes each and every one of us who we are. When I say, "We are fundamentally the same," it never occurs to me that I am like you, only that you are like me. And it is safe to assume that you are thinking the same: that I am like you. What we end up with, as discussed in chapter 1, is a total elision of meanings. We also have a fundamentally narcissistic construct in which I assimilate you to me rather than recognize you in all your differences (however much those might make me uncomfortable). It is no wonder that so much of the "identity politics" of the past decades has focused on recognition. For by denying difference in the name of civil peace, we are at the same time denying the recognition that we all crave: a recognition of ourselves as individual, separate, and unique—by definition, different.

The goal of any attempt to live together differently must therefore be to test just how far we can build both trust and a common store of knowledge across different communities. Can we, as a group made up of individuals who are members of different communities of belonging, nevertheless construct a minimum framework of trust in some small arenas of knowledge and understanding? In slightly different terms: can we learn to grant moral credit to people who are different from us? Can we learn to live with less-than-perfect knowledge of the others and, despite being excluded from their histories, languages, and memories, still have enough trust to allow the construction of a shared world of reference on which to draw when events divide our different communities?

To what extent can we grant moral credit to the other, to him or her who is not a member of our group, and so share some common frame of understanding and knowledge despite being members of very different communities, tied to different myths, obligated by different commandments, and loyal to different particularities? This is no small undertaking. For communities of trust are those of shared moral dispositions, familiarity, sameness, and shared experience in which, in situations of risk, community members grant moral credit to one another, and the value of peace trumps that of abstract justice. In contrast to such communities, most of us share a more anonymous public realm with strangers of dissimilar experience and disparate moral values. In this realm, in which others are experienced as potentially dangerous, requiring the enactment of security measures, and in which the highest virtue is justice rather than peace, we invoke a language of rights to regulate our relations with one another—something we would be loath to do in either our family or our church.

To build such trust across communities it is necessary to construct a set of experiences that are shared but, at the same time, to leave room for all particularities. The most quotidian and mundane matters—religious dietary restrictions, prayer commitments, and other communal obligations—must all be respected. We can build trust by making these experiences public and also sharing them, even as we remain loyal to our own particular communities of trust, belonging, and knowledge.

Shared experience, what we call "embodied knowledge," must be central to any attempt to construct new communities of understanding across different communities of belonging. Shared experience—which includes that of one another's particularities, not just the common conditions that all may experience (hunger, thirst, exhaustion, etc.)—provides the necessary basis for constructing frames of knowledge across our different communities of belonging.

Here we come again to our stress on shared practice rather than simply shared ideas or meanings, focusing on *knowledge for* rather than *knowledge of*.

Conditional knowledge, which is always framed toward specific purposes, can be shared across communities, even as our categorical propositions, our "assertive" knowledge, remain firmly rooted within different communities of belonging.

Through such shared practice we may seek two outcomes: (a) a wider circle of trust, composed of those to whom we may grant moral credit, and which includes those who may not be members of our moral community; and (b) the very reframing of the knowledge necessary to work in and share a world with the other, from *knowledge of* to *knowledge for*, from those propositions that we categorically assert to those that embody conditional knowledge relevant to some shared purpose. Both, we can hope, will bring us to a point where experience precedes judgment rather than the other way around. We, the authors, have found that predicating action or practice on this idea of *knowledge for* and on a wider circle of trust creates a container, or space, in which new, creative, and imaginative ways of living with difference can emerge and thrive.

REFRAMING SELF-OTHER RELATIONS

Developing a practice based on the principles we have outlined here is a slow, cumulative, and not always conscious process that necessitates the experience of straddling boundaries. Individuals retain their membership in, and terms of meaning as provided within, their "truth communities," but they also come to recognize that these memberships provide only partial, fragile, mutable, and heavily freighted interpretive frames for events in the world—frames that are marked by Bacon's idols of the tribe, marketplace, cave, or theater.[8] One way we can achieve this recognition is through some sort of intentional action that opens us to the realization that the frames of meaning we bring to our interactions need not be set in stone. This realization is essentially what happens when we are placed in an environment that does not deny difference but actively engages with it.

One year, for example, we arranged for the fellows of the summer school to attend Jewish Sabbath services and then have lunch with different families in the community whose religious worship they had attended. The fellow from Tajikistan had lunch with an observant Jewish family. Before eating, the family members followed the traditional practice of ritually washing

A Pedagogy of Community

their hands and then refraining from speaking between that action and the blessing over the bread; at the table they also sang in Hebrew both the obligatory prayers and traditional hymns for Shabbat afternoon, as is typical in an observant Jewish household. Sitting at this table, not at all sure what was going on, not quite understanding (before it was explained to him) why no one answered his questions when he voiced them in the time between the handwashing and the blessings over the bread, our fellow was suddenly taken back to his childhood in Tajikistan. He recalled how, as a child, when his parents moved to a new apartment, they took with them their neighbor, a Christian woman who had nobody to look after her. For years this Christian woman lived with our friend's Muslim family, ate with them, and sat with them when they prayed and observed their other ritual obligations. Never until this Shabbat afternoon had it occurred to our fellow that it might have been strange for this Christian woman to sit at a Muslim family's table and witness their prayers and customs, which in some ways were shared (the common culture of Tajikistan), but in other ways were quite dissimilar. Any number of times afterward, the fellow mentioned with wonder how the experience of the Jewish Shabbat had given him insight into a critical aspect of his own childhood. Being the "outsider"—welcome, respected, feted, and honored though he was, still the "outsider"—at the Shabbat meal allowed him for the first time to appreciate what it must have been like for this woman who had spent so many years at his parents' table.

In a sense, the fellow's experience of the Shabbat served to "other" his own past and allowed him a new insight into the experience of his neighbor of long ago and the meaning of commensality—not to mention hospitality—across different traditions. A shared practice led to new sets of meanings, new ways of interpretation, in this case of the past. It also extended—retrospectively—the workings of empathy.

Such cases abound when the opportunity is presented. In the summer of 2003 we sat down for a meal in a Sarajevo restaurant. All of us were hungry, it being well past dinner time, and immediately fell ravenously on the food placed before us, though the food that was being prepared for the religiously observant Jewish fellows from Israel (fish, cooked in aluminum foil to meet their dietary requirements) was not yet ready. As a result, these observant Jews could not eat with everyone else; again, all were very hungry. The other person who did not eat right away was the Palestinian Israeli Muslim, who refused to touch his food until his Jewish colleagues, who had traveled with him from Israel, had been served too. The significance of this act was not fully felt until after the program was over, when the Orthodox Israeli woman, who had an eight-hour layover in Budapest on her way back to Israel from Sarajevo, told her husband over the phone that rather than stay in the airport, she would spend the time in Budapest itself and do some shopping and see the city. Not expecting that she would travel alone, he asked who would accompany her. She said she would go with Ahmed and Salam, the Palestinian Israeli fellows, who were on the same flight. Her husband was shocked; and as she reflected on his reaction, it dawned on her how much she herself had changed in the two weeks—previously such a reality would have been inconceivable to her too.

A Croatian-American fellow experienced a much more radical case of such reframing during her time in Bosnia and the fellows' visit to a former hospital in the city of Stolac, which had been turned into a torture camp. As she said, the experience of standing in the physical place where members of her collective, her affinity group, had perpetrated crimes against humanity had the profound effect of othering her from herself and reframing her own sense of group belonging and self-understanding in relation to her group.

Seligman experienced a much less extreme case when asked to lead prayers in an Orthodox Jewish synagogue in Newton, Massachusetts. The rabbi and community had agreed that he could bring a group of international fellows to morning prayers to give them some sense of the experience. He was already leading the prayers when the group entered, about ten minutes into the service. All of a sudden all the other congregants fell silent, ceasing the usual murmur of voices that is an integral and enveloping aspect of Orthodox Jewish prayer. At that moment it became clear to Seligman that one group to which he belonged (the synagogue and, by extension, the Jewish people) was distancing itself from and demonstrating some mistrust of another group to which he also felt a great responsibility and loyalty (the fellows of the school). The experience confounded a previously unproblematic frame of meanings of collective belonging, and it forced further reflection on the very nature of shared ties, social responsibility, group membership, in-group/out-group identities, and the nature of being an other.

Figure 6. Part of the Kostana Hospital in Stolac. Renowned as one of the leading bone hospitals in the Eastern Bloc, it became a prison and place of torture during the Bosnian War. Photo by David W. Montgomery, 2006.

What this type of experience makes possible is a redefinition of the purposes toward which explanation is oriented. To hark back to the aphorism on explanation mentioned in chapter 1, the mind then, we can say, comes to rest in a different place. Distancing our collective representations of who we are and our own commitments to our own traditions (which are in no way weakened or questioned) from the process of idea formation allows us to redefine those purposes toward which explanation is oriented. These are no longer defined by the collective purposes of each and every participant's own "in group."

We thus begin to localize our ideas and circumscribe our explanations in response to what is most or more immediate, without engaging our own particular collective philosophy of history, humankind, God, and existence. We learn to live, if not without the latter, at least without the latter forming the foundation of each and every decision involving the other. By distancing these grand or meta interpretive grids from every environment-which-is-in-need-of-an-explanation, we create a space where alternative and competing practices among members of differing and even mutually exclusive interpretive communities can construct a common life (even while remaining mutually exclusive in their truth claims and all that follows from such).

A concrete example is perhaps in order here. In the Jewish tradition, one of the fundamental principles regulating relations with gentiles is known as *darchei shalom*, the ways of peace. Famously, this is interpreted to mean that Jews must fulfill obligations of neighborliness to their gentile neighbors, even if not explicitly commanded to—indeed, even when explicitly absolved of the obligation to treat the gentile neighbor in the same manner in which they treat their Jewish brother. Most contemporary understandings of this principle view it as purely prudential, obligating Jews to act in such a way so that the gentiles will have no reason to complain of Jewish behavior. Thus, for example, without such a concern there would be no need to return lost property to a gentile. Such is the usual, "on the street" understanding of this term that one would find in many Orthodox and ultra-Orthodox Jewish communities. Yet there is a great debate over the concept of *darchei shalom* and of the purely prudential understanding of its force, going back to the time of the Talmud (circa sixth century C.E.). In fact, rabbis from then through modern times have recognized that this very limited understanding of *darchei shalom* is problematic and have offered a much richer and more value-laden interpretation of its obligatory nature. Indeed, the Babylonian Talmud itself contains a ruling that not returning lost property (to a gentile) is a "violation of the Holy Name."[9]

The point, however, is that one can find in the tradition what one wishes to find, and one's scholarship will develop accordingly. Moreover, one may well be so much under the sway of contemporary idols of the tribe (note: the tribe at any given moment is not coterminous with the tradition) or the cave as to blind oneself to the richness of other possible interpretations and understandings that the tradition permits or even encourages. This point is especially relevant, because often people who stand within a tradition—Jewish, Catholic, Muslim, Hindu, Protestant, and so on—claim to be obligated by their acceptance of transcendent dictates and revealed texts. It is these obligations, they assert, rather than any prejudice, failure of judgment, idols of tribe, marketplace, cave, or even grandmothers' stories for that matter, that direct their behavior. What we are suggesting is that this is often not the case; one can in fact accept and live comfortably within a heteronomously ordered tradition and still be open to experience and to the

A Pedagogy of Community

implications of experience, as well. We would add that all this is encompassed in the very meaning of *halacha* or *sharia* (both of which mean "way" or "path") and was also the original meaning of the Christian religion.[10] For if all were finished, complete, and wholly assured, no *way* would be called for, only a binary and, in the nature of the case, finalizing decision, which would make all that followed meaningless.

All of this brings us to a knowledge focused on particularities and, hence, experience, or what we are calling shared practice. Experience, as Dewey has taught us, is the central component in thinking. "To learn from experience" he tells us, "is to make a backward and forward connection between what we do to things and what we enjoy and suffer from things in consequence. Under such conditions, doing becomes a trying; an experiment with the world to find out what it is like."[11] In this process we cannot separate the intellect from experience, and the attempt to do so leaves us with disembodied, abstract knowledge that all too often emphasizes "things" rather than the "relations or connections" between them.[12] This is of precious little help in our attempt to connect the multitude of disconnected data that the world presents into a framework of meaning. Meaning, after all, rests not on the knowledge of "things" but on the relations between them, which in turn, as Dewey so brilliantly argues, can be assessed only through experience—because only through experience do we bring the relevant relations between things into any sensible sort of juxtaposition. The relevant relations between fabric, wood, staples, hammer, stain pot, brush, and so on become relevant only in the construction of the chair. Without the experience of chair-making, the relations between the components—even the definitions of the component elements—are open to endless interpretation. Moreover, if I were building a light glider, the relevant relations—of tensile strength, thickness, suitability of material, and so on—would be different. Meaning, emergent from experience, can be supplied only by the goals toward which we aspire; and experience, as opposed to our simple, passive subjugation to an event, is always in pursuit of a practical aim.

How, then, we may ask, are these insights into the nature of experience and of thinking relevant to the sharing of practice but not of meaning? Having "bracketed out," or suspended, our received impressions in search of new judgments based on experience of a particular and embodied nature, can we say anything about the experience of shared practice that leads us to new types of judgments and conjectures? Can these new ideas, or even the process of arriving at them, in turn be formalized in any way and used as tools for further experiments in judgment formation? If so, can they then be carried forward into different organizational settings and institutional arenas?

Perhaps the best way to begin is to define the "backward and forward" motion that is achieved in the process of reframing. The *backward motion* refers to our existing preconceptions and uncritical knowledge base, often of a generalized nature. This knowledge is not tested by any real experience but is only the received knowledge of the tribe, cave, marketplace, and so on—meanings writ large, as it were. The *forward motion* is, clearly, our continued process of conjecturing and idea formation, now to be informed by the particular experiences of a shared practice and not solely by the "received wisdom" of our respective tribes. In short, we learn to act (according to our newly formed conjectures and judgments) rather than react (according to our received prejudices and cognitive grids).

From this point it becomes clear that the "thing" upon which we are acting and which is in turn acting upon us is not a block of wood or a screwdriver, nor the deciphering of a text or a geometry problem, but rather our ideas of ourselves in relation to people who are different from us. A small matter, it would seem, when put so simply. Yet it goes to the core of our existence and is on a par with what Dewey was referring to when he discussed the painful process of suspending judgment and living in the suspense that results. By suspending judgment, we are, after all, suspending one of the prime activities of the "discriminating ego."[13] Holding judgment in abeyance, we are in effect reigning in the ego's will to dominate the given situation through explanation. We are, in fact, bracketing out meanings and applying ourselves primarily to the immediacy of the shared experience rather than preexisting interpretive frameworks.

One critical component of this process, especially of our own attempts to understand its working along collective lines, is the role of symbols. A symbol acts as a medium, an intervening substance that, in blurring the boundaries between the self and its object, also enables the eventual possibility of perceiving objects outside the self. Symbols are the critical link that allows us to perceive the other, through a process of not quite incorporating the other within our internal space. They allow both the blurring of boundaries and their reconstitution. In the context of our theme here, the relevant symbols are not crosses, flags, six-pointed stars, or the like but rather those very *ideas* we form, that place "where the mind rests" in our regard of the other. While not reducible to an image, they nevertheless provide a code or grid, framing both ourselves and the other in a web of significance and meaning. In Dewey's terms, we are referring to those ideas which provide the supplementary information we need to make sense of our meeting with the other.

Symbol systems (which are essentially cultural systems) thus function as mediating structures that enable the very relation between self and world. But if we return to our example of the Jewish laws of relations with gentiles, or that of how, in one program, a Christian Evangelical fellow came to reframe his understanding of missionary activity as something that was destructive of civil peace in a multireligious city like Birmingham, England, and so could be delayed until the Second Coming, we see that these systems are themselves open to endless interpretation and divergent understandings. Their own boundaries are fluid, to be determined by the conjectures, judgments, and goals that define the situation within which they are invoked—that is, by practice. Yes, they may well *mediate* our relations with the world, but let us not confuse that with any final *definition* of either us or the world! Holding such definitions in abeyance—a process that demands the suspension of judgment, the mental pain of such suspension, and the blurring of boundaries—allows a malleability in our approach to these cultural and, by definition, collective systems. This flexibility in turn permits us, at the best of times, to think through our relations with the other in a way that would not otherwise be possible. New conjectures, new judgments, a new experience of thinking are now possible, as the experience of difference is disembodied from existing judgments, conjectures, and "idols."

An interesting illustration of this process of thinking through a situation in new ways that require holding existing understandings in abeyance took place in Bursa, the first capital of the Ottoman Empire, where the school fellows were invited to share in the welcoming of the Jewish Sabbath one Friday night with one of their members. There were fifteen people in the room (ten Jews, four Muslims, and one Christian). According to Orthodox Jewish observance, ten Jewish men are required for a full quorum, or minyan, at which all prayers can be recited. For non-Orthodox denominations, women also count toward the minyan. In this case, the ten Jews constituted a legitimate minyan for the non-Orthodox Jews present. But since not all of them were men, in the eyes of the one Orthodox Jewish member of the group there was no minyan. However, the non-Orthodox Jews still needed to count this Orthodox man to meet their required ten for the minyan. There ensued a vigorous argument between the Jewish fellows and staff about how to deal with the situation. In the end the Orthodox man simply said, "Do what you want"—that is, "Count me or not, as you will"—though he refused to lead prayers. Now, the person who did lead prayers had no idea if this man, standing at the back, gave the appropriate responses to those prayers for which a minyan is mandated or not, but in a sense it did not matter. This group of ten Jewish men and women found a way to pray together and welcome their Sabbath even though they could not agree on their collective status (i.e., whether there was a minyan or not). They shared a practice (prayer) without sharing an understanding of whether this particular practice was formal public prayer (with a minyan) or simply a set of multiple private, individual prayers. It is, furthermore, interesting to speculate whether it was the presence of non-Jews in the room that caused the actors to find a solution, and whether the solution would not have been reached had there been only Jews in the room. In that case the end might well have been a stalemate and not a resolution. The presence of the other may indeed have been essential to enabling the Jewish participants to open up new interpretive frames, somehow parse the difference of meanings, and yet share a practice.

It is perhaps significant that this incident happened in Turkey of all places, with its associations of Ottoman tolerance (of Jews) and continuing modern challenges in relation to minority issues—of Kurds, Armenians, Alevis, Greeks, and others. A living monument to such challenges and to the role of symbols therein is the Hagia Sophia (Ayasofya), built between 532 and 537 C.E., a church until 1453, a mosque for the next 481 years, and converted into a museum under Atatürk in 1934–1935. The Hagia Sophia was, indeed, a primary symbol for Eastern Orthodox Christianity, then for the Islam of the Ottomans, and finally (secularized) for the modern Turkish state established by Mustafa Atatürk. Today, many are lobbying to return it to one of its original incarnations, as either mosque or church (current Turkish law prohibits

Figure 7. Hagia Sophia (Ayasofya).

Figure 8. Hagia Sophia, in Istanbul, was a Christian cathedral between 537 and 1453, a mosque between 1453 and 1931, and since 1935 a museum. Figure 7 shows Christian mosaics; this image, Islamic motifs. Photos by David W. Montgomery, 2007.

its use as anything other than as a museum). Significantly, a small minority, including the murdered Armenian journalist Hrant Dink, argued for its being turned into a place for both Christian and Muslim worship (on Sunday and Friday, respectively), as well as for secular tourism (the rest of the week).[14]

While those who are lobbying for sharing the site are a minority, they represent precisely the type of move we are arguing for: recognizing rather than suppressing difference, sharing sacred spaces (see chapter 6), and negotiating boundaries in the face of the other. Significantly, too, they demonstrate that symbols themselves are fungible and can be negotiated, and their valence can be not only questioned but also changed. Such an edifice—church, mosque, museum all in one—would serve as a multivalent symbol of tolerance in the face of difference. Allowing the expressive symbolism of Christians, Muslims, and secularists would make it a monument for living with difference and tolerating its boundaries.

If empathy and living with difference are to be a permanent and integral aspect of our relations with others, they must emanate from experience and practice rather than a particular ideological position or a priori interpretive framework (even one stemming from the received wisdom of liberal individualist precepts). In other words, they must be born of experience rather than ideology. Dewey famously claimed that "ideas are not genuine ideas unless they are tools in a reflective examination which tends to solve a problem."[15] Characteristic of such ideas are "a willingness to hold final selection in suspense [as well as] alertness, flexibility, curiosity." In contrast, "dogmatism, rigidity, prejudice, caprice, arising from routine, passion and flippancy are fatal."[16] The first characterization, we posit, is a pretty good description of our story from Bursa, just as a Hagia Sophia shared among different communities of belonging would contribute greatly to such practice and experience.

A Pedagogy of Community

CHAPTER THREE

A Community of Pedagogy

Watching a movie about homosexuality was shocking for me. I always avoided learning about this group and why they are different. By having a discussion about this issue and watching the movie, I believe I came out with a different perspective of the issue and am open to learning more. I cannot say I am a true supporter, because frankly I am not, as I think it is against nature, but I find myself accepting and respecting this community more.

STORIES OF REFLECTIVE PRACTICE

In previous chapters we explained what we mean by crafting a space where one can learn to live with difference. In this chapter we introduce the methodology through which we implement our vision of learning to live together differently. Reflective practice is at the core of this methodology and is actualized though careful scheduling of group members' time and activities together. Our aim in the program is to create a shared experience. We do this through a combination of different methodologies, chief among which are deconstruction, facilitation, and practicums, or site visits—all of which constitute modes of experiential learning. We begin with examples of what we mean by *deconstruction*, which as a pedagogical practice—and despite the very different contexts—is not that far removed from the type of "decoding" that Paulo Freire describes and advocates in his seminal book *Pedagogy of the Oppressed*.[1]

Standing amid the roofless ruins of the old Coventry Cathedral in the West Midlands of England, our group of Muslims, Jews, Christians, Sikhs, and secular individuals remained silent, awed by the magnitude of the devastation caused by the Luftwaffe's bombing in World War II. We had come from Birmingham that morning, stopping en route in Stratford-upon-Avon,

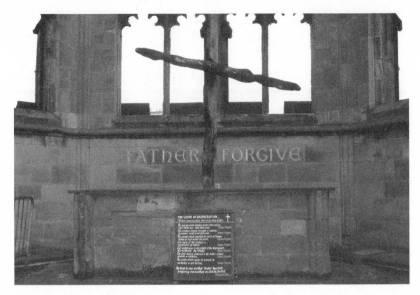

Figure 9. Coventry Cathedral.

Figure 10. The ruins of Coventry Cathedral include an altar plaque with the Litany of Reconciliation. Photos by David W. Montgomery, 2008.

the birthplace of William Shakespeare and a major tourist attraction. The group was based in Birmingham and was addressing a specific theme: "The Good City: Living Together Differently." Birmingham, the United Kingdom's second-largest city, is ethnically and culturally diverse. In fact, it is expected, by the next decade, to be a city of ethnic minorities with no ethnic group forming a majority. Stratford-upon-Avon is a smaller town, a showcase for England's grand history and theatrical tradition. The ruins of Coventry Cathedral are a lasting symbol of the suffering that World War II inflicted on Britain. The move between these three sites impressed upon our group the rich history, complexity, and diversity of contemporary life in England.

In Coventry, we visited the magnificent new cathedral, whose architectural continuity with the ruins of the old was a potent symbol of the endurance of the Anglican Church. There we encountered the narrative of the suffering of the English people during the war. As we toured the many structures making up the new cathedral, our guide, a young German volunteer, took us to the star-shaped Chapel of Unity, where ecumenical services are held. In the center of the saucer-shaped mosaic floor lies a dove of peace. The room is designed so that round objects can roll from the edges toward the dove. The guide explained that this intricate mosaic symbolizes the hope that all of humankind will come together in unity and peace. About thirty of us congregated in the chapel—among them Jews with head coverings and beards, Muslim women with headscarves, and many people of color. Our guide distributed golf balls to each one of us and asked us to let them roll onto the mosaic, toward the center, in an experiential exercise that he called "unity of peace." When one golf ball did not roll properly and got stuck, he casually pushed it with his foot until it joined the other balls in the middle of the dove.

Wasserfall left the chapel pondering the powerful image of the guide kicking the ball while speaking about togetherness and unity in peace. Juxtaposed with the gurdwara (Sikh temple), mosques, and churches of Birmingham and the medieval beauty of Stratford-upon-Avon, our young guide's act seemed like a casual erasure of diversity in contemporary England and in our group. Jews and Muslims in the group shared her feeling, and the moment made a lasting impression not only on the fellows but on the organizers as well. In our deconstruction session the next day, our local host, a Birmingham vicar, decided to use this example to discuss the place of difference in the Anglican Church. He explained that the dove does not just represent peace, as our guide had told us; it also signifies the presence of God through the Holy Spirit. The dove thus connects to the Trinity, with Jesus as the savior unifying all in God's love.

"What then was the concept of unity that our guide put forward in the chapel?" asked our local host. As we debated the meanings of his act, it became clear that our guide spoke only of Christian unity, though he presented it as a universal feature. Underlying his message was the belief that unity can be attained when all humankind accepts the universalism of Jesus and his message of peace. Another question then arose: could this Christian vision of unity recognize the diversity of contemporary Britain as represented by our group? Even though we were a group of people with visible signs of belonging to other religions, the young man's Christian narrative had not taken that difference into account. On the contrary, what had been highlighted in this powerful exercise was the casual dismissal of difference experienced by the minorities in the Chapel of Unity. The guide had called upon us to feel united in a Christian credo; at the same time, he had symbolically erased any discordant voice by casual kicking the wayward ball. We all reflected, during this "deconstruction" session, that in the case of the chapel, the relationship between unity and diversity was a forced one.[2] The actions of the guide contrasted powerfully with his words. For the Christians among us, this incident symbolized the power of the Anglican Church. For the Muslims and the Jews, it emphasized that their own difference was not taken into account and was subjugated to a powerful narrative of Christian unity. Their experience in the chapel made them aware of their singularity, while the Christians felt the dissonance of seeing their basic sense of universalism not accepted by the minority.

+ + + +

Wide awake in the warm Kigali night, Wasserfall heard the muezzin call. It startled her at first, because she was completely unaware of the existence of a Muslim community in Kigali. As part of the first Equator Peace Academy,[3] we had come from Uganda to experience firsthand memory and community in Rwanda. After two days of visits and lectures on the history and memory of the genocide, we had not heard a word about the Muslim community in Rwanda. Our group included people from sixteen countries, mostly in Africa, and a handful of Westerners. The next morning, still thinking of the muezzin, she started asking organizers and participants what they knew about the role of the Muslim community, who made up about 4 percent of the Rwandan population, during the genocide. Participants from different African countries, mostly Christians of various denominations, did not know much but assumed that being a Muslim during that period was not the most important factor, and that Muslims had behaved as other Rwandans had. Tutsi or Hutu ethnic identity was what had mattered most, participants thought. Muslims, in their minds, behaved as everyone else had, and behavior by Rwandans of all religions during the genocide could be explained only as ethnic cleansing. They did not believe that religious affiliation changed people's behavior in any way. Not one person in our group had a different view of the matter. The Ugandan organizers themselves were not sure about the role of Muslims during that period.

Our guide, Peter Celestine, a Catholic priest based in Kabale, Uganda, has written about the role of the churches in the genocide. Celestine explained to the group that Rwandan Muslims had actually harbored Tutsi in their mosques and saved the lives of fellow citizens during the massacres.[4] This information came as a surprise to most of the group and was talked about during our stay in Rwanda and Uganda. Visiting the churches where massacres had happened, while learning at the same time that a minority of people belonging to another religion had behaved differently, helped the group both to experience the importance of our taken-for-granted assumptions in shaping our memories and to reflect on the power of the theories and beliefs that cloud our memories; it was a great learning moment in the group. Two years later one of the organizers, when visiting the United States, remembered how important it had been to learn that members of a different religion had acted with compassion and not according to the wide ethnic divide. She explained that it had allowed her to shift her perception of Muslims and Christians alike.[5]

Figure 11. Rwandan church that was the site of a massacre in the 1994 genocide. The structure on the left, behind the church, is an ossuary holding the remains of those killed while seeking shelter in the church. Photo by David W. Montgomery, 2012.

WHAT IS REFLECTIVE PRACTICE?

Reflective practice is a process that focuses on slowly revealing the ways we perceive social reality *as* we experience it. As social actors, we live within grids of understanding and within categories and assumptions. These stem from both past experiences and theories about our experiences. Reflective practice helps us become aware of, and rearrange our perceptions of, our social roles and expectations. Donald Schön explains that the problem of dealing with the uncertainty of our social (or scientific) experience starts with posing a question and learning to reflect as we implement solutions.[6] At CEDAR we ask a basic question: how do people learn to live together differently without shedding their most basic beliefs and, at the same time, maintain the mental and cultural space necessary to encounter people who believe and act very differently than they do? It is not easy learning, as the many religious and ethnic conflicts around us attest. CEDAR programs focus on enabling participants to practice the skill of meeting differences without erasing them. They create social and learning containers to help individuals reflect as nearly as possible *in* and *at* the moment while keeping in mind the historic and cultural aspects of their actions and learning.

A Community of Pedagogy

The steps of this reflective practice are deconstruction, facilitation, experiential learning, and internal evaluation. These social containers are designed so that we can move from the plenary to different small groups that allow participants to reflect while acting and experiencing. Doing and thinking are complementary.[7] Actions and thinking are part of our human repertoire as we seek solutions to the questions that circumstances throw our way. The ability to integrate our thinking and acting in a smooth pattern allows us to understand the meanings of our actions and to act in a meaningful way. These containers are designed to help us reassess, stop, and reflect as we experience our own social selves and the social selves of others in action.

In the earlier example of the Chapel of Unity, an act experienced during a site visit produced dissonance for people from different religions and so created a question, a query. It stopped some of us in our tracks. A Christian scholar, who is also a clergyman, added more historical knowledge in the form of the background meaning of the symbol of the dove. We became aware of the ways in which people from different religions might experience the concept of unity, which is central to the Christian credo. The group then used this experience to uncover some of the taken-for-granted assumptions of all those involved. We learned that Jews and Muslims experienced the universal unity in peace as an erasure of their differences. Jews and Muslims cannot become "one in Jesus," because they do not accept Jesus as their savior. For Christians, becoming aware of the erasure that is implied in their most sacred universal credo opened up a way to perceive their own complexity. Reflecting on this dissonant act in our group of difference helped all of us integrate the action of the guide with our own taken-for-granted assumptions about the Anglican Church. Coming to terms with the feelings of discomfort that this act created for the minority was done by cognitively deconstructing the experience from as many points of view as possible.

Reflective practice implies a constant, process-oriented, and systematic action. Reality is complex, and no simple cause-and-effect formula can explain our experience of reality. CEDAR's unique approach integrates reflective practice into the habits of an internationally diverse group composed of religious and nonreligious individuals from diverse cultural, ethnic, and national backgrounds. Since the important work of Dewey in the

1930s and Schön in the 1980s, many peace-building activists, evaluators, feminist theorists, social psychologists, and others have used reflective practice as a central tool for learning and as part of the core of their theory of change.[8]

Lederach and others see reflective practice in their intercommunal work and value the role it plays in fostering peaceful change in situations of deep conflict. For Lederach, reflective practice is a method all can use to bring about change in one way or another. His call to leap into the "moral imagination" is based on the assumption that reflecting on conflict situations will allow us to change our behaviors. For Lederach, the practitioner grasps previously unseen opportunities by way of reflective practice. But this is not an easy process, and Lederach created a specific tool kit to "foster . . . reflection, an explicit building of knowledge and development of theory."[9] His reflective approach to peace building puts the accent on experience. Lederach and others working in the field of reflective practice strive to empower people working in conflict areas to see that their experiences in the field are as important in building knowledge as the knowledge brought by social theorists.

Schön's initial insight is that reflective practice constitutes a complementary process of knowledge building, because it integrates experiential and embodied learning with cognition. For Schön and Lederach, reflective practice is a way to give people in the trenches a voice within the professions. It legitimates concrete knowledge of people in the field who seek and implement solutions tailored to the needs of a given conflict year after year. For Harold Saunders and his team, an iterated use of reflective practice within the same group leads to further understanding among longtime foes. For all, reflective practice is a means *to* and *for* change. Feminists use reflective practices (called reflexivity) to focus on power relationships in research situations and to bring about societal change through awareness of the inequality of these relationships.[10]

While drawing on previous understandings of reflective practice, CEDAR's approach shifts from stressing individual reflection to stressing the importance of the group in creating and shaping personal or cultural knowledge. This, then, allows people to become aware of their own cultural assumptions. Reflective practice is not just an individual process but also a collective practice of immense power in a diverse group of people. We learn to see our assumptions about others as stemming from our own sense of collective belonging.

How to live together without ignoring or erasing our differences in the midst of an international cohort is the question that forms the backbone of our reflective practice. It allows us to integrate experience and reflection as we seize those opportunities for increased understanding that always arise in diverse groups. Reflective practice is the concrete way that we operationalize the three modes of learning in the school: cognitive, experiential, and emotional.

CONFRONTING ASSUMPTIONS ABOUT "MY OTHER": REFLECTIVE PRACTICE AT CEDAR

Self and other are not static categories. In CEDAR programs, we discover the power of our collective assumptions as we meet people whom we define as "our others" in the group. Defining who our others are is a journey in itself. As people spend two weeks learning to live with a group of very particular individual others, they learn that their assumptions about those others do not match their experiences. Reality unfolds in the course of the program, and we are forced to reassess our assumptions about the other and our own group belonging.

+ + + +

At the beginning of the 2007 program in Istanbul, a young Sunni Turkish woman reacted with anger to the portrait of her country in the film *Journey to the Sun*. This 1999 Turkish movie portrays the journey of a young Turk who treks southeastward, toward a Kurdish village, to bury the body of his Kurdish friend. His attempt to bury the body in the ancestral village is fruitless. The powerful last scene, the end of the journey, takes place in an empty space under the road sign announcing the entrance to the village. A lake is all that is left of the destroyed village.[11] The casket is seen floating on the lake that replaced the village, as the young Turk watches the sun set. This movie, shown at the beginning of our program, provoked the young woman's anger. A Sunni Turkish professor was supposed to introduce the movie, but at the

Figure 12. Group work, Bosnia, 2006. Photo by David W. Montgomery.

last moment he could not appear. An Israeli film critic, a speaker at the school, was asked to step in and present the movie as well as organize the discussion following the screening. The young Sunni Turkish woman erupted in anger, accusing the organizers of presenting a highly negative portrait of her country, and accusing the Israeli speaker and an American Jewish organizer of political biases. She also claimed that by showing the difficulties of the Turkish state, they were avoiding the Israeli–Palestinian conflict. The Jewish organizer explained that two years earlier, in 2005, the school had been held in Israel and had focused on that conflict then. The subject of the current program in Turkey was the legacy of Ottoman rule there with regard to ethnic relations in contemporary Turkey, and the Israeli–Palestinian conflict was, therefore, completely off topic. The conflict between Kurds and Turks was at the core of this year's theme, the legacy of the Ottoman Empire. As the organizer finished talking, a quiet young Kurdish woman raised her voice and explained that the movie actually depicted the plight of her people in Turkey very effectively. As a small child, she had seen her father mistreated as he was taken to jail. This intervention made a huge impression on all the participants and on the Sunni Turkish woman in

A Community of Pedagogy

Figure 13. Group work, Uganda, 2012. Photo by David W. Montgomery.

particular. By the end of the program her attitudes had changed palpably. She became very friendly with both the Jewish organizers and the young Kurdish woman. The program ended with the young Kurdish woman's family inviting the organizers and the Sunni Turkish woman and her family to eat in their house. Everyone sat on the floor eating traditional food,

Figure 14. Group work, Indonesia, 2012. Photo by David W. Montgomery.

Figure 15. Group work, England, 2009. Photo by David W. Montgomery.

A Community of Pedagogy

Figure 16. Group work, Israel, 2010. These images depict various instances of group work in CEDAR programs.

listening to the two families take small steps of recognition toward each other's past.

+ + + +

At the same school in 2007 there were Muslim fellows from Bosnia, Jordan, Albania, Pakistan, Germany, Turkey (Sunni, Kurd, and Alevi), and the United States. From the outset one could sense an underlying current of frustration among the different Muslim participants. The organizers slowly came to recognize that not all was well within that small subgroup. We heard complaints and reports that one person whom the subgroup had appointed as prayer leader was, subsequently, not followed in prayer by the group members. Others reported that they were not fully accepted in this small group of Muslims. They had different assumptions about what practices make for "a real Muslim." They differed on how Muslims should behave in private and public—for example, some felt that even a small sip of arak, tasted out of curiosity, rendered the person unfit to be a prayer leader. Some of the Muslims in the group refused to eat the food served by the Alevi community we visited on the outskirts of Istanbul. The Alevi are part of Shi'a

Islam and, with a population of 10 million, make up about 15 percent of the Turkish population. These difficulties and frustrations were not voiced publicly, but they surfaced in small groups and private discussions. At the end of the program, however, one Muslim fellow who had been hurt by his coreligionists made his feelings very clear. Fellows had decided to use one of the last hours of programing to express something about their experience at the school, taking turns of two minutes each. This fellow chose to remain silent and asked all participants to sit with him in silence for his two-minute turn. He symbolically and powerfully expressed his feelings of hurt at having been silenced and having his Muslim identity erased. He also wrote of his coreligionists' unwillingness to accept him:

> I came with some preconceived notions of the different groups of people and faith. It was learning for me to find out that the groups that I thought I would have no problems joining were the ones that were the hardest to be part of; I was just not accepted. The ones I did not want to join were the ones that were welcoming. Borders are very difficult to pass or break, [sic] it means that you absolutely have to accept, be accepted.[12]

+ + + +

These two examples highlight taken-for-granted assumptions about communities of belonging and the nature of each one's "other," as well as the ways in which these are challenged through the CEDAR experience. Our methodology seeks to uncover these assumptions as they are renegotiated in the group. The Sunni Turk, for example, considered the choice of movie a conscious effort to depict her country in bleak colors by people she perceived as outside her moral community. She interpreted the scheduling of the movie as a political threat from a group that she labeled the "Zionist enemy" because of their common identity as Jews or Israelis. This focus on the "enemy" allowed her to gloss over her own country's history of intragroup conflicts as borders were redesigned after the fall of the Ottoman Empire. When the young Kurdish fellow shared her own citizenship and history with her, the Sunni Turk had to listen. Everyone sat enthralled by the declarations of both women. The Turkish woman clearly saw, as she faced the young Kurd, that the screening of the movie was not a "Zionist" challenge but rather the challenge of her own history. She learned to see her own country's

Figure 17. A prayer ritual at an Alevi center in Turkey. Photo by David W. Montgomery, 2007.

history through the eyes of a fellow citizen who is also a Kurd. She reassessed her perceptions of Jews as well, finding them more complex than she had envisioned, and realized that the movie depicting her own country's history of conflict could not be equated with Israeli propaganda. In the group and during ensuing discussions and experiences, she came to understand her own assumptions about Israelis, Jews, and Kurds.

On the other end, the Kurd's resentment against the Turk softened as she learned to identify her own taken-for-granted assumptions. When she encountered the Alevi community, another minority group, during the program, she, along with other Sunni Muslims, had refused to eat the food served by that community. She felt sick to her stomach, but her sickness abruptly ceased as we left the community. At the end of the program, she expressed her awareness that she had treated the Alevi minority community as the Turks had treated her own Kurdish community—namely, as impure and not worth socializing with. She also evolved from seeing herself as a victim of the Turkish government's brutality to perceiving herself as someone who had inflicted her prejudices on another minority. This shift from being a victim to recognizing herself as one who had created victimhood in others was a powerful learning experience, allowing for space and recognition of the Turkish viewpoint that in turn helped her create space for a relationship with the young Turkish woman.

Another Alevi Turk, a fellow in the group who sat quietly though all this drama, also expressed an understanding of the personal aspects of Sunni prejudices against his community at the end of the program. His wife's Sunni family and prejudices toward the Alevi had created feelings of hurt for all. He understood the power of taken-for-granted assumptions and could see for the first time how, from the point of view of his wife's family, her marriage to an Alevi like him had hurt her parents. The program made him understand, if not accept, the personal grief his wife's Sunni family experienced and the power of taken-for-granted assumptions. For him, the program ended with an emotional phone call to his wife. For the other two women experiencing their differences in the program, it ended with the traditional Mediterranean practice of a shared meal mentioned earlier. Wasserfall could not but see this meal as a stand-in for the traditional *sulha*, the coming together of different offended parties after a dispute.

For the Muslim who had not been accepted as he expected into the small subgroup of Muslims, the program ended with his growing awareness of his own assumptions about the boundaries of his community of belonging. These boundaries had shifted ever so slightly for the two weeks of the program as, to his surprise, he found himself welcomed within the Jewish and Christian subgroups but not among his coreligionists. It made him grasp his own "othering" of other religious communities to which he did not belong. He had assumed that as a Muslim he would be unwelcome among non-Muslims of his native land, and that was not the case. This was an unforeseen turn of events and a major learning moment.

Reflecting together on our collective religious and other boundaries, we were surprised to feel connected to people whom "in real life" we might see as enemies or just aliens. Encountering others with whom we would never associate outside the group is powerful; we expand the boundaries of our community. Being asked to experience and reflect with them is an opportunity to face difficult aspects of our own group belonging.

To reflect on the cultural assumptions we make during our experiential learning, we need to face what is generally left unsaid. As explained in chapter 1, unstated assumptions usually direct precisely where the mind comes to "rest." By bringing assumptions to the awareness of the group, we challenge where our minds rest and expand our vision of whom we define as our other. It is the director or the local host who brings this knowledge to the group, since doing so requires a deep understanding of the situation as well as of the overall goals of the program. For example, in Birmingham in 2008, it was the Sikh organizer who helped the group become aware of what was left unsaid during our visit to the Sikh gurdwara. The group was quite taken by the welcome and the delicious vegetarian meal served. We learned that people from all walks of life and religions are welcome to eat and share in their beautiful space. Service to humanity is worship, and feeding whoever comes to the temple is one of the main activities of the community. The beauty of the space and the inclusive philosophy had our group enthralled by Sikhism. The next day, one of our local hosts, a Sikh herself, explained that although Sikhism is based on service and is welcoming to outsiders, Sikhs exclude their own women. These exclusionary practices regarding the female members of their own community were not presented during the visit. By referring to the unspoken, underlying sexism in her community, she challenged the sense of inclusion that we all felt during our visit to that community. The reflective pedagogy—the incessant reflection on our assumptions about what constitutes self, others, and how realities are created—is what binds participants together. As we face these moments of comprehension, we are obliged, for a moment at least, to reassess our own assumptions about our criteria of belonging.

An excellent example of this is the Jewish prayer service discussed in chapter 2: during the 2007 school, the group spent Shabbat in Bursa but lacked enough male Jews to constitute a prayer quorum, causing the group's Jewish members to consider counting female Jews for their quorum. For the Orthodox man this was not an option. For the one liberal Jewish woman, on the other hand, the idea of not being counted here in Bursa, the first Ottoman capital, a former center of Jewish life where only a tiny Jewish community is left, was unthinkable. She became angry. A discussion followed, in which the Jewish woman became frustrated and refused to allow the ritual to take place if it was not to be considered a public prayer. Moreover, she argued, they were in a group involved in working out how to live together, so how could they, in this subgroup of Jews, erase women and not find a way to welcome Shabbat within their community? A compromise was found: an

Figure 18. A visit to a Sikh gurdwara in England. Photo by David W. Montgomery, 2008.

observant man led the prayers, and the Orthodox man did whatever he had to do. (It was not clear in the end if he indeed responded to the call for prayer which signals that the group praying is considered a quorum.) From the Orthodox man's point of view, the turn of events was a compromise. It had to be explained to the observers that he allowed the other Jews to count him in "their" quorum, which from his point of view was not a quorum. The Jewish woman was satisfied that the group marked the ritual as public, and she was willing to live with the residual ambiguity of the situation.

This conversation was fascinating for the Muslims in attendance. They were impressed that the controversy happened in front of them. The Jews had not kept silent about their differences in front of the Muslim and Christian others. A number of Muslim fellows further revealed that the fact that women in Judaism were so outspoken was news to them. Ironically, earlier that day, a Muslim woman visiting the group was denied entry to the mosque for Juma prayers, because in Bursa women do not pray in the mosque (she prayed outside). The juxtaposition of the Jewish practice, and debate, with the incident at the mosque provided a rich moment for all involved to reflect on their own assumptions about religion, community, gender, and the politics of gender exclusion.

Experiential learning emphasizes the "here and now of concrete experience."[13] As we have seen throughout, this form of learning is very different from academic learning, where referencing past scholarship is a core aspect. Meeting the *context* of our learning is as important as the *content* of our learning. It is during these moments when life interferes that important learning happens. Chapter 1 told the story of Anata in 2005, which became a group exercise in learning about how our assumptions lead us to give or refuse moral credit to certain categories of others. Awareness that our perception of reality is clouded by our assumptions about who does or does not have moral credit grows during these informal aspects of living together. It is then that we are surprised, uncomfortable, and able to renegotiate to whom we give or refuse moral credit, which in turn helps us reflect differently on the situation. The young Turkish woman in the story of the Istanbul school in 2007 described earlier learned to grant moral credit to the Kurdish participant and thus expanded the boundaries of her group of belonging.

It is the doing together, the experiencing together, and the informal parts of the program—yoga, dancing, singing, and all other physical activities linked to our work in the group—that allow us to engage in deep learning and restructure our parsing of reality, at least for these two weeks. But it is not only in the informality of living together that learning happens. The program choreographs daily scheduled opportunities for reflective practices.

SCHEDULED EXPERIENTIAL LEARNING
Facilitation

We envisioned facilitation as one of the program containers that would allow participants to connect general and theoretical cognitive learning to personal stories. Each participant is asked to actively connect her personal story and circumstances with the general theme of the program. It is a space crafted so that each one can integrate private and public forms of knowing. Our practice of facilitation has changed through the years. We moved from whole-group facilitation sessions and processes in Israel and Turkey to a small-group structure in subsequent years. When a facilitator joined the team after Turkey in 2007, the goals of the facilitation shifted from just providing a safe space to processing the experience and helping to integrate the learning.

Figure 19. A group facilitation in Yogyakarta, Indonesia. Photo by David W. Montgomery, 2012.

At the start of the session, the fellows are divided into five or six groups, each of which is designed to maximize diversity. The groups stay together for the length of the program and meet for an hour and a half of highly structured time to address a topic or question posed by the staff. Initially, each person in the group addresses the topic or question for six minutes. During that time, others' questions or responses are not allowed; the speaker has the full attention of the group. That stage generally takes about thirty minutes. The second round, in which each person speaks for three minutes, allows the speaker to share thoughts and feelings evoked by listening to others present their stories. The last part of the session is a fifteen-minute general and free discussion. Five or six such meetings are scheduled, one every two days of programming.

Over time, as we developed the facilitation container, staff removed themselves from these sessions. Staff members design the facilitation questions at staff meetings. Good questions are difficult to formulate, because they need to allow for deep reflection and the integration of the personal and the public. Staff also try to create synergy between these sessions and the

A Community of Pedagogy

general learning and to develop questions that follow a trajectory from the very general (who each participant considers her trust communities and communities of belonging) to the more detailed questions about belonging. Participants are asked about situations in which they feel like outsiders in their group of belonging, and also about experiences of conflict between different groups of belonging. The timing of these different questions parallels the experience in the group; for example, questions about situations of conflict are asked around the beginning of the second week of programming, which is the point in the group trajectory at which feelings of discomfort surface. The facilitation program ends by focusing on separation from the group and reentering the home setting.

Practicum/Site Visits

We have experimented with many forms of experiential learning during our fourteen years of programming. Each site visit and activity is designed to maximize fulfillment of the program's goals for meeting in groups and reflecting on living together differently. We do not use site visits as show-and-tell opportunities, but rather to allow participants to reflect on the experience—sometimes with the locals and sometimes as a group after visiting. We are not tourists, even when we visit beautiful tourist spots, such as Bali in Indonesia. (There, for example, we reflected on the outcome of tourism for the locals and for ourselves.) We make a point of visiting places of worship when they are in use, so that our fellows from the same community can participate in the ritual if they so choose.

By creating opportunities for our group members to participate in the ritual, we also give others in the group the opportunity to observe fellow participants in their religious environment. This in itself is a strong learning experience. Seeing your friend, the person with whom you have shared meals, gone shopping, and told your story, stand up and take the Eucharist or become a prayer leader in a mosque or church can be surprising, to say the least. You suddenly perceive him in a different light, and the closeness you experienced in the daily activities might be either suspended or reinforced. You understand what it means to perceive your friends from the group as members of their different faith communities. The program gives all of us opportunities to cross and recross boundaries of our different communities

Figure 20. A practicum visit to the ruins in Nicaea, Turkey, site of the first ecumenical council of the church. Photo by David W. Montgomery, 2007.

of faith. Part of our pedagogy is creating these opportunities and becoming aware of crossing these boundaries. Ultimately, you learn from the slow process described in chapter 2 that sharing a narrative with people is possible without forgoing your own community of belonging.

SCHOOL RULES

The two rules briefly discussed in chapter 1, which are our only two rules of engagement, allow us to create a safe environment. As we start the program, the director introduces these two rules, the necessity for which emerged during the first summer school, in Mostar, Bosnia and Herzegovina, in 2003. The rules were established following an evening program on the subject of women and purity (and rituals of purity). The program was titled "Women and Water" after a book by Wasserfall on Jewish rituals of bodily purity, and it involved a panel of speakers: Wasserfall, a Muslim woman, and a Christian man. The event, which took place at the civic center in Mostar, was scheduled, as usual, rather late in the evening, after a tightly packed day of activities. Mostar in 2003 was still very much a ruined city, not yet rebuilt and with reminders of the war still evident. As the evening progressed, it became clear that a number of men in the audience were having difficulty with the theme of the panel, especially the discussion and description of intimate details of women's anatomy. As the evening wore on, a number of men left, including some summer school fellows and staff. All were Muslims. By the end of the evening, few Muslim males were left in the audience, and their departure had a visible effect on everyone in the room.

Later, some of the school fellows and staff who had left claimed that they had been tired; one had indeed traveled to Sarajevo and back that same day to fetch his luggage, which had been lost; others arrived late owing to prayers, and left, so they claimed, for the same reason. Be that as it may, there was a good deal of anger at the departure of so many Muslim men from the discussion, and it was decided to discuss it openly the following day. The next morning, however, word of what had happened spread rapidly and was taken up by some colleagues from an Italian university who were joining us. One of these colleagues, a well-known Italian feminist scholar, was indignant about what had happened (she had not been at the event itself but had been informed of it by a student of hers who had been present) and called the men who had left "Nazis" more than once. To many, this seemed too much. To be sure, being disrespectful of one's female colleagues was unacceptable behavior, and leaving en masse in the midst of a discussion of gender-related issues was also improper behavior, but not at all to be compared to Nazism. The hyperbole was shameful and, of course, dangerous. Whatever else it did, it absolutized differences and boundaries: if a person did not share one's ideas of gender equality and women's status in all matters, then he was a Nazi. In fact, if anything was an example of a totalization of difference, an inability to exist in a complex and multidimensional reality in which one could disagree with certain things but not with others, this was it. Calling these men Nazis and thus denying their humanity, simply because hearing women discuss intimate female matters made them uncomfortable, was surely going too far.

In any case, it was in the discussion following that evening that the group accepted the principle that no one has a monopoly on suffering and, therefore, no one group can claim moral superiority or privileged access to a moral good, a claim that so often goes with such an incident. Over the course of the next two summer schools, this principle and its elaboration from principle to practice—that is, to the two rules stating that we must conduct ourselves *as if* we do not have a monopoly on suffering, and we must be present at all events—became part of the opening clarification of ground rules at every school.

Because we have always brought together highly diverse groups of fellows—Bosnians, Serbs, and Croatians; Albanians and Kosovars; Tajiks and Pakistanis; Turks, Israelis, Jews, and Palestinians; Catholics, Protestants, and followers from the Eastern Church; men and women—it has been essential to define the shared space of our interaction as a space where no one group can make claims to any sort of special status. Clearly, meeting in what are often highly contested spaces, such as Jerusalem and Mostar—or even Roxbury in Boston—sometimes makes it difficult to abide by this rule, but it has generally carried the day as a working principle for group cohesion.

Every one of us carries a history of our people's suffering and perceives our people's suffering as the worst in history. Learning that everyone feels like that is a difficult and slow process. CEDAR programs do not ask people to change their feelings, but ask them to behave for these two weeks *as if* they did not hold this claim as truth.[14] Even if we believe intellectually that our suffering does not entitle us to a moral claim on others, in practice some of our buttons will inevitably be pushed. As mentioned in previous chapters, this feeling exists for all of us in different forms. Facing it and reflecting with a group of others can help us learn the basic skills of living together with difference. The first rule is not to arrive at a situation in which you feel that your interlocutor owes you for the past suffering of your group of belonging. People in the groups come from parts of the world ridden by conflicts, whose histories are full of communal trauma. In this group, we are asked not to front our suffering and expect that others owe us because of our history. When somebody owes you because of your suffering, there is no space to encounter her. It is only when we reign in our feelings and allow different narratives to surface that we can meet our others. We learn quickly that we all have the same attitude, and that to learn to live together differently we need—at least for these two weeks—to hold these strong feelings in abeyance and allow for the magic of the encounter to unfold.

The second rule of the program is that one cannot choose à la carte from a menu of activities but needs to attend all of them. One fellow coined the phrase the "gift of your presence" to describe the product of this rule. Being present with and to your fellows is a gift she thought allows you to experience difference in action. To create a community, one must be part of it; you need to show up. Throughout the program, we call for all to be present during all activities. People learn quickly that the benefit of being present is feeling connected to and part of the group. As one fellow reported, it came as a great surprise to discover that by being a full, active, and present member, he also learned to become a listener. The art of listening deeply to others was a major and difficult skill for him to learn. In facilitations and other activities throughout the two weeks of the program, we create situations in which listening is at times more important than speaking. These two rules help us learn to bracket out some of our assumptions; they provide a mental space in which we can hold on to our own sacred beliefs while still giving space to others.[15]

As described throughout this book, feelings of discomfort arise in many situations. The question of the impact of emotion on our reflective patterns is beyond the scope of this chapter, but discomfort is a strong emotion that we have seen surface again and again in the programs, as fellows start reflecting with others on meeting locals, encountering new situations, and the meaning of fellow participants' behavior. In Indonesia in 2012, for example, many of the program activities caused unease. Encountering the issue of Indonesians' silence and their reluctance to speak out in the program created discomfort for our very verbal Westerners. Visiting the *pesantren waria*, the transgendered Muslim religious center, was a difficult experience for people of various religions from both the East and the West. Experiencing the blending of features of Javanese culture with different Christian churches was hard for some Christians. For some secular academics, it was the school itself, which is not a regular academic environment (but does engage academic issues), that created feelings of unease. All of these instances, as well as many others mentioned in previous chapters, are examples of crossing or blurring boundaries or categories of belonging. Our reactions to this blurring of boundaries seem to be very important as we negotiate space with others, and these reactions can be threatening as well. Experiencing a blurring of boundaries in fact exposes us to different group narratives that do not always fit nicely with our own and, therefore, trigger feelings of disquiet. Some Christians questioned how Javanese church members can be Christians when they

Figure 21. The tabernacle at a Catholic church in Java, Indonesia. Photo by David W. Montgomery, 2012.

worship Jesus in a Hindu temple. Many in the group questioned how Muslims who call themselves religious can claim to be women when they have the genitals of men. Some of the academics started asking how this "school" can be a respected academic program when participants are asked to reflect on their feelings.

As we reflect in the group on such examples of discomfort that arise, as we go through the experience, we learn about ourselves as well. We learn the slow process of what we, the authors, have called "decentering." The collective and its narratives do not take precedence in our group. One Croatian fellow reported her experience in facing the atrocities carried out by her own people in Stolac, Bosnia: "The moment when we all stood in front of the bone hospital [where these atrocities had been committed] was different for me than anything I wrote about before because it went beyond the cognitive level of understanding. It was a moment of 'othering' my own group—when my own group became the Other to me."[16]

By combining the three modes of learning—cognitive, experiential, and affective—without privileging any one of them, the school provides the context in which change can arise. Like this fellow, we may all suddenly grasp the opportunity to see our own group differently. This opportunity will change the way we relate to our own boundaries of belonging. As B. K. S Iyengar, one of the most influential fathers of modern yoga, claims, "self-knowledge" is not always comfortable. For him discomfort is a precursor of change.[17]

This nexus of discomfort-learning-change has recently become a source of contention on American college campuses, because some student organizations have demanded that faculty and university administration members post "trigger warnings" on curricular material that may upset and discomfit certain students, such as Shakespeare's *The Merchant of Venice* and Virginia Woolf's *Mrs. Dalloway*. Whether we can really grow and learn without passing through a stage of discomfort is, however, debatable. Greg Lukianoff, president of the Foundation for Individual Rights in Education, has pointed out that the move to post such warnings in college syllabi "is sort of an inevitable movement towards people increasingly expecting physical comfort and intellectual comfort in their lives." He goes on to note, "It is only going to get harder to teach people that there is a real important and serious value to being offended. Part of that is talking about deadly serious and uncomfortable subjects."[18]

Learning from discomfort implies learning to live with the ambiguity of the world.[19] The Croatian fellow quoted earlier did not reject her own group of belonging, but she did come to see the conflict and relations between Croats and Bosnians in a far more complex and morally challenging manner than before. Discomfort allowed her the necessary space to grasp a new alien narrative and perhaps integrate parts of it into her own.

CEDAR programs present us with learning tools that enable us to see others as well as ourselves differently. Only after experiencing these different narratives through reflective pedagogy can we integrate the experience into new collective "narratives." When we use what is at hand to allow our pedagogy of community to unfold, we discover that feelings of discomfort are powerful teachers.

THE LIMITS OF OUR APPROACH

During our stay in Bosnia in 2006, we spent about a week in Stolac, a small town in Herzegovina. Many Muslim refugees from the 1992–1995 war had

Figure 22. Rebuilding sites destroyed during the Bosnian War in Stolac. Photo by David W. Montgomery, 2006.

begun the difficult task of rebuilding their houses, mosques, and neighborhoods that were destroyed in the war. Their existence in the town remained tenuous. Stolac in 2006 was still very much a divided city, where children from the different communities attended the same school at different times, and Muslims and Croats patronized different coffeehouses. UN troops were still posted in that location and maintained a difficult balance. Croatian and Muslim citizens lived in a de facto apartheid. As a group, we encountered hostility from the Croats because we were housed with Muslim families, our local hosts being one of the families who had spearheaded the return of the Muslim population to their ancestral home. In 2006, the group witnessed acts of aggression by the Croats toward their Muslim neighbors. Urine was voided on the wall of a rebuilt Muslim house, and accelerating cars forced a group of fellows off the road. We never actually met the Croatian population, and our local hosts offered no explanation; they assumed that all understood the Croatian aggression. Our group was composed of people of different religions and included some Croatian-born Americans. Participants asked why it was not possible to encounter the Croatian viewpoint.

A Community of Pedagogy

We were hosted by Muslim families and ate in Muslim restaurants. One free evening, a small group of fellows decided to cross over and eat at one of the Croatian restaurants. We had a pleasant encounter with the owners, who were friendly to the disparate group, and we brought back our story of the encounter to the full group. Our Bosnian organizers could not fathom why some of the fellows would want to meet the Croatian citizens of Stolac, whom they considered the aggressors and who by all accounts had destroyed the Muslim houses. This was quite a difficult moment for the whole group, as well as for our local organizer, who felt that the group was insensitive to the atrocities committed by some Croatian citizens.

Only after the group had moved on to Boston was it even possible for some reflection and self-reflection by group members on the events of Stolac. We realized then that, for the Muslims of Bosnia, the ground of Stolac had in some sense been hallowed by the deaths of their compatriots. In such a space, charged with such meanings, reflective pedagogy was not appropriate (probably not even possible). As one lecturer remarked, it would be akin to discussing the German narrative of World War II in the middle of Yad Vashem (the Israeli memorial to the Holocaust) or Auschwitz.

On sacred ground, when facing memories of the dead, there is simply no place for deconstruction or narratives of the other. In places like Yad Vashem, Stolac, or the Rwandan churches, where hundreds and thousands were murdered, one cannot present or ask for the narrative of the perpetrators. In spaces that are felt to be hallowed ground, one cannot hold one's suffering in abeyance; suffering is too raw and present. Reflective pedagogy is thus limited by geographical and temporal proximity to actual suffering. The process of meeting your others cannot be done in a graveyard.

GOING HOME

At the end of a program, we feel part of a community of pedagogy with a diverse group. We have learned to engage with others, but we are also happy to be returning home to a familiar situation. Experiencing the two-week program is an exercise in building a new culture. Coming home means reintegrating ourselves, and integrating this new culture, into our existing communities of belonging.

Home implies, if we are lucky, safety and comfort. We crave it; and because we need to rely on our taken-for-granted assumptions to get on with our lives, reassessing everything all the time is not feasible. We could not live without knowing that when we put the key in our door, the same old smells and the same old furniture await us. We need to know that our familiar beds are where we left them in the morning and that our families will embrace us when we return. We need to know that our communities are still there, warts and all. Familiarity is what home means, and it is comforting to let down our hair and relax. Meeting our boundaries allows us to expand our notions of self and otherness. It is also essential to feel connected to our own familiar core. We need to balance memories and familiar assumptions with discomfort and with creativity. We need to be comfortable and set in our ways, but we also need to learn that these very set ways bring unexpected baggage. As we learn to see the porousness of our boundaries, our return home reaffirms these essential boundaries with a different awareness that may change the way we engage with our neighbors.

There is thus great hope in reflective practice. We feel hope when we feel content, because we did what needed to be done. Even though the results may not be those we wanted, we do feel contentment in a deep sense. CEDAR's reflective pedagogy is a step on that path. It makes sense. "Hope is definitely not the same as optimism. It is not the conviction that something will turn out well, but the certainty that something makes sense regardless of how it turns out."[20] Working within the framework of a reflective practice has helped CEDAR create a structure within which fellows are able to encounter, even if only for these two weeks, the power of facing down their assumptions and reshaping their vision of themselves and their others. The experience offers great promise that something can shift in the ways in which each of us interacts with others.

CHAPTER FOUR

Ethnographies of Difference

For the first time as a Christian, I felt like a minority. This experience
opened my eyes to how other people who do not belong to my
community of belonging feel in my community of belonging. Since then,
where possible, I am conscious of the presence of other people in my
community of belonging.

Difference is a nuance central to experience. Visiting an unknown country
brings exhilaration, at least when you can control the terms of your experience of difference. In previous chapters we explored the pedagogy and
structures that CEDAR has created to encounter and face difference. Here we
touch upon some of what lies behind the experience of difference in the
program.

Being in an unknown country, it turns out, is but a minor aspect of the
differences fellows encounter. The context of the country and the yearly
topic are important only as a field upon which we can engage with difference. The yearly group itself becomes a laboratory. As we meet our fellows,
we encounter the boundaries that divide "us" from "them." When the synergy of the program's components is just right, moments of deep understanding happen when least expected. The group becomes the tool with
which we (re)assess our reactions to what we bring to the experiences we
make with others. As we see the impact of our taken-for-granted assumptions on our surroundings in real time, these moments are filled with possibilities for exploring our group's boundaries. We start by seeing each other
as unknown, foreign, maybe even exotic. And as we start creating connections with each other and become "the group," a "familiar" environment is
constructed. But as the program unfolds, we learn more about one another

in the new situations we encounter, and the familiar again becomes alien. Meeting our fellows in different situations, we are confronted not only by what separates us, or what unites us, but also by some of the basic assumptions held by our own groups of belonging. We are on the way to creating ethnographies of ourselves in difference, to seeing how it is that we actually encounter difference.

THE IMPACT OF POVERTY: ROMA IN BULGARIA

"Do not take any valuables. Make sure you wear closed-toe shoes. Have a policeman guard the bus, or the gasoline will be stolen." These were instructions given to our group by a visiting Bulgarian lecturer on the morning of our visit to Stolipinovo, a district in the city of Plovdiv, Bulgaria, inhabited by Roma. We had also been instructed by a visiting anthropologist to try to engage in acts of connection with the local population, such as buying cigarettes, drinks, or other small items in neighborhood shops. Roma, who identify as having Turkish ancestry, constitute the majority of Stolipinovo's inhabitants. With twenty thousand people (some estimate the population at about thirty-five thousand), the neighborhood is one of the most populous districts in Plovdiv.[1] When we arrived, children were playing in the dust; men bustled in small groups; and women washed clothes in front of their apartment buildings, many of whose stairwells had been burned out. As we walked through the neighborhood, we found ourselves in an area across from the rundown apartments, where Roma have built illegal housing. We walked on mounds of detritus as women and children from the neighborhood came to tell us their stories. They spoke about not having electricity, water, and other basic needs. As we took in their extreme living conditions, they described unemployment, hunger, insufficient medical care, and segregated schools. They spoke about being chronically deprived and suffering from poor health. Dogs wandered through the debris, and we were told that there is no working sewage system for the district and that electricity is sporadic.[2] The shock of seeing the neighborhood was plainly visible on many of our fellows' faces. We regrouped before lunch, feeling a need to discuss in smaller groups what we had just experienced.

A Palestinian Israeli recalled a different kind of poverty that she encountered at home, and wondered about the responsibility of the Plovdiv munici-

pality. A Ugandan fellow described the situation of the Roma as "social differentiation," acknowledging that class differences are evident all over the
world. He also noted that the children of the Roma did not look malnourished
but acknowledged that in his country, the situation of the poor is not as tragic
as that of the Roma in Stolipinovo. A fellow from Indonesia mused about the
responsibility of the state and commented that the poor in his country do not
reach this level of deprivation. Another Indonesian fellow spoke about the
shame of a society that parks the poor in ghettos and does not integrate them
into neighborhoods. Others questioned the reality of poverty among the
Roma. Two women, one from the Balkans and the other from an African
country, spoke of the special moments they had experienced meeting the
Roma. Taking pictures together and kissing the children or speaking with the
inhabitants was an exceptional experience, they volunteered.

The room was filled with the unease of having to deal with confusing
feelings. A fellow from the First Nations of Canada expressed her deep feelings of conflict about the visit. Many sections of her community resemble
what the group saw in Stolipinovo, she said. She compared our visit to other
visits that she had experienced while living on a reserve (what in the United
States is called a reservation). She remembered being on the "other side," on
the Roma side, when well-wishing strangers came to watch some of her
people's ceremonies. She felt torn about being part of a group that looked
upon the Roma as strangers. Another fellow, a Frenchwoman, questioned
the legitimacy of our presence there and asked if the Roma we met knew
who we were. Did we make an effort to explain? The thoughts expressed by
these two women caused group members to reflect on their own reactions
and consider whether they were rooted in prejudice. Were they based on
certain assumptions about people living in extreme poverty? Did we have to
make an effort to enter another's view of the world to understand the experience? Was the shock and dismay expressed as a way to estrange us from the
Roma further? Were people distancing themselves from the Roma to distance themselves from some of the extreme living conditions of the poor in
their own countries? Was it a way to push the Roma and the poor outside the
boundaries of human community?

The consensus in the group before the two women spoke had been that the
level of poverty in the participants' respective home countries was not as

problematic at that faced by the Roma in Stolipinovo. They had looked to blame the Bulgarian government and local racism. The native Canadian and member of ATD Quart Monde felt a deep sense of identification with the Roma and guided participants in the discussion to view them as just one example of a distressed population.[3] This move not to erase the poor, and not to blame the situation merely on unfortunate decisions by the Bulgarian government, made the group uneasy, however. As soon as this was expressed, the lens of group reflection returned to the group itself. What is the legitimate attitude when we meet extreme poverty? How do we confront the outsider-insider divide when poverty is the topic? How do we face poverty in our own countries?

"There is poverty everywhere," commented one fellow, who asked, "How then am I supposed to react?" The unease of the group was palpable as we faced the fact that most of us never really deal with poverty in our home countries. We learned in the discussion that continued among the group that poverty may indeed be the ultimate form of difference, one that most of us never really take into account. Poverty is a boundary that is troubling for most of us to encounter. The intervention of the two women made us reflect on our own behaviors at home. It brought up the issue of poverty as an uncomfortable boundary.

THE LEGACY OF SPIRITS: TRADITIONAL HEALERS IN UGANDA

The smoke billowed, the drums beat, and we all stood mesmerized by the agility of the possessed man who danced through a burning fire. His body glistened from the heat as he reached out for some money and reduced it to ashes with a flourish. Not minding the heat on the soles of his feet, he reached his arms to the sky as he danced to the sounds of the drumming. Every eye was on him. Many had stood by when an older woman healer had shaken and spoken words of the spirit that possessed her. This man's dancing, on the other hand, beckoned to the onlookers. As he spoke the words of the spirit that possessed him, he spread ashes on the inner wrist of each person who came forward. A sea of different-colored arms spread around him, seeking to receive some of the good fortune embedded in the ashes.

Our group of thirty people had started from Kampala, Uganda, on a long day of visits to the bush.[4] Our first stop was the encampment of Prometra's traditional healers.[5] The site is well marked from the main road and consists of a large multipurpose building at the end of a dirt road, along with a few small houses scattered at the edge of the forest. Many come from Kampala and elsewhere for treatment. Students from the Uganda Martyrs University come regularly as part of their introductory class in psychology and healing. The main healer and a founder of Prometra Uganda, Yahaya Sekagaya, a former dentist in his early forties, first explained the mission and vision of the school for healing. He then introduced the symbol of African traditional healing, a pot with many holes. In African tradition, the pot holds water and the holes in a pot represent the issues with which the community and the individuals have to deal. The main role of traditional medicine, in his view, is to help fix those holes so that the community can be whole again.

After our visit to the main building, Sekagaya led us to the forest. After some walking, we stepped into a clearing. We were asked to remove our shoes, because we were entering a sacred space, one filled with spirits. We were told that healers are a conduit to the spirit world; that they provide a bridge to spirit healing; and that as spirits possess the healers, the healers may speak in languages previously unknown to them. The ground in the clearing was covered with tarps, and a canopy of trees swayed overhead, sheltering a small group of local healers from the midday sun. About ten locals sat on the tarps in a loose circle. As they saw us file in into the clearing, they set their drumming to a fast pace. The mood was joyous and welcoming. Our host, Sekagaya, sat in the middle of the circle, while our group stood around and watched.

The ceremony started. One by one, local traditional healers stood up from the circle and became possessed; some shook, some danced, others just stood and started speaking to different members of our group who came forward. As the beat accelerated, spirits of their ancestors descended upon the healers. Before our very eyes, the traditional healers became mediums though which healing flew to those in need. One person was told that his journey to learn about himself had brought him to Africa; another was told that her spirit was "possessed," which was translated by Sekagaya as meaning "conflicted" in Western terms. Another person was told that he needed to settle a rivalry at home. This man had shown skepticism beforehand and was shaken by the instruction. Most of our group, though uninvolved, nevertheless stood

Figure 23. A spirit possession in the bush in Uganda. Photo by David W. Montgomery, 2012.

mesmerized by the dance, the drums, and the fire. A few skeptics held back and hovered at the edge of the circle.

The majority of our group were African Christians, for whom this healing ceremony triggered deep dissonance and questioning of their roots and beliefs. A day earlier we had listened to an African anthropologist explain the place of traditional healing in African religions. Our speaker had talked forcefully about what he called an abuse of these religions. He contended that the healing scene we would be witnessing was not authentic. African healers of past generations had not abused the practice for their own publicity. The legitimacy, legacy, and abuse of African religions had been debated in the group. Some wanted to renew the bonds with traditional healers, while others felt it threatened their Christianity. The question of how modern Africans were to balance these seemingly opposite worldviews was on everyone's mind as we entered the healing ground. As we left, participants debated the place and legacy of spirit healing in Uganda.

On the bus back from Prometra, people sang religious Christian songs, such as "How Great Thou Art." One of our fellows, a cleric, whose voice had

Ethnographies of Difference

resonated in all our group's bus rides, prayed with intensity to the "Lord Jesus for forgiveness for having gone to where we went." This prayer was remarkable in many ways. "Gone to where we went" might be interpreted as meaning the physical encounter with the traditional healers, but the deeper meaning might be that some of us, by participating in the ceremony, had encountered "spirits" and "gone" to a place where Christians, in her mind, are not supposed to step.

THE PHYSICALITY OF CULTURAL RESPONSES: TRANSGENDERED MUSLIMS IN INDONESIA

A handful of days into the program in Indonesia, as we continued to learn about the diversity of the country, a certain level of comfort was emerging in the group. We had already visited a few *pesantrens* (Indonesian Islamic boarding schools) and thus had a rudimentary knowledge of the workings of Islamic schools in Java. We had even visited a church and mosque that share the same address, so we also had a basic understanding of religious cohabitation, collaboration, and acceptance. However, arriving at the *pesantren waria*, located in a small house in a crowded tiny alley, was something different. The entrance to the pesantren through a small door leads to a large main room with space for up to twenty people to socialize or sit on the floor and study. The inner house is composed of two other smallish rooms, a kitchen, and a small courtyard.

When we stepped out of the bus on a hot July afternoon, we were met by music and by five warias in full regalia. They were heavily made up, wearing mostly colorful female Indonesian dress. The small alley had been transformed into an outside sitting room, with a canopy spread across to shelter the group from the sweltering sun. A handful of young boys and men sat at the entrance to the alley and welcomed us by playing Indonesian traditional music. We listened to the recitation of Qur'anic verses by a Muslim waria, viewed a Hindu dance by a Christian waria dressed in traditional Hindu dancing garb, and then met in small groups with the different warias. In each group, an Indonesian staff member served as a translator, since the warias did not speak English. The waria in our small group was dressed in a long, flowing dark dress and a headscarf, was in her fifties, and had a well-defined philosophy of life. She explained that the soul of a human being is

Figure 24. A Qur'an recitation at the *pesantren waria* in Indonesian. Photo by
David W. Montgomery, 2012.

not gendered, and that God loves the warias' souls and not their bodies (or
the bodies of any others). She felt she was a woman trapped in a male body.
She expressed her luck to be able to live as a woman and was beaming as she
explained that she was married to a "manly man." She was very proud of her
husband.

As the fellows listened to the woman, they expressed definite uneasiness
as well as real interest in all that she said. Encouraged by the warias, they
asked questions, trying to understand who these people were. Nevertheless,
the shock of meeting the warias was plain to see on some fellows' faces. A
Muslim scholar in our group commented that the Qur'anic recitation we just
had heard was very traditional. He was impressed by the knowledge of the
woman who had chanted it. Our host was pleased by this recognition of the
waria's religious skills, because these transgender women view themselves
as devout Muslims. There was lots of nervous laughter among the group.
Some people shifted on their chairs; and although they tried to repress it,
their unease was apparent as they looked down to avoid looking straight into

the warias' faces. Some fellows, on the other hand, embraced the waria and seemed to be happy and enjoying the singing and dancing.

Waria (derived from the Indonesian words *wanita,* meaning "woman," and *pria,* meaning "man") is a term in Indonesian culture for a person who is physically male but behaves as a woman; some think of the waria as a third gender.[6] The warias refer to themselves as women and are employed mainly in beauty salons, in nongovernmental organizations, or as sex workers; few other employment options are available to them. The community around the pesantren has been largely supportive of the group, because it sees that their activities are moving in a "positive" direction, meaning that people come there to pray and learn about Islam, not to solicit or push a waria agenda.

Each year before Ramadan, the warias visit a public grave from the 2006 earthquake in which fifteen warias rest. They do this because no one else will pray for them. It was in response to their desire to pray together and visit the waria graves that the founder of the pesantren waria found a religious leader willing to guide the waria community. Since the pesantren opened in 2008, the warias have learned how to recite the Qur'an and do daily prayers, and they study together on Mondays and Thursdays. The group did have LGBT members; but as media attention grew, the lesbians and gays left. Most of the women we met were proudly married "to manly men."

The founder of the pesantren made clear that the nature of the group is to support one another in living a waria and Islamic life, but the school readily accepts any kind of religiosity and has Hindu waria members as well. When the warias come to the pesantren, they come to learn like any other student at any other pesantren; and if they behave in a way unbefitting a religious student, they are either asked to stop or requested to leave. Warias are human beings and have the same rights as others, she says, and they also have faith. They view their gendered way of seeing the world as given by God, and thus, when warias worship God, it is up to God to accept their prayers or not.

But of course it is precisely the issue of acceptance that is the source of discomfort in relation to the waria. The immediate community may be accepting, but the larger community is certainly not. The warias spoke of being harassed, discriminated against, and beaten. For this reason, some members of our group were moved by the struggles the warias faced and felt themselves in solidarity with them. Others, however, struggled with the idea that one could be a waria and religious, that one could be studying the Qur'an by day and employed as a transgendered sex worker by night.

A week later, in one of our group discussions, fellows started speaking about the genuine discomfort they had experienced during the visit with the warias. Some described having felt that they wanted to take a shower— although they had not acted on their desire, because they believed it would have been shameful to do so. Others expressed disgust but felt ashamed of those feelings. Still others loved the visit and expressed a real connection to the warias. Most, however, felt that the juxtaposition of waria and religion was not credible. They perceived the women as homosexuals and had difficulty accepting the behavior. The visit became one of the most-talked-about events of our fortnight together, and for many it was an encounter they could not ignore.

DIFFERENCES THAT SURROUND:
STORIES OF BOUNDARIES

These three stories describe people encountering their boundaries of acceptability in real time. Encountering the Roma with this particular group highlighted the discomfort of facing extreme poverty. However, because someone from the First Nations was present, fellows rethought the narrative they told themselves. Visiting the traditional healers introduced the discomfort of facing the legacy of past traditions that "gnaw" into the present. In this case the group did not discuss the matter publicly, but at least one person found that the encounter helped her rework her own narrative of belonging. In meeting the warias, fellows encountered a blurring of the markers of gender differentiation.

In each of these examples, members of the group had to make sense of the experience, and the discomfort they felt played an important part in enabling them to revisit their previous narrative. In the process of approaching our boundaries, we become aware of our own taken-for-granted assumptions because others in the group challenge our perceptions. And because for these two weeks there is nowhere to escape to (remember the first rule[7]) this process in turn creates the need to reexamine these assumptions, both alone and with other fellows. As we saw in chapter 3, finding the "sweet spot" where there is some discomfort, but not too much, is key to learning.[8]

Ethnographies of Difference

The instructions we received as we prepared to visit the Roma did not make sense. Rather, they pointed to the fact that some ethnic Bulgarians perceive the Roma as dangerous and outside the boundaries of acceptance. The filth of the streets and amount of detritus was real, but the fear of catching a disease was certainly overblown, as was the fear of being robbed during the visit. The interesting learning point in this story is that most of our fellows separated themselves from the situation of the Roma by explaining, in one way or another, that their home situation was quite different; "their poor" did not live in such abject conditions. Only when the fellow from the First Nations connected herself to the Roma did the discussion start to change. Fellows listened to her because they had formed a relationship with her; so when she related her personal upbringing to the plight of the Roma, she was able to question our behavior and our assumptions. The discussion moved from an assessment of the Roma's situation (which could not be done in the time allocated and in light of the lack of expertise) to an assessment of our reactions. We were able to start asking questions. What did taking pictures of the Roma represent? Do we really know how poor people live their lives? Do we always tend to create strong boundaries when we encounter poverty? The discomfort and the confusion shed light on the ways in which we avoid seeing the poor and, instead, make them invisible.

In our second story, the singing of the cleric created deep conflict for African Christians. Because logistics prevented the visit from being followed by a group discussion, it is difficult to assess the impact on the group as a whole. In individual discussions, some fellows explored the difficult legacy of traditional spirit healing for African Christians. The next day, our only Buddhist fellow asked to lead the group in a meditation on the bus, which made people uncomfortable. They responded to their discomfort by joking and discounting the intent of the meditation. The reactions of the group, coming after the visit to Prometra, led this fellow to an identity crisis. For someone with roots in Africa, coming to Uganda was all about finding family roots. After the incident at Prometra and the fellows' reactions to the Buddhist meditation, however, it became clear that Africa was not home for this fellow; even though her family origins might have been in Uganda, today being a Buddhist with roots in East Africa was pretty much the sum of it.

In our third story, the group discussion and informal discussions led some people to question their reactions to seeing the warias through the prism of the warias' sexuality. Some highly religious fellows expressed dismay about their own reactions, acknowledging their discomfort and questioning their reduction of a person to an act. They did not know how to reconcile their feelings with their different beliefs and emotions. Homosexuality is always a category of behavior that elicits great unease among at least some of the fellows. For a number of years we screened the movie *Trembling before G-d*, which depicts the struggle of gay Orthodox Jews, women and men, to remain within the Orthodox community. The movie, combined with visits to different communities such as the waria, helps fellows find compassion within themselves, be willing to hold contradictory feelings, and refrain from rushing to privilege their own biases at the expense of respecting the other person's being.

The program creates spaces, or "containers," in which reactions to political and social encounters are public and, as described earlier, happen within a group of difference. This approach enables fellows to become their own ethnographers as they explore the social context in which their own beliefs and perceptions play out in the group. Fellows become aware of the categories they use to parse their social worlds. They see these categories for what they are: much-needed, indeed essential, mechanisms that allow smooth social interactions with others in their social world. Like all categories, however, these resonate strongly with the fellows' own communities of belonging. Thus, while they constitute part of an individual's taken-for-granted world, at the same time they are also heavily freighted with untested and unquestioned social and moral assumptions.

Although reassessments of these categories are always difficult, they also allow space to see the world from another's viewpoint. This is the first step in learning to live with difference. It is not just encountering difference that is important; it is also being willing to engage with differences without fearing them, as well as reflecting with others on the impact of difference on "us" and "them."

DIFFERENCES WITHIN

As we have argued, difference is an essential aspect of social life; no matter how much we search to find commonalities and sameness, we will always

Ethnographies of Difference

discover that somehow and somewhere, in an exchange with another, we are different in meaningful ways. This recognition of difference registers our identities as members of a particular group of belonging. It is essential to our social selves. The recognition of difference is political and particular and ecumenical; it is intelligible and confounding. We need to be part of groups; we need belonging; we need boundaries.

Furthermore, boundaries need to be maintained. That does not suggest, however, that people should go about the tasks of boundary maintenance in a clear or rigid way. Rather, there is a great deal of creativity, fluidity, and fungibility in both how boundaries come to be and how they are maintained. What this means is that while societies may set up conditions highlighting certain aspects of boundaries—be they religious, ethnic, regional, racial, or class-based—boundaries ought not necessarily be defined in the ways they have in fact come to be defined. Here one can think of the nation-state as a clear example of seemingly natural identities that are nevertheless historically modern in their construction. Connecting identities to the reification of the physical boundaries of the state is part of the legacy of both the Peace of Westphalia and the French Revolution. But it is only one option for how collectivities could be organized; both local and transnational movements offer competing visions of where boundaries could (or should) be.

As the earlier vignettes described, for many fellows it was the time with the Roma, African healers, or warias that clarified some of their boundaries, sometimes in very real moments of self-discovery. The differences between these groups were not characterized, or even internalized, in the same way by all; but in the experience of difference, the boundaries became real, prompting tangible feelings of comfort and discomfort. It is thus in confronting boundaries that the affective nature of experience can challenge the cognitive rationalization of a purported sameness.

There are various ways of characterizing what it means to think about the nature of experiencing difference. The early stages of encountering difference can be impersonal, focusing on facts and the various contexts of people engaging with others. It is only when one is influenced by the difference that it becomes more personal. For example, a non-Muslim may know something about Ramadan and fasting, but the implications of Ramadan become more real when the non-Muslim tries to go to a halal restaurant for lunch and finds it closed. Such encounters lead to greater awareness of difference and the implications that difference entails. Only through direct experience can we recover the original "innocence of the eye," in John Dewey's phrase, and so begin to get some sense of the "language" of what is, to the believer, not only Ramadan but also Islam as a civilizational project.[9] We begin to have experience (as opposed to simply abstract knowledge) of Islamic injunctions and prohibitions, of its idioms, of its forms, not just of its substance. We learned this from chapters 1 and 2, which Dewey summarizes in saying that "what counts is what we do, not what we receive."[10] As he explains, actively engaging, as opposed to passively receiving, the world forces us outside of ourselves and permits empathy with its "true meanings." This is the real significance of our personal experience of difference: an engagement with—and hence the possibility of empathy with—the immediacy of an other's existence, with that which cannot be said, described, or defined but only pointed to and acknowledged.[11]

In describing the immediacy of experience, Dewey has said, "If existence in its immediacies could speak it would proclaim: 'I may *have* relatives but *I* am not related.'"[12] What he means here is that while one can draw inferences or comparisons between, say, lighting Christmas lights and a Hanukkah menorah, or Ramadan and Lent, or washing one's hands before approaching the realm of the sacred in Buddhism and in Islam, the particular experience of the one or the other is in fact ineffable and indescribable. Think back, or better, feel back to your own childhood experiences of Christmas or Hanukkah or Ramadan, or standing before an ancestral altar in China, and you will immediately recognize what is not encompassed when the forms of such experiences are discussed in a comparative religion or sociology class, or in the latest popular book on religion that you may have picked up. What is lacking in these academic (and pseudoacademic) works is, precisely, the experience—not only of the past but also of the present. For, when lighting the Christmas lights with our own children, we connect back to our childhood and the plethora of memories, emotions, interwoven personal and communal associations, and meanings that the act evokes. The experience of difference, then—not merely knowledge of but also experience of—provides some small opening into that world of the other and, with it, as we say, new potentialities for empathy.

Ethnographies of Difference

In some sense this reflective part of engagement is akin to ethnography, in which one examines the social context of people's lives. As active observation—embedding oneself in the social world of others—ethnography is influenced by these social worlds and therein permits a fuller understanding of the implications of the happenings and events being experienced. In writing ethnography, it is often the case that the particulars of an experience are seen as yielding generalizable insights, such as when one family's fast is perceived as serving as a model for understanding Ramadan. While most ethnographies are carried out by an outsider engaging in an insider's world, CEDAR's pedagogy aims to facilitate living with difference by creating an ethnography of difference that is personal. The process of ethnography that we explore here is an ethnography of the self, a process of self-reflection in which one sees oneself in relation to others, as well as in relation to the categorical biases through which one views the world.

Of course, there are other ways of describing this sense of reflexivity, but looking at it in terms of an ethnographic self emphasizes the nature of discovery often gleaned from more distant observations. Observations are always more formative when experienced as moments of (self-)discovery. In these moments of discovery the world is seen anew: the Evangelical Christian at the Metropolitan Church in Birmingham sees that he can relate to gays and lesbians, whom he sees as morally wrong, through a narrative of suffering; at the same service, a Mainline Protestant realizes that he cannot participate in the Flower Communion because the invitation to communion has been opened to all, including those who do not believe in the sacrament of communion. Both the narrative of suffering and the essence of communion as a rite open only to a Christian community of belonging were evident to both of these individuals before the Metropolitan Church experience, but they were seen in a clear and dramatic way only through these experiences.

Here, too, we may go back to the work of Dewey and the discussion in chapter 2 on the difference between science and art—the former providing signs, or directions, that point us toward experience, the latter being constitutive of it. Through experience we realize the constitutive nature of what was hitherto simply a focus of cognition (and hence simply a bit of information). Now the knowledge is deepened by experience, and the constitutive, world-sustaining meaning of the event is made clear. While as Christians we may have taken communion for decades and understood the critical role that suffering plays in our theology, confronting these as boundary issues in the presence of the other offers us a whole new perspective. What was taken for granted is now problematized and, as a result, open to the mind's gaze. Whether through meeting an other whose activities we consider an abomination, or stepping outside a communion that we consider a sham, we find that our ideas of ourselves—in these cases, of ourselves as Christians—are challenged and a new self-reflexive stance is established, critically, within the context of the group experience. This, then, may lead to a new level of understanding, of ourselves as well as of our other. For gaining insight into the immediacy of experience is a two-way process, not only of the other's but of our own as well.

In the opening vignettes, we saw how encountering the Roma led someone from the First Nations to identify self-reflexively with doing to the Roma what others had done to her. The visit to the healers at Prometra and the subsequent prayer for forgiveness by a Christian fellow prompted the reconsideration of personal identity by another fellow. Though having long held African-ness to be an essential component of it, the latter fellow was clearly different from the other Africans in the group—in part because of having Buddhist religious leanings and in part because of having grown up in a non-African context. In the face of the warias, a Muslim fellow who grew up amid diversity in his religious community found himself torn by the waria experience, on the one hand believing intellectually that it was good for the warias to have a community in which to practice and study Islam, yet on the other feeling dirty and in need of a shower because of the discomfort that being in their presence aroused for him.

Another fellow, a self-proclaimed secularist, came believing she had no boundaries and was accepting of all, but she later realized otherwise. When members of the Indonesian group were given the assignment, at the first facilitation, to discuss their community of belonging, she asked, "What if you do not have an 'other'?" By the end of the program, however, she recognized that she did indeed have boundaries, and that religiously committed individuals were beyond them, were in fact her "other."

Moments of discovery are created through relationships, shared activities, and reflections on the other that come about through living together with difference. It is in these moments that the other is met—not merely encountered, but seen for what the other is: a reminder of what constitutes my boundaries. Moments of discovery are outcomes of where we meet the other. And in my engagement with the other, there is always a notion that the other's presence requires a policing of my own boundaries, lest that which is essential to me be lost. This is more of a social fact (in the Durkheimian sense) than what many liberals claim of unity and universal sameness. Lest we see this otherwise, the case of the fellow from the program in Indonesia who realized the defining character of her secular beliefs and Balkan identity only when faced with others who held different beliefs and had different identities reminds us that there are limits to what can be shared. We cannot accommodate everyone and still be who we are.

As we noted in the preceding chapter, facilitation is a space in the program during which fellows can start processing the experience of being in the program. It is a highly structured time when people are encouraged to listen and not only speak. With the aid of a prompt, people are asked to connect the general issues being discussed with some of their feelings and their own narrative. For example, what does it mean for each of us to be in the program and learn about the Roma in Bulgaria or the divisions in Bosnia? How can learning about living with difference be integrated into the story of my own community?

Facilitation provides a space where fellows can explore with others those things that seem most alien and unfamiliar, but there is also a space for them to explore the experience themselves. In a sense, we encourage fellows to do their own ethnography of difference: they can reflect in different groupings on the context of their engagement; they can parse out the distinctions that they make in a new way. Facilitation helps people (re)define their experiences of difference and integrate them into their own narrative.

Facilitation, then, is a space where fellows can recognize and acknowledge their personal relationship to the issues being confronted. It allows the conditions necessary to prepare an ethnography of the self with respect to the experience of difference. Recognition, and acknowledgment, of the emotive character of experience is essential to doing such ethnographic work. Allowing a space to explore what one *feels*, rather than simply what one *thinks*, is central to recognizing our preexisting frameworks of understanding. It opens one up to self-discovery and to recognizing the role of difference in maintaining our own group boundaries. And while *thinking* can be an act that mitigates *feeling*, it need not be such. Our contention is that to live with difference, one needs to both think and feel. To that end, a safe space for exploration is needed. We seek not only an awareness of the presence of difference but also an ethnography of difference that provides context for the impact of particular categories and boundaries on us and those with whom we interact.

DIFFERENCE AS PEDAGOGY

All of the vignettes presented in the book show some engagement with difference, whether this entails fellows struggling to make sense of it, overcome it, or find a new way to accept the inevitability of it. In fact most, if not all, social engagement takes place around the nature of difference, whether in assessing compatibilities and incompatibilities of the other or the contexts in which moral credit can be granted. Thus, while we have talked about the reflective approach of ethnography that sheds light on the lived context of difference, we see difference not only as an artifact of social life but also as a pedagogy in and of itself.

What we mean by *difference as pedagogy* is that difference holds the potential to teach us about ourselves and those around us. Part of CEDAR's approach to seeing difference as pedagogy is inherent in the structure of programming and the opportunities for collective interaction that this structure creates. The CEDAR structure—its intellectual, experiential, and affective components brought together in deconstruction, facilitation, practicums, reflective practice, and the diversity of the assembled group— allows fellows to explore their understanding of their group's taken-for-granted categories and also provides a space in which to construct their own ethnographies of difference.

In doing so, as we have already discussed, opportunities are created for moments of discovery. The structure enables these moments of discovery when the time is right for the person; discovery is not merely an act of meeting difference but also of being willing to engage with difference. It is possible, of course, that nothing will happen—some fellows have resisted fully engaging with the program—but the structure of the program establishes conditions in which people are likely to be engaged by what they experience. For those who are open to the pedagogy, we find that the CEDAR structure gives the reflective distance necessary to parse out distinctions of difference in new ways, to see one's agency in making distinctions, and to realize the socially constructed nature of what brings people together and pulls them apart.

This is not to suggest that everything is merely a matter of structure. The success of engagement is always uneven, as the vignettes here illustrate. The Roma and waria interactions are examples that worked—fellows collectively engaged with the challenges these experiences presented and the ways in which they pushed their boundaries of comfort. There were emotional exchanges that revealed the sense of exposure entailed in realizing one's discomfort; and in such instances, the potential for learning that is inherent in recognizing difference finds traction. In relation to the waria, perhaps the most interesting outcome was the fellows' informal discussions regarding acceptance of the former's sexual behaviors. A number of religious fellows questioned their own tendency to essentialize a person by one character trait. They became aware that developing relationships with people very different from them, as was being done in the group, complicated the process of distancing oneself from the other.

Likewise, the issues of poverty that arose from time spent with the Roma led many to believe initially that their own group of belonging did a better job taking care of its people than the Bulgarians did in taking care of the Roma. But it was group members who used to live in poverty and had experienced marginalization who became the catalyst for others to rethink their relation to poverty and reflect more critically on poverty in their home communities. Poverty is a definitive boundary that the group came to realize is also a neglected one with which most rarely engage. It is usually seen as an aspect of life, but the intervention of the First Nations fellow brought the Roma experience closer to the group, to the point where poverty could be seen as both a debilitating and defining boundary that is present, yet often overlooked, in all the communities from which the fellows came.

In the cases of both the transgender Muslims and the Roma, fellows did not know immediately how to square their feelings with their belief systems, but a process of ethnographic reflection began that included the group. In terms of group reflection, the Prometra experience was less productive. For some, it was no doubt emotionally challenging and individually transformative, but the group did not discuss or collectively engage with what happened and what the experience meant. The Prometra story touched on the legacy of differences within a group of African Christians in the context of traditional African healing rituals, led to the questioning of how much freedom one group has to define a legitimate way of being African, and challenged many fellows' conceptions of spirits and the spirit world. But the opportunity of the experience to challenge the group was largely underutilized.

Again and again we have seen that confronting one's boundaries is a charged emotional as well as intellectual experience. As such, the emotions need to be recognized no less than the thoughts and ideas engendered by the encounter with our boundaries. Indeed, emotions are not merely responses to boundaries being crossed; they also act as precursors to, or provide context for, a response that should be critiqued in ways that an ethnography of difference allows. And so, in the course of the program, tensions do emerge out of unplanned confrontations with personal boundaries. These, however, are then reintegrated collectively and become part of the collective experience (among other ways, through facilitation). Creating a diverse environment that does not privatize difference opens up the self-reflexive potential inherent in all of us.

The experience of difference can be both decentering and productive. The self-reflective space that the CEDAR pedagogy creates allows for a recognition of taken-for-granted assumptions inherent in *knowledge of*, assumptions that can limit the creative potential of *knowledge for*. It allows one to see the part of oneself that connects to the group, and to see how this connection relates not only to the everyday lives of those in the program but also to the complexities of home and the communities of belonging to which all will return. The establishment of a community around difference, and outside our groups of constituent identity, creates a belief that different ways of being together are possible. These ways may entail a good deal of discomfort, but they can also afford greater respect for what it means to live together

in difference. We eat together with all the inconveniences of different dietary restrictions, we acknowledge the religious worlds of others, and we find
ways to connect to others through a process of recognition. In other words,
they allow one the opportunity "to see the other; to see the other see you;
and to see yourself seeing the other."[13]

CHAPTER FIVE

Living with Difference

An Italian teacher spends two weeks with Muslims, Orthodox Christians, Protestants, and Jews in Bulgaria—and on her return to Rome begins a campaign to reform multicultural education at her school: to stop sweeping difference under the carpet and to allow the school's many families to encounter the varied and different communities they actually are.

Difference, and the challenge of living with it, surrounds us. Differences can be parsed in countless ways—for example, religious, ethnic, gender, or nationality—and this parsing is often a political act. As such, it influences the social environment in which people live—the resources to which they have access, the possible futures they fear, and the distinction they make between neighbor and stranger, safety and danger. As we noted in chapter 1, Tone Bringa effectively captures this parsing of difference, and the fluidity it entails, in her documentary *We Are All Neighbours*. Set in the village of Višnjica, just outside Sarajevo, during the Bosnian war, it shows Catholic Croats and their Muslim Bosniak neighbors sharing coffee and looking out for one another, until Croatian military units launch an assault on the Bosniak residents. After that event the differences of Višnjica are parsed in new ways, and neighbors who once felt safe are now presented as unknown—and dangerous—strangers. There was no inherent reason for these differences to emerge as they did in Višnjica, but in the face of the threat of war, establishing difference—"we are not like them" or "they are not like us"—seemed prudent.

In earlier chapters we focused on the ways in which CEDAR's pedagogy transforms the group during its two weeks together. Central to this process is the fact that the religious, economic, racial, ethnic, regional, sexual, and any other assorted differences that individuals bring to the CEDAR program are not privatized but rather constitute part of the collective encounter that is essential to the pedagogy. For example, when we meet the religious obligations of members in the group, we do not have one person go to his or her place of worship to pray while others go to the market, as normally happens when religious difference is privatized. Rather, the group goes to each place of worship together to allow the members of that group to pray there. This allows the fundamental context of difference to be both recognized—one or more fellows leave the group to be part of prayers with their coreligionists (another group of their belonging)—and shared (we are there as a group).

Such experiences have caused many of the fellows to look at the other for the first time in a way that respects their fundamentally opposing ways of seeing the world. By going places together and being present in these activities together, fellows acquire an appreciation for the gravity of diversity often overlooked when differences—such as one Muslim's obligations to pray, or one type of Muslim's apprehension regarding praying with a Muslim of another type, or yet another's wish not to pray at all—are generally seen as private matters. In this context the role that the privatization of religion plays in our understanding of what is and is not shared becomes part of the public experience of the group. It is in this public experience that difference, and the discomfort often experienced in bumping up against it, can be recognized.

Religion often plays a part in this awareness. Not because religion is a theme central to all of the programs, for a myriad of themes have been discussed across more than a decade of schools. Themes of ethnicity and belonging (2011, 2012, 2014), tradition and modernity (2013, 2015), nation and nationalism (2003, 2005, 2007), civil society (2004, 2006), and ways of living with others (2008, 2009, 2010) have all been topics central to CEDAR and its affiliates' programs. But in talking about these themes with a group that does not privatize difference, religion always seems to come into play. As one of the least negotiable forms of social ordering, religion gives us grounds for appreciating the limits of building community on sameness. After all, saying that Jesus is the Son of God is very different from saying he is a prophet or a heretic. All of these understandings point to different interpretations of the world that are irreducible to sameness and, quite simply, cannot be shared. Thus, the theme of a gathering can be anything, but when one brings together people from different places with different views and different experiences, the role of religion as a lived category in peoples' lives becomes a salient marker of distinction that cannot be elided. And our argument is that it need not be elided.

The move to privatize religion emerges, as we have already suggested, from the particular historical and social context of Western post-Enlightenment thought. To those for whom religion is not a lived category, it becomes the norm that religion and public life are to be separated, and that religion is to be presented in its most neutered form—as a dangerous artifact of how people used to see the world, a force that secular education and a neoliberal economic system will mitigate. This is not, of course, how everyone sees the world. Among those for whom religion *is* a lived category, their religious community of belonging influences both their view of the world and their behaviors. Engagement with difference affords the opportunity to create a self-reflective space where one can appreciate the various forces that influence how another sees the world.

In chapter 2 we noted various discussions about how to accommodate religious interests in the case of Hagia Sophia. Some have advocated having Muslim prayer services on Fridays and Christian services on Sundays, while allowing the building's continued function as a museum—which the secularists support—on the other days. Such an arrangement would reflect a compromise of the varied understandings of history by allowing all these groups to retain the distinctness of their essential terms of meaning. Central to any such sharing of space is the recognition of the difference inherent in the groups who would worship or otherwise use the space. In having people share space, it would be misguided to assume they share meaning.

Recent efforts in some American universities, such as Bowdoin College and Vanderbilt University, display the extent to which liberal agendas push a vision of sameness that is exclusionary because of its very goal to be inclusionary. As universities try to rid bias from campuses, some campus groups "have refused to agree to the college's demand that any student, regardless of his or her religious belief, should be able to run for election as a leader of any group, including the Christian association. . . . One Christian group balked after a university official asked the students to cut the words 'personal commitment to Jesus Christ' from their list of qualifications for leadership."[1] For a Christian group, confessing belief in Jesus is certainly not an exceptional requirement of those who would lead a Bible study group, just as confessing belief in the teachings of Muhammad or familiarity with the Torah would not be exceptional for a Muslim or Jewish study group, respectively. For the religious group, this seems a bare minimum requirement. Members of the groups being banned claim they are not excluding people from participation but only saying that, to lead, one should hold certain views. The universities that have imposed requirements of acceptance do so based on claims of diversity and equality of access. Laudable as such claims may be in some contexts, people making these claims do not appreciate the nature of difference, pushing instead for a conformity of sameness.

In a sense, this is the Flower Communion from Birmingham writ large. As discussed earlier, members of the Metropolitan Church, in an effort to make the diverse CEDAR group feel included in their church service, held a flower communion in place of the more traditional type of communion. While they clearly understood that non-Christians would be uncomfortable participating in a communion of wine and bread, they believed everyone could participate in the exchange of flowers placed on an altar. But as it turned out, both Christians and non-Christians in the group were uncomfortable with the compromise. The reality is that liberal agendas can be just as uncompromising as those they seek to critique; *not all exclusion is prejudicial*, and certainly the very nature of group building involves exclusion. The task before us is to recognize our biases—be they couched in a liberal, conservative, capitalist, socialist, libertarian, or any other ideology—and find a way forward. Some differences are, after all, essential to our very being.

Communities, of course, do not differ simply along religious lines. In terms of noting the challenge of living with difference—and of accessing resources, sharing space, and living together—ethnicity, regionalism, and race are equally divisive and almost ubiquitous markers of difference.

Despite the multiple differences of religion, ethnicity, and regionalism here in the United States, race still stands out as one of the most defining differences of our political life. Seventy years after it was written, we are still caught in the throes of what Gunnar Myrdal described in his *American Dilemma*. And while the 2009 arrest of Harvard University professor Henry

Louis Gates Jr. by Sergeant James Crowley as Gates attempted to break into his own home (on returning from a trip to China to find the door jammed) ended in a benign "beer summit," other meetings between white police officers and suspected black males have ended rather less felicitously.[2] In 2009, Gates and Crowley joined President Obama to share some beer in the White House Rose Garden; in 2014 and 2015, however, what is widely considered to be discriminatory treatment of black men by white officers ended in tragic violence on several occasions.

In Milwaukee in April 2014, Officer Christopher Manney fired thirteen or fourteen shots into Dontre Hamilton (whom relatives claimed was schizophrenic) and killed him; in November 2014 in Cleveland, twelve-year-old Tamir Rice was shot—within two seconds of the squad car driving up to him—as he played with a lifelike toy pistol in the park; in August 2014, John Crawford III was fatally shot in an Ohio Walmart while he was chatting on his cell phone and swinging a pellet rifle in his hand; and, also in August, eighteen-year-old Michael Brown was shot to death in Ferguson, Missouri, as he was being arrested by police. All these black men were shot to death by white police officers. The fatal choke hold put on asthmatic Eric Garner—also black—in November 2014 by a white police officer in New York who ignored his screams of "I cannot breathe" is yet another example of violence perpetrated on black men in the United States by white officers of the law. And in April 2015, the death of Freddie Gray while in police custody set off riots in Baltimore that reflected broad social frustrations about race and discrimination.[3] At least for black men, who make up 6 percent of the population but 40 percent of the murder victims, racial differences are of primary importance in defining their life chances and well-being.[4]

While race is not the subject of this book, the nexus of difference and new ways of knowing (knowledge *for* rather than knowledge *of*) very much is. For this reason, and against the background of so much violence against black men perpetrated by the officers of the state in 2014, it makes good sense to recall a city where no such violence occurred but might well have— certainly twenty years ago: Boston, Massachusetts.

In the 1980s, Boston was still reeling from the court-imposed integration of its school system a decade before, as well as the immense interracial tensions that this decision brought in its wake. Youth violence and gang-related murders rose over that decade, and gunshots were being fired on a nightly basis. The police department was seen as racist, impudent, and overbearing, and while its heavy-handed response led to a drop in violence, the department was totally delegitimized within the black community as a result. To say that the police view of black men was jaundiced is to be complimentary. The situation reached its climax in 1989, when Carol Stuart, a pregnant white woman, was horrifically murdered while in her husband's company (he was shot in the stomach but survived) as they were driving home from a prenatal class at a hospital located near a largely black community. The immediate police reaction—instituting a "stop and frisk" policy and "tipping kids upside down" in that neighborhood—inflamed racial tensions in a city that was already split along racial lines.[5] (In fact the husband had murdered his wife and shot himself as part of a cover-up. He later committed suicide by jumping off a bridge before he could be apprehended.)[6]

By the mid-1990s, however, relations between the police and the black community had turned a corner, and collaboration between the police and leaders of the black community remained in place through a series of fraught events. For example, in March 1994 a police SWAT team broke into the wrong apartment during a drug bust, causing Accelyne Williams, the retired black minister who lived there, to die of a heart attack. A year later, a black undercover officer was badly beaten by police officers in a case of mistaken identity, and an assistant district attorney was shot to death in his car by a black gang member. Any of these events could have led to a return to the negative relations between police and black community that had characterized earlier decades. What prevented this from happening was, by all accounts, the formation of what has become known as the Boston TenPoint Coalition—a coalition of black ministers and police officers who, essentially, set aside their claims to "knowledge of" in order to work together toward a circumscribed but important shared goal: keep the next kid from being killed. Boston, a notoriously racist city, was, in fact, now a city with a working coalition that brought white police officers together with black ministers.

Christopher Winship, a sociology professor at Harvard University and a CEDAR founding board member, has studied and written widely on this coalition between black ministers and white police officers. As a result of this coalition, black communal leaders conferred legitimacy on the police even as the overwhelmingly white police force slowly lost its almost visceral distrust of the black ministers and the black community at large.[7] For example, the Reverend Eugene Rivers, who together with the Reverend Raymond Hammond and the Reverend Jeffrey Brown played a critical role in the formation of the TenPoint Coalition, had, until then, maintained famously hostile relations with the Boston police, who were in fact convinced that he was one of Boston's major drug dealers.[8]

What brought the ministers to work with the police is itself a long and fascinating story, one focused on the May 1992 shoot-out and stabbings by members of rival gangbangers at the Morning Star Baptist Church during the funeral service for a dead gang member, as well as on the 1991 drive-by shooting of the Reverend Rivers's own house, in a dangerous area of Dorchester. Of importance for us here, however, is the fact that cooperation was established between previously hostile social groups without any previous ideological transformation. As Winship puts it, "No leadership from above demanded that the two parties negotiate a more constructive and effective relation for the good of the city of Boston. There were no meetings involving the two groups in which a master plan was created. There was no attempt to follow the example of other cities or other groups."[9]

In fact, it took quite a few years for the sides even to realize that they were working in partnership with each other. Neither side decided to revise its view of the other, or even to *trust* the other before their joint work. In fact, when black ministers began to patrol the streets at night on their own, "in collar," they were at first accosted by police officers who assumed they were pimps and drug dealers (who else would be out on the streets in the middle of the night?).[10] What happened was a gradual change in the attitude of each side toward the other as a result of shared practices, such as eventually patrolling the streets together and working together with probation officers and the judiciary. Each side was willing to bracket out what it "knew" of the other in order to work toward the common goals of safe streets and a drop in youth homicides. They did not start by revising their truth claims about their antagonists (and make no mistake about it, the black ministers and white police officers were engaged in an antagonistic relationship) and then work together. They began by working together, and that shared experience led them slowly to reframe their knowledge of the other. The community came to grant legitimacy to the police—even instituting a yearly award for best policing—and the community leaders came to play a role in deciding what would become of youthful offenders. Trust followed on the heels of shared experience; it did not precede it. Indeed, as Winship explains, the cooperation was combined, but not joint. Work toward the common goal led to willingness on each side to scale down its epistemological claims from claims to *knowledge of* to *knowledge for*. The result came to be known as the "Boston Miracle."

What these ministers and police officers achieved in Boston was a problematization of their own categories: they began to question their own taken-for-granted assumptions, and doing so led them to rethink their attendant worldviews (at least with respect to the other). Interestingly enough, this problematization appeared only as their own categories no longer sufficed to make sense of the situation—analogous to the discomfort that is a precondition for learning, discussed in earlier chapters. The result of this discomfort was a new awareness and reflective stance, which ultimately led to the creation of a shared past on which future proactive interventions could be based, as they were in 2006, in turn enabling Boston to avoid the type of outrage that was triggered by the violence in other cities in 2014.

Sadly, this type of reflexivity and disaggregation of knowledge claims appears to have been sorely lacking in the cases of police violence that occurred in several American cities that year. To gain a better appreciation of the prevailing situation, consider what lawyers call a "hypothetical"—a case study, in this instance of a real person in a real city, though not one involved in the violence of 2014—just to get a sense of the manifold types of difference that are often masked by purely racial categories. What was achieved in Boston was, after all, the ability of both sides to view the complexity of the other and eschew the simplistic typecasting of difference, a process whose absence arguably led to many unnecessary deaths. This hypothetical involves Jaylen (fictional name, real person), in the city of Pittsburgh.

Jaylen works as a valet at a restaurant in the affluent Pittsburgh neighborhood of Shadyside, where he parks cars that cost more than what he makes in a year. For transportation, he relies on the city bus, a friend, or quite often, walking; when (or if) he saves enough, he wants to buy a car that confers the status of "making it" in his neighborhood. He grew up in nearby Homewood, nearly the mirror opposite of Shadyside.[11] Shadyside is nearly 78 percent white; Homewood is 94 percent black.[12] Shadyside has expensive boutique shops; Homewood has boarded-up facades and discount stores. People visit Shadyside for leisure; people leave Homewood if they can. Jaylen has a high school diploma, a girlfriend with whom he has a two-year-old daughter, and a warm smile that puts customers at ease. Despite his outgoing personality, he feels he goes largely unnoticed at work—"just a black man parking a white man's car." If he walks down certain streets in Shadyside, he feels suspicious stares from residents and shoppers, as if "they are watching because I don't belong, waiting to make sure I leave." He does not like talking about his home life, especially with white people. He lives with his mother, girlfriend, and daughter, but he does not know where his father is. Most of his peers work minimum-wage service jobs in nearby, mostly white neighborhoods; some have been caught up in street violence, others are incarcerated. Like many Pittsburgh natives, he is proud of his home city and has no desire to leave. But it is also the case that he has no real opportunity to leave. When asked what makes Pittsburgh a great place to live, he simply says it is where he grew up, his roots. His Pittsburgh is deeply influenced by the racial divides of the neighborhoods. And just as he does not always feel safe in his own neighborhood, he also feels unsafe in the supposedly "safe" white neighborhoods.[13]

+ + + +

Pittsburgh used to be known for steel. By the early 1900s, the city produced upward of half the country's steel annually and was a thriving center of industry. In the early twentieth century, immigrants, mostly from Europe, lent the city a predominantly white, working-class feel.[14] During the 1940s and later, the Great Migration of 6 million blacks from the rural South to the Midwest, Northeast, and West utterly changed the racial dynamics of the city.[15] The vast majority of those who came to Pittsburgh then worked as laborers in the steel industry. The city's economy was strong, with good jobs to be had and a steady labor supply. During World War II, area steel mills worked around the clock to produce materials for the war effort; and after the war, steel was redirected for both export and domestic use. Some of this economic success was visible in the black community as well, which was relatively successful in Pittsburgh compared with other major urban centers

Figure 25. Homewood.

Figure 26. Shadyside. Photos by David W. Montgomery, 2015.

in the north. In other words, the black community in Pittsburgh has not always been poor, and some of the poverty now seen in places like Homewood is relatively recent.

The success of the steel industry made Pittsburgh one of the most polluted cities in the world, described by James Parton in 1866 as "hell with the lid off."[16] In the years after World War II, the city tried to address the pollution problem with various clean air initiatives and projects to high-light the cultural accompaniments of the city. The collapse of the steel industry in the 1980s did much to improve air quality, but it also resulted in massive unemployment and migration. Owing to tremendous shrinkage of the industrial sector, which occurred in much of the Rust Belt, many in Pittsburgh who had moved there to work at industrial jobs as part of the Great Migration were now left without jobs and suffered great economic hardship.[17]

Reeling with plant closures and unemployment, the city shifted its economic base, from one dependent on industrial skilled labor to one focused on health care, finance, high technology, and education.[18] As a result of these efforts, by the first decade of the twenty-first century Pittsburgh came to be viewed as a model of city redevelopment. According to various magazines and rating guides, Pittsburgh is one of the "most livable cities" in the United States and the world.[19] However, what makes a city "livable" depends on which residents are being asked and what their skin color is. Certainly, Pittsburgh is a better place to live if your skin color is white.

While distinctions are seldom black and white, in some cases they are. Lower incomes, restricted opportunities, weaker schools, and higher crime rates are all characteristic of the predominantly black neighborhoods in the city—for example, two-thirds of the homicides are committed in the area from the Hill District through East Liberty, Homewood, and the East Hills.[20] In 2012 the average homicide victim was "a 30-year-old black man with some involvement in crime. . . . The average offender was a 26-year-old black man with some involvement in crime."[21] In other words, most violent crime is black on black.

There is very little racial integration in these neighborhoods, which have become either ghettoized and black or gentrified and white—in the latter case pushing the poor farther out into suburbs, with longer commutes to minimum-wage jobs and less access to public transportation. This, of course, is not the goal of the city but something that belies the spoils of living in "a most livable" city.

Racial issues are not new but rather a persistent dynamic of urban life in America.[22] One effort to overcome the dynamics of racism is a program cosponsored by the American Anthropological Association: "RACE: Are We

So Different?" This exhibit, which was mounted in Pittsburgh from March to October 2014, aimed to push individuals to question the utility of racial categories, and it accomplished this by recounting stories of suffering and the various misconceptions that accompany these categorizations. The point is not to say that all are the same but, rather, to say that racial categories obscure more reliable explanations of difference.[23] In other words, difference is more than biology.

Inherent in discussions of race is the struggle to overcome the privilege (or at least the perception of privilege) others enjoy. This status can be economic—access to schools, jobs, and futures that are tied to the opportunities with which someone is born—but it is also psychological: the internalization of a category that some segment of society deems relevant. The story of racial differences in the neighborhoods of Pittsburgh can be one of ethnicity— black Americans versus black immigrants from Africa.[24] Or it can be one of regionalism—in which part of town one lives and works—or something different, such as skin color, which travels with you wherever you go.[25] In other contexts, other differences become salient.

In Birmingham, England, for example, stories of not belonging, similar to Jaylen's, have a South Asian and often religious hue. While many of the city's residents are immigrants, many others have lived their entire lives in England and see themselves as British more than as Indian or Pakistani. Not long ago, this issue of belonging became front-page news when Birmingham schools were accused of fostering an Islamist (that is, non-British) set of values.[26] What remains troubling is the seeming inability of state actors to find a creative way to bring communities together across racial, religious, and other lines of difference.

+ + + +

History plays a role in creating communities of difference, but the communication of those differences is carried out in a contemporary context. For Jaylen and others in the United States, the experience of race is of a past-mediated present; as we come to recognize a difference between shared space and shared experience, we begin to see as well that the ways in which communities become divided determine different opportunities for work, leisure, and even finding a spouse. In Pittsburgh and elsewhere, it is not uncommon for people to be in the same public space and yet not share it, tacitly accepting the public biases of their black or white identities and thus passing one another in the commons. Biases are thus not just collective stereotypes but also individual prejudices, which need to be recognized for what they are so that the two groups can learn to live together.

Like race, ethnicity and regionalism can become cultural markers of difference when accompanied by segregation and division. Cities do this in different ways: Nicosia, Cyprus, is divided by a physical border and checkpoint that separate Greek and Turkish Cypriots; Tel Aviv-Jaffa is not one city despite what its name implies, since Jews are moving into increasingly gentrified and gated communities; and Pittsburgh is demarcated by both the ghettoization of black neighborhoods and their impending (white) gentrification. In the continuing sectarian violence in Iraq, one's neighborhood, Shi'a or Sunni, is all too often the factor deciding if one will live or die.[27] But of course, as the genocide in Rwanda made clear, divisions are not necessarily religious (though, here too, as discussed earlier, the Muslim minority did play a noble role, saving Tutsi from the genocidal wrath of their Hutu neighbors). Different locations are subject to different dynamics. Throughout the book we have looked mostly at religious differences, but as this chapter shows, race too is a form of difference from which tensions and conflict have emerged, in the United States and elsewhere. As long as we shy away from engaging with the substantive differences that define us as unique individuals and members of separate communities, all differences can be turned into points of contention and opprobrium and, in particular circumstances, can provide reasons for violence.

CEDAR schools and pedagogy emphasize providing new opportunities for engagement with difference, through which individuals can experience their own biases and hence subject them to some reflection. Doing so, we believe, leads to new forms of practice—in fact to a shared practice in situations that we do not fully control, thus creating a new space of potential trust across differences, with all the obligations that such trust implies.

This trust is an integral part of all CEDAR programs. To the individuals who organized the Balkan Summer School on Religion and Public Life, it is the key to everything CEDAR stands for. In the words of Borislava Petkova, creating a space of "sharing and belonging" for "collective engagement" (in

John Eade's terms) is what provides the conditions for trust and for the emergence of a group that solves problems through a process of shared practice. As Milena Katsarska notes, "Working together as a collectivity, rather than according to preconceived ideas or recipes," is at the core of the feeling of shared purpose, sense of belonging, and commitment of CEDAR practitioners. Of course, this shared practice must also be accompanied by a great sense of responsibility. After all, involvement in an educational enterprise such as this carries with it a real risk of loss, which on some level always accompanies change. This sense of loss may emerge when a shared practice leads us to challenge our preconceived ideas and opinions and we come to realize that others can be right—indeed, that others have "the right to be right."[28] Because this risk of loss is substantial, so must be the responsibility taken by school leaders and all others who participate in CEDAR programs. And because the problems with which CEDAR fellows engage are, in the words of Desislava Dimitrova of the Balkan Summer School on Religion and Public Life, the "defining problems of our everyday lives," this responsibility is also a matter of ongoing daily life, not just a two-week program.[29]

Not surprisingly, many of the people attracted to CEDAR's practice and principles struggle with this very responsibility in their own communities. One such person is the Reverend Paul Gwese, who joined the program as a fellow in Bulgaria in 2011 and subsequently sent more and more of his colleagues from Zimbabwe to CEDAR programs with the aim of organizing affiliate programs in Zimbabwe. Gwese was born in the eastern highlands of Zimbabwe, and his background strongly emphasized relations with his "inner community."[30] Both his parents were devout Christians, and he attended church regularly, as they required. He was active in the church, and the Anglican priests in his parish saw leadership potential in him, though his teenage years were like those of other children in his village. However, it was the influence of his family and the support of those priests that led him on his faith journey and, eventually, to the Anglican priesthood.

Gwese attended seminary in Harare and shortly thereafter began to serve in a more traditional parish, which was seen as politically volatile because of the changing racial dynamics in the country at the time. During the colonial period, the parish was in an affluent, white-only suburb. Later, as blacks bought houses and moved in, some whites saw them as intruders. The tensions of racial politics presented themselves in the church community, and Gwese had to minister to a divided congregation.

Not all communities are as racially divided as his first parish, but all have divisions that are difficult to manage. Today in Zimbabwe, for example, the rising gap between rich and poor manifests itself on a weekly basis. Gwese explains,

> At the end of the day, on a Sunday morning, or on a Sunday evening, they [rich and poor] all come together to congregate in the same parish. They share the same communion plate. They share the same cup. But when they go home, this one is going to drive [his] Range Rover; and this one is probably going to walk back home, because he cannot afford even to get into the public transport, which only costs fifty cents. So as a priest, I am in a very challenging position, where I have to give hope to this one, who cannot even buy a loaf of bread; and I also have to somewhat highlight to those with so much, that, remember: God didn't give you [wealth] so that you can throw [it] in the [trash] bin—but to use what God has given you to remember those without.

Gwese must thus construct—in his own church, under one of the most enduring and most repressive authoritarian regimes in today's world, amid a huge economic depression that affects his congregants unequally—a space of shared belonging across serious economic, political, and tribal differences. In a sense this has always been the mission of the church, and Pope Francis has explicitly embraced it for Catholicism. The view from the Vatican is not necessarily the same as that from the Anglican diocese of Harare, however; nor are the resources that need be mobilized in pursuit of such an aim.

Gwese recognizes that an appreciation of all the differences in his parish is central to his ministry, as is the need to serve all others openly, regardless of his own assumptions. He recalls his time as a student in England: "I realized that there were people who lived a life that was different from mine. What I thought was abnormal, to them was normal. And I thought they thought the same thing about me, that I was a strange person because we have varied views about issues of religion, issues of moral persuasion. But . . . you cannot dismiss and judge a person by who they are. At the end of the day, they are also people created in the same image. I believe I am created by God. . . . Humanity is broad, and the way we live is also broad. . . . The world does not end with my perception. The world is bigger than I think it is. . . . I don't live in my own world, but I am influenced by others." In order to develop this vision and make it part of the message of his fellow Anglican priests in Harare and beyond, Gwese has in fact introduced CEDAR methodologies (a stress on difference, a combination of different ways of knowing and learning, facilitation sessions, etc.) into the annual Anglican priestly retreats. These sessions, and the continued participation of Anglican clergy in CEDAR programs outside Zimbabwe, are setting the stage for developing such programs within the country.

Gwese's experience of CEDAR has allowed him to push beyond his own community of belonging (his parish and church) and engage with many of the different communities in Zimbabwe, including the Muslim community. He considers himself committed to his community, but he also recognizes that his responsibilities extend beyond that community. Without such feelings of responsibility, the type of situations we have recently experienced in relation to issues of race in this country, and to issues of religion, ethnicity, and national belonging abroad, may repeat themselves in his country as well, because political and tribal divisions can overlap in a volatile mix.

As noted earlier, this overlapping of differences is often a recipe for conflict. It might be race and class in Pittsburgh and elsewhere; religion and ethnic identity in western Europe and the Balkans; or nationalism, ethnicity, and religious practice in central Asia, to name just a few global crisis points. In all cases, social identities are overlaid in a manner that makes empathy, fellow feeling, and the ability to see oneself in the other more and more difficult, if not impossible, to attain. It is precisely in such situations, however, that it is vital to build a set of shared practices across communities.

Another individual whose initial involvement with CEDAR programs gave rise to a strong commitment to bring the programs home to his own religious community and world of belonging is Anver Emon, a professor of law at the University of Toronto and a longtime CEDAR collaborator. The son of immigrant parents who moved to the United States from India in the 1960s, Emon experienced difference at an early age as a young South Asian Muslim living in Los Angeles.[31] His family sought to integrate into a new country at a time when Islam in America was maturing through the building of mosques and community centers. Immigrant, Muslim (Shiite), Indian, dark-skinned—the differences were multiple, and to simplify their lives and "fit in," his parents began to see themselves, and present themselves, as Sunni so that they could at least in some ways be part of the majority community (that is, the majority of Indian immigrant Muslims).

Perhaps as a result of his background, Emon is extraordinarily sensitive to the importance of the problems faced by all communities of belonging and, indeed, to just how loaded this term is, how fissile and how implicated in the dynamics of both inclusion and exclusion. And so he recognizes "communities of belonging [as] the place for comfort and the potential for being that source of comfort—but [at the same time as having] the potential for [causing] other forms of suffering that they can perpetrate in the name of belonging."

And while it is impossible to ignore the suffering that membership in certain communities can entail, or the exclusion that membership in any particular community always involves, Emon recognizes that "you need to find a way to be in the world that you inhabit with your difference. . . . When you don't know where you come from, then you cannot face the larger polity with dignity when they impose upon you their presumptions of who you are. You internalize what everyone else thinks you are without really knowing what you are. To raise my child [sic] with difference is to help them find the place from which to stand so that they can face the world around them with dignity." Of course, such a place of belonging is also a place of boundaries; but as Emon remarks, boundaries can be things that you "bump up against," not always and necessarily places of danger.

This approach to difference and boundaries profoundly informed the program Emon developed at the University of Toronto's Connaught Summer Institute of Islamic Studies in 2013.[32] There, he and others brought graduate students in Islamic studies from all over the world to experience, on the most personal of levels, the great diversity of Islamic communities—from Salafi to gay and lesbian to Shiite to Ahmedia to Ismaili, as well as from secular to strictly observant Islamic communities. Among the explicit goals of the program were the desire to develop the university's relationship with Muslim communities in Toronto and the wish to "provoke a critical self-awareness of the relationship between researchers and their research."[33] Emon also creatively developed CEDAR pedagogy to fit the Islamic project. Thus, organizing study sessions of the fellows together with the different Muslim communities in Toronto, he set out the principle that no one "has a monopoly on truth" (changing slightly the CEDAR principle that no one has a monopoly on suffering). This became a powerful tool to explore not only different textual readings within different communities but also the difference between academic and community readings of texts and their attendant obligations. Emon and his colleagues are in fact engaged in an important experiment: bringing CEDAR practices and principles into the university. We cannot know where this will ultimately lead, but the results have been positive enough that plans to extend this intervention in additional directions are under way.

In different places and at different times, however, the bumping up against boundaries that Emon describes can be terribly dangerous, and it is appropriate to ask what CEDAR pedagogy can contribute in such circumstances. We ended chapter 3 by noting the limits to CEDAR pedagogy, but as the two-week program is adopted in increasingly diverse places and circumstances, it is more than right to query how this transition can be effected. A third CEDAR fellow, Margaret Angucia, a Ugandan educator and activist, posed this question with a deep sense of urgency against the background of the wars of the Lord's Resistance Army in northern Uganda.[34]

Angucia grew up in a Catholic family in a simple African village in northwestern Uganda. Both her parents were teachers, and although they were not rich, they were able to meet the family's basic needs. While Angucia was in primary school, the Ugandan Bush War was ongoing, and people in her region were displaced. Later, the Lord's Resistance Army insurgency further affected the region, displacing more people and taking men away to the fighting. She tells the story of an abducted ten-year-old boy from the village of Mancura in northern Uganda, who, when identifying himself, gave the rebels the clan name of his neighbors rather than that of his own; when he escaped, the rebels, seeking vengeance, came there and massacred ninety members of that neighboring clan while sparing the boy's own. This episode plunged the two clans into lasting conflict, which has prevented some people from returning to their villages. The boy is now grown up and not living in Mancura anymore, but his clan members are still suffering, prevented from returning to the village by the claims for compensation made by the other clan, demands that they cannot fulfill given their own poverty.

Together with Father Maximiano Ngabirano and Esibo Omaada, both of the Uganda Martyrs University, Angucia has established the Equator Peace Academy (EPA) within the university. The EPA ran its first program in 2012 and its second in 2014. This last, devoted to the problem of refugees in Uganda and titled "Coping with Difference in a Foreign Land," has set the stage for continuing work with and research on refugees, for the university's commitment to refugee well-being (vocational and language training), and for an additional program, in 2016, dealing with displaced persons in East Africa and the area extending up to Juba in South Sudan.

Like Emon in Canada, the team in Uganda developed its own program and ran it according to East African principles. They built on and developed CEDAR principles and practices, adopting the program's general orientation to difference, knowledge, and the importance of community in the making of a self. But they also infused CEDAR pedagogy with the knowledge and traditions of East Africa, where most of the staff and fellows were from. Group exercises and modes of reflection were imported from work on tribal reconciliation methods; African imagery and metaphors took the place of Western ones; and as the African team took over the major programmatic roles in the school (running facilitation, deconstruction, and academic presentations), it became clear that CEDAR pedagogy can be easily adapted to local needs and knowledge.

A good example of this process took place one Sunday as fellows rode the bus from Kampala to western Uganda to spend time in a number of refugee settlements. They sang exuberantly on the bus, expressing a feeling of group belonging and well-being. However, the songs, whether in English or any number of African languages, were all Christian. When one non-Christian in the group pointed out that 20 percent of the folks on the bus were not Christian, and that perhaps other song choices might be appropriate, the singing stopped altogether and a somewhat (at least for some) awkward silence ensued. Both EPA and CEDAR staff present realized that this would be an ideal opportunity to discuss some of the most pressing issues of social inclusion, integration, and sharing public space. How in fact could they live together differently? That is, how could they build an inclusive model of community that would give voice to minorities while still conveying a sense of shared community, as opposed to merely parceling out differences in different symbolic or material spaces, as so often happens in the United States with, for example, the celebration of Hanukkah, Christmas, and Kwanza?

Deconstruction on the bus the following day was led by Ngabirano, who asked people to reflect on what had happened and why the singing stopped as soon as the Christian nature of the songs had been pointed out.

Some Christian participants noted that they too had been uncomfortable during the singing; they really felt that it was a continuation of worshipping, but they had not known how to engage with the issue. The only Muslim present explained that he had been raised as a minority in a Catholic school, has some family members who are Christians, and knew all the songs. He did not think twice about his minority status. He was not aware of the worshipping aspect of the songs. They were just familiar songs. The discussion that followed engaged with the difficulty, from the majority viewpoint, of integrating the minority and the meaning of becoming aware of minorities' needs and their presence. For the minority, who had earlier that day attended a Catholic service, continuing to sing Christian hymns on the bus felt like too much. People reflected on their boundaries, and on what the different responsibilities of the minority and the majority are in such a situation.

A Christian fellow noted that it is very difficult to become aware of group boundaries when the minority is silent. A secular woman explained that it is also the role of the minority to create space for themselves. She wondered why she did not feel like advocating for herself in this situation. Another minority person questioned why the group was unable to sing pop songs or any other songs. She added that, as soon as it became clear to her that these were religious songs, she "checked out" and waited for them to stop. Speaking up for the minority is also quite difficult, and highlighting one's minority status could bring anxiety. Wasserfall explained that we each bring our history to our encounters with others, and some of these feelings might be of insecurity and fear. The "better to stay quiet" syndrome, as she dubbed it, might stem from a collective history of victimhood.

Ngabirano explained that it is also important to become conscious of what is lost when we realize that there is a minority in our midst. Is the feeling of kinship and comfort of being in the majority lost for the majority when a minority is present and needs to be integrated? The group then began to question and debate what we may have to give up, or let go of, in order to be part of a group of difference.

One of the many fascinating aspects of this discussion was that it led the group to question Africans' felt need for new procedures when they meet strangers (that is to say, the Western political science models in which so much of this type of discussion is often framed). Some argued that they already have traditional knowledge that would allow them to navigate majority-minority relations. Ngabirano explained that Africans have all internalized the hegemony of individualism. Singing Catholic songs in this setting was, in his mind, an outcome of this individual approach. The individual self was finding a way to express a personal sense of sacredness through the singing. Africans, he contended, have forgotten their African traditions of living in communities with lots of people around. The African tradition is sensitive to strangers and tries to integrate them in a more communal way. The community approach is not taken for granted anymore, he continued; people nowadays forget to look first at the group before acting and, instead, take their own individual needs as motive enough for their actions. The majority, according to him, was expressing itself through a Western individualistic model and expected members of the minority to take care of themselves as individuals as well. No one thought in terms of what kind of songs would be appropriate to sing on a bus whose passengers were Christians, Jews, a Muslim, and a member of the First Nation peoples of North America. The focus of each one of the singers was his or her own relationship to his or her own religious community, not the group expression of togetherness. There is a place and a time for both; what is appropriate in church is not necessarily appropriate on a bus trip in very mixed company. This is not to say that Christian songs were inappropriate on the bus, but that having *only* Christian songs—and not giving space to the Jews, Muslim, First Nation member, and others—was exclusionary.

Ngabirano ended the discussion by reminding us that one of the two rules of the school is that "there is no monopoly on suffering." The present discussion, he said, adds a variant on that theme: there "is no monopoly on victimhood." Some of us bring past experiences of communal victimhood to our meetings with strangers. Becoming aware of our own cultural baggage in real situations will help us learn how best to create communities of difference, he added. To become truly a group of difference where all voices are heard, we need to restrain the focus of our individual desires and take a more communal approach. Learning to focus first on the group composition and needs might help us on this road.

This example shows EPA staff adopting the CEDAR methodology and expanding on it. By developing the idea that their own culture has the tools needed to create a group of difference, EPA staff were in fact reclaiming their tribal past and integrating it into the present situation. This incident was one of those teaching moments when reflecting on the discomfort brought new understandings. As the group deconstructed the singing on the bus, they became aware that to form a community of difference they would need *knowledge for*—to know what will make people uncomfortable. In that particular situation they needed *knowledge for* in order to learn to work together. African Christians reflected that their African traditions allow them a way to connect with their present situation. They discovered that there are traditional ways to include strangers. Their traditional communal African model teaches individuals to act from the viewpoint of the community in question. Singing in that model is not only a personal expression of individual worship but also an expression of being together. This awareness changes the terms of the togetherness. East Africans have communal knowledge, a cultural background to draw upon when in a mixed group; put in these terms, CEDAR staff helped people see the possible road ahead as they all learn to live with difference in the African context.

This sense of communal obligation is critical to Angucia's notion of selfhood. For twenty years she served as a nun, and although she eventually left the convent, she was never canonically released from her vows. She continues to live her vows, seeing her time in the convent as formatively preparing her for life, and she believes that those in CEDAR and equivalent programs are obligated to work with the communities with which they interact and not just learn from them. Returning to the case of the two clans of the village of Mancura, is the solution to purchase a cow and so settle the compensation demands? Is it to get the elders of the village involved in discussing and solving the problem? She does not know, but she is sure that some level of "community outreach" is part of CEDAR's own responsibilities to the communities with which it engages: "I am conscious of the fact that there are huge things out there that you cannot always change. But there are certain things that you really think will help. You need to do something here. I don't want to be teaching and doing research for the sake of the university or for my sake. I really, if I could, want to get a concrete relationship between the university work and the life of the people. And I think that will be my kind of contribution."

Significantly, this notion of an "engaged pedagogy," which goes well beyond the formalism of so much of contemporary higher education, is at the center of many people's commitment to CEDAR pedagogy and practice. It is what inspired the visual anthropologist Elizabeta Koneska to see the school as a place to address Christian-Muslim relations in Macedonia, and what led the historian Yuri Stoyanov of the University of London's School of Oriental and African Studies to see it as an alternative to the ever-increasing academic propensity to teach, in his words, "the global rich."[35] For him as for many others, CEDAR practices allow us both to return to more traditional notions of pedagogic "calling" and to explore new forms of pedagogical experimentation and innovation.[36]

DIFFERENCE AS AN APPROACH TO COMMUNITY

Central to the approach of the individuals quoted in the previous section is a sense of responsibility to their own communities of belonging and an awareness that all such communities also exclude. Merely ghettoizing different communities does not address the need to live with one another that all communities have. What we, and they, advocate is, rather, an approach to community that respects the centrality of what gives community its character: that which makes us different. Making the transition from the two-week group to the broader community in which fellows reside is a huge challenge for fellows to negotiate. Part of the broader goal of the program itself is to give a basis, a *knowledge for*, living together differently with and within communities that represent the plurality of views held in any place. Gwese, Emon, Angucia, and others have all taken the CEDAR experience back to their own realms of engagement: the Anglican Church in Zimbabwe, around which Gwese is planning CEDAR programs; Islamic studies programs at the University of Toronto, which Emon organized in 2013; the ongoing Equator Peace Academy, which Angucia, Ngabirano, and others have established in Uganda using the CEDAR model; and the development of a Balkan network in Bulgaria, Macedonia, Turkey, and elsewhere. All have taken from the CEDAR experience the idea that a different way of structuring relations is possible through reflective practices, experience of the program, being together with difference, and being present in the presence of the other.

This was made only too clear in the December 2014 program of the EPA. During the EPA trip to the refugee settlements in western Uganda—Mbarara, Oruchinga, Nakivale, Rawmanje, and Kyak II—we visited with some of the nearly four hundred thousand Congolese, Sudanese, South Sudanese, Somalians, Rwandans, and others who wait in an eternal now, an endless present, without past or future, sometimes for decades. Stripped of everything, prevented from owning any real property, with no agency, no community, no markers of belonging, nor even a shared language with their host communities or with one another, the only orienting markers of life are those provided by the so-called international "community" through the distribution of humanitarian aid (mostly health provision and foodstuffs whose quantities are determined in an office in Geneva rather than locally), which comes with the ever-repeated idioms of UN-speak. Even the signs announcing the settlements were marked with such international "stamps." Any discussion with refugees, for which permission must be sought well in advance, is always with both men and women to preserve "gender balance," though the women often do not speak at all. Any discussion in any of the settlements, which are often just camps, is replete with current mantras such as "provisions against SGBV" (sexual and gender-based violence), the continual reference to which, using just the acronym, betrays its mimetic, rather than substantive meaning. One has the strong feeling of participating in a ritual rather than a discussion.

Even more telling is that in all these settlements and camps, the only things that are named and notated—that is, repeated in writing—are those belonging to or donated by the international community. Every bag of rice is stamped, every can of vegetable oil marked, the laws of fraud posted on every other fence (the fences mark the boundaries of the land administered by the United Nations High Commissioner for Refugees within the camps). None of this is unreasonable in itself, but it stands in jarring contrast to the

Figure 27. Signs announcing the Nakivale Refugee Settlement in Uganda in 2014. Photo by Megan Carson.

lack of all other forms of signage and notation anywhere else in the camps. No signs or markers exist in any space, or on any edifice anywhere, except the ones saying that a specific building was constructed by Contractor X under Contract Y at the behest of the United Nations High Commissioner for Refugees, or that something was donated, or that, in the case of vehicles, it is owned by such and such an agency from Denmark or France or Great Britain, and so on. The only reality that is reproduced is thus the reality of the humanitarian aid and the abstract human-rights concerns (reproduced, as we are attempting to show, both verbally—in the mantras of a certain type of speech, where certain words and expressions continually reappear—and in written forms, in the camps' signage). The actual lives of the people living in these camps, sometimes for generations, have all the permanence of a plastic bag sweeping across the Ugandan plateau.

In essence, in these cases—and they repeat themselves across East Africa and in too many other places the world over—there is an ever-expanding reproduction of agendas and worldviews set in the offices of the UN and other agencies in western Europe and North America. In these internationally constructed agendas, there is precious little thought given to the actual lives of hundreds of thousands of refugees lived over the course of decades, devoid of a past or of a future toward which they can orient their lives. In this sense, what many are experiencing today in Africa and elsewhere is but a new form of colonialism, which in its classic nineteenth-century iteration sought to reproduce its structures, worldviews, hierarchies, and agendas. The cognitive and physical grids set in the metropole spread the world over, with little concern for their impact on the daily lives of people—except as these could be integrated into the metropole's own model. All would be Englishmen, or Frenchmen, . . . or, in any case, Westerners.

What resulted from our visit, however, was the development, with local camp commandants, of alternative ways of imagining life in the camps. Through discussion with EPA fellows and staff, camp commandants came to understand the importance of establishing incentives to structure a "future" into the lives of the refugees. These incentives included, for example, vocational and language training, ways to foster attachment to and pride in their dwellings (through something akin to a government "buy back" of refugee housing when they leave resettlement camps), and perhaps even giving them a "voice" by organizing local radio programs that would allow them to represent, share, and thus maintain their past.

Such ideas and initiatives emerge out of the thick, local, and experiential nature of EPA and CEDAR programming, which requires the suspension of assumptions and taken-for-granted realities and truth claims and forces us instead to approach reality with new insights and initiatives. This represents the most viable and socially beneficial way to "scale up" CEDAR programming and introduce it to wider social and institutional realms—whether to the realms of refugees in East Africa, to tribal reserves in North America, to the sphere of police-community relations in the inner cities of the United States, to the field of intercommunal relations in Cyprus, or even to churches with religiously conservative attitudes toward gays and lesbians.

It is through the experience of difference that we have the opportunity to deepen our understanding of the self—and of the other—and to strengthen our awareness of the limits of what can and cannot be shared. Knowing that this unique experience in difference occurs within just two weeks, we nevertheless feel as Aristotle did about the importance of viewing tragic drama: it is a means to broaden the pathways of empathy and so, crucially, of knowledge as well. In the best of circumstances, a full appreciation of difference leads us to a position of humility with respect to our existing epistemological claims, yet not necessarily to relativism or to questioning our values.[37] Maintaining the tension between an epistemic humility and our own value commitments can lead not only to fresh understandings but also to new initiatives that can bring CEDAR pedagogy to broader institutional realms.

The CEDAR experience of creating community around difference and building community outside our groups of constituent identity creates an opening, as well as an understanding of how different ways of being together are possible. These ways may entail a good deal of discomfort, but they can also engender greater respect for what it means to live together in difference. As we look to the communities in which we all live, difference always presents itself alongside opportunity.

CHAPTER SIX

On Boundaries, Difference, and Shared Worlds

Through having to negotiate the reality of nonkosher food in Israel, some Jewish fellows in the 2010 program were faced with the reality that what they understood as their own "home" contained myriad others.

THE PROBLEM OF BOUNDARIES

In 2011 we ran the program in Plovdiv, Bulgaria. At one of the sessions the anthropologist Elizabeta Koneska showed her documentary movie *Shared Shrines*, about a devotional shrine in Macedonia used by different Muslim sects as well as Eastern Orthodox (and other) Christians.[1] The response of our participants was fascinating. Many of the Russian Orthodox fellows were outraged at such a violation of boundaries, which is how they interpreted the fact that so many religious groups prayed in the same shrine, an act they saw as sacrilege. Religiously obligated Sunni Muslims from Kosovo and Bosnia expressed a similar reaction. On the other hand, a number of secular participants applauded the movie, seeing it as the necessary overcoming of all particularities and boundaries in some new universalism. From the organizers' perspective, what was so interesting was how people reacted to this documentary film—they saw it not as providing new information on lived religion in the Balkans but as evincing some moral agenda regarding which they had to take a stance (either for or against). What everyone was struggling with, however, was clearly the issue of boundaries.

Boundaries represent one of the most important and recurring themes of all CEDAR programs. A major, explicit, and stated goal of the school is the "decentering" of self; and the question of boundaries and their repositioning has been a critical component of school dynamics. Boundaries by definition impose constraints. And by constraining, they differentiate, limit, restrict, define, and break the flow of what would otherwise be a fractal universe (of thought, emotion, sensuous perception, or physical reality). They constitute the frames of a reality. They are given in the past. This pastness, the givenness of a past imbued with authority, is what Hans Gadamer has noted as the ground of our very existence in time. All innovation and creativity can progress only in reference to this past and its givenness.[2]

Consequently, the traditional or the given—that is, what we think we already know—is what we take to be authoritative. It is what defines the field of our vision, including our innovative and revolutionary visions. Boundaries, the origin of our categories and symbolic differentiation of existence, are always given in the past (included in what we already know, or think we do). The ground of our existence is always an already given reality that provides the boundaries in and through which we experience reality.

The future, of course, can bring new frames. It can reorder what is in the frames. It can, in Gregory Bateson's terms, turn existing frames into "muddles." And that is precisely the risk that is inherent in the future and future-directed action, which a good portion of CEDAR programs is dedicated to achieving. The future represents the potential for creativity, which means breaking apart and reordering what is already framed in one particular way, or pattern, or set of patterns. Boundaries are reframed, limits breached, constraints torn down, clichés unpacked; as a result, new meanings emerge. This is always a risky business, but a necessary one, for individuals as well as for all societies. The very openness of the future thus carries the potential to question existing categories and the boundaries through which they are constructed. Though given, boundaries are never uncontested, and the inherently open-ended nature of this contestation makes working on boundaries an endless project, part of the continuing human enterprise.

To some extent the integration of existing boundaries with future possibilities is the "boundary work" of each generation, but in another sense it is also the work of each and every individual. With this work, which we must note is often accomplished with a good deal of discomfort, the dialectic of past and future is filtered through two major, if contradictory, impulses. On the one hand is the impulse to absolutize existing boundaries, on the other is the impulse to overcome the constraints of all boundaries. In the nature of things this first impulse is usually associated with a certain "pastness," or orientation toward the past, while the second is more future directed. When past and future are integrated by either making existing boundaries absolute or overcoming them completely, the boundaries themselves are lost, dissolved into absolute totalities or absolute negations. Their very quality as boundaries—that is, entities that both separate and connect, divide and unite, differentiate and bring into mutual relation—is overcome and lost. Lost, too, are what resides on these boundaries: sentiments, hesitations, affects—and, most tragically, human beings.

We see this all the time, not just in the great sweep of history, with its wars and mobilization of public sentiment for or against some real or imagined enemy, but in our personal relations as well. We tend either to solidify as one group against an other (group or individual) or to erase all borders, proclaiming an all-embracing sameness in which all difference tends to get lost or, at the very least, minimized and trivialized. Often, of course, these processes develop concomitantly, creating an insurmountable boundary excluding one group and melding all differences among those on "our" side of that boundary. We did this as children playing on the street; we do it as adults at meetings; and we most certainly do it in our media as we report on "others" of one stripe or another. Psychological work on this is legion.[3]

Boundaries are also by their nature ambiguous, both because they are defined by the center of meaning and order that they circumscribe and because they are perennially open to what lies beyond the order-giving power of that center.[4] As well as being ambiguous, they are dangerous—a truth we know from generations of anthropologists working in the traditions of Mary Douglas and others.[5] We also know this truth from the treatment of marginal groups, whose marginality is precisely vis-à-vis the margin, or boundary, of whatever the dominant group may be. And we know it as well from many centuries, if not millennia, of bloody wars, which have so often been fought over the violation of a boundary.

The opening story illustrates both the discomfort that we often feel upon approaching boundaries—our own and those of others—and the two quintessential "modern" solutions to the issue. The first inclination, to erase all boundaries, is represented by those secular individuals who applauded the movie as the panacea to all the world's problems. Simply deny all particularity, or difference, they say. All religions are the same, as are, by implication, all people; therefore, we should not dwell on differences but rather celebrate the oneness. The second approach, demonstrated by the response of our young Russian Orthodox and Muslim members, is to reify the differences and boundaries between ourselves and others into untranslatable essences. Both are modernist responses in that both absolutize boundaries—either by totally doing away with them or by conceptualizing them as unbridgeable walls.[6]

Both responses should remind us of the discussion of tolerance in chapter 2, about the moves to either (a) do away with the difference by claiming an overriding sameness or identity or, (b) by contrast, make the other and the objectionable so beyond the pale that there is no need for tolerance. Either solution results in a retreat behind impenetrable boundaries rather than an attempt to straddle them.

These two modernist responses see boundaries as razor-thin entities, reducible to individual units and markedly devoid of constitutive collective characteristics.[7] In this understanding, modernist social and political concepts have essentially obviated the need for what was traditionally understood as tolerance. In its place a whole new conceptualization of the self and relations between selves has developed, predicated on the inviolable boundaries between autonomously constituted agents, which are maintained by the rights of each.

In contrast, learning to live with difference involves an approach to boundaries very different from either of these two modernist responses and based on something closer to tolerance. Tolerance is a virtue that has everything to do with boundaries and margins. It does not have anything to do with all-out threats to who we are, whether external or internal, physical or symbolic. Rather, tolerance concerns behaviors and beliefs that exist on the "margins" of the group's identity. Jews and prostitutes, legally defined in medieval canon law as tolerated entities, were good examples of precisely this type of marginality, as were lepers, sometimes Muslims, beggars, strangers, and so on. All existed on the borders or margins of society, neither beyond nor fully within.[8]

We can thus posit societies with "thicker" boundaries—that is to say, societies where a great number of individuals, behaviors, and attitudes are considered marginal. As opposed to these, we can also posit societies with relatively "thin" boundaries—that is, societies with little room for marginal behaviors, attitudes, and points of view. Hence, the thicker the boundary, the greater the number of issues of tolerance and intolerance that emerge and become relevant, as the chances increase that one will come into contact with behaviors and beliefs one finds objectionable and which make one uncomfortable without necessarily threatening one's physical existence. Tolerance is such an important theme in societies with strong group identities, because these societies have very thick boundaries, with very wide corporate identities and group definitions, which necessitate tolerance, however often and tragically they may be defined by its absence or failure.

Contrary to the way we generally think, modern societies—defined, say, by the Déclaration des droits de l'homme et du citoyen, the U.S. Constitution, Article 9 of the European Convention on Human Rights, or Article 10 of the Charter of Nice—are in fact less about being more tolerant than about doing away with group boundaries. This point is best summed up by Count Stanislas de Clermont-Tonnerre in his 1789 speech to the French National Assembly quoted in our introduction, which denies any group identity to the Jews.[9] In a sense this has been the project of all modern states, in their liberal form even more than in other more romantic-national forms. The statement applies not simply to Jews but also to every corporate group, and certainly to those who consider themselves "truth communities." Within the public sphere, boundaries are parsed into razor-thin edges, and individuals interact not as members of groups but as bearers of rights (citizens' rights, social rights, human rights, and so on). Group identities in the public sphere have thus been replaced by individual identities, and the problem of tolerating difference has been replaced by the legal recognition and entitlements of rights. Thus we can say that the modern world has elided the problem of tolerance, *obviating the need* to be tolerant rather than *making* people tolerant. It has replaced tolerance with rights.

While tolerance is all about the type of relations that exist on these boundary lines of group identity, much of the economic and political thrust of the modern world order is actually about replacing group identities with individual ones and replacing tolerance with rights. In the process, tolerance goes from being a community-centered act to an individual, almost psychological attribute or personal characteristic.[10]

While this approach may have characterized nineteenth- and twenti-eth-century realities in parts of Europe and North America, we are currently witnessing a return to group-based identities and, especially, religious com-mitments in many parts of the world. Moreover, the growth of transnational identities predicated on religion, ethnicity, and nationhood, but not depend-ent on statehood, is calling into question the type of individual identities that stood at the core of the revolutionary European idea of citizenship in the eighteenth and nineteenth centuries. The social realities of many places in the world, both in Europe and beyond, however, raise serious questions about the adequacy of a rights-based approach to living with difference and with those who exist on our borders.

We suggest that at the core of these developments lies a hidden and unresolved challenge—namely, our inability to deal with the existence of what may be termed "radical difference" and the challenge it presents to the way we negotiate boundaries in our societies.

TRUST, CONFIDENCE, AND DIFFERENCE

Most current approaches to difference, including religious difference, rest on a set of pretty clear assumptions, which include the secularization of the political realm, the privatization of religion, and the removal of substantive differences and divergent claims to the Good from the public arena. Increas-ingly, however, we have come to find that the secular public sphere is not devoid of its own claims to the Good, and that these claims are in fact among the most contested in the contemporary world. Thus, and to take but one example, the secular-liberal vision of society rests on a particular under-standing of humankind as composed of autonomous, self-defining moral reasoners. It is precisely this idea of moral autonomy, however, that is con-tested by billions of church-, mosque-, temple-, and synagogue-goers the world over. For these religiously committed individuals, people are not mor-ally autonomous but instead live under heteronomously enacted and revealed laws. The secular, liberal claims for moral autonomy are thus not as neutral as they are presented to be.

Beyond the problem of current visions of the public square is the fact that removing competing claims to the Good really does more to displace the problem than to solve it. As we have come to see, this situation leaves us with an extremely "thinly" defined public sphere to which the commitment of many individuals and communities is highly mediated. On the other hand, hidden within or at the boundaries of this public sphere are very "thick" moral communities, many with highly rigid definitions of the Good, along with clear boundaries of membership and loyalties.

Removing moral claims from the shared sphere of our interaction does not in fact seem to leave us with a "usable" space for our common life. Rather, it appears to leave us with two separate spheres of shared interaction: in one, defined to a great extent by the state and its institutions, we interact according to abstract and increasingly impersonal rules of justice defined by rights. These rights are, however, far removed from a second, more intimate, and more manageable sphere of public trust in which we grant one another a certain degree of moral credit predicated on our shared communal, religious, ethnic, or racial pasts. The discourse of the first realm is of rights and state sanctions; that of the second is of trust and solidarity, care and compassion, loyalty and commitment.[11]

Thus, that public reason on which our constitutional social order is based is precisely what has also left us bereft of a sense of belonging. By a *sense of belonging*, we refer to claims that can be made on us, or that we can make on others, that appeal not to a sense of abstract justice or right but rather to a shared sense of solidarity, trust, and mutuality based on a shared "past." As the Boston ward leader Martin Lomasny related to Lincoln Steffens at the beginning of the twentieth century, "I think that there's got to be in every ward somebody that any bloke can come to—no matter what he's done—and get help. Help, you understand, none of your law and justice, but help."[12] Robert Merton famously quoted this comment to explain the perseverance of the political machine in American political culture.[13] Legalized assistance, doled out by cold, bureaucratic organizations (welfare agencies, settlement houses, legal aid clinics, public relief departments, etc.) was seen as involving a loss of self-respect. In an impersonal society, the political machine provided, in Merton's terms, humanized and personalized methods of assistance that did not degrade the recipient. What the comment gets at is the chasm between a regime of enacted, abstract rights and life in a human community of mutual care and shared belonging.

The human need for empathy, trust, and solidarity is of course recognized today, as in the past; but these things are to a large extent accepted aspects of the private realm, whereas the public arena is ruled by the dictates of an increasingly abstract reason. Consequently, in many Western societies the division of public and private realms parallels the divisions between truth and trust, reason and empathy, justice and mercy. Of course the extremely complicating variable in today's world is how religious communities have come to represent that side of the equation associated with trust, empathy, and mercy. Whatever else they are, religious communities are decidedly not universal, which is precisely where they come up against the rules of an abstract and universal reason. The 2012 ruling of the German High Court in Cologne that male circumcision constituted "bodily harm" and hence violated a child's right to self-determination when imposed by his parents is an excellent example of just such a problem and of the way the demands and obligations of a community of belonging (in this case, Jewish or Muslim) can be seen as running up against the abstract rule of individual rights.

Here we should recall the words of two nineteenth-century thinkers who had something of value to say about religion. According to the first, "Religious distress is at the same time the expression of real distress and the protest against real distress. Religion is the sigh of the oppressed creature, the heart of a heartless world, just as it is the spirit of a spiritless situation. It is the opium of the people."[14]

Karl Marx was right—in fact, more so than he himself realized. For he believed that the abolition of particular historical conditions would lead to the abolition of the "illusion" of religion. He did not realize that religion and religious distress constitute the human sigh par excellence, the sign of a distress that is rooted in our very existence, not one that can be transformed from within history. In our current conditions, at least part of that distress is rooted in the aforementioned divide between the terms of truth and the terms of community, between the demand for justice and the demand for mercy.

The second thinker whose thoughts on religion are pertinent here is Emile Durkheim, the founder of the discipline of sociology. For Durkheim, religion was "a unified system of beliefs and practices relative to sacred things, that is to say, things set apart and forbidden—beliefs and practices which unite in one single moral community called a Church, all those who adhere to them."[15]

Every student of the social sciences is familiar with this quotation, and it is indeed quite relevant to our current project. For if a liberal constitutional order is predicated on secularism and the workings of a public reason, then the sacred has little claim on the public realm; and when it makes such claims, it is reviled as fundamentalism. If this is the case, however, it is difficult to make a claim for moral community or, again in the terms posited above, for maintaining the terms of empathy, trust, and solidarity among those whose relations are structured by the self-same legal order.

We thus find ourselves at the core of a conundrum. We have an idea of the public order as (a) secular, (b) predicated on the idea of the morally autonomous individual, and (c) oriented toward the preservation of different sets of individual rights rather than the realization of an idea of the Good. At the same time, more and more communities within the nation-state are made up of individuals who do not understand themselves to be morally autonomous but rather see themselves as enacting different sets of God-given commandments; those individuals are not at all secular and have very clear ideas of a public Good—indeed, a divine Good—that trumps the legal recognition and assurance of individual or citizens' rights. The result is the establishment of two competing arenas of social interaction, expectations, mutuality, identity, and commitment. One can be defined by what we call *trust*, the other by what we term *confidence*.[16]

Communities of trust are those of shared moral dispositions, familiarity, sameness, and shared experience in which moral credit is granted to community members in situations of risk, and in which the value of peace trumps that of abstract justice.

In contrast, the realm of confidence refers to a collective of rights bearers of dissimilar experience and disparate moral values in which justice is the highest virtue and others are experienced as potentially dangerous, requiring the enactment of security measures.

We can usefully schematize the two models as follows:

Trust	Confidence
Shared dispositions	Multicultural values
Moral community	Community of rights bearers
Value of peace	Value of justice
Familiarity	Strangeness
Sameness	Difference
Shared moral dispositions	Disparate moral values
Shared experience	Dissimilar experience
Moral credit granted to communal members	No credit granted, knowledge demanded
Others experienced as a risk	Others experienced as a danger
Risk leaves room for doubt	Danger requires security
Our group	Other group

(For the social scientists among us, we note that we are fully aware of how much this categorization recalls the classical distinctions drawn by nineteenth-century sociologist Ferdinand Tönnies between *Gemeinschaft* [community] and *Gesellschaft* [society]. Our quibble is with the notion that one historically came to replace the other; we believe that both continue to exist concomitantly, that in fact in some sense one even produces the other.)

Increasingly, in the contemporary world, communities of trust are markedly diverging from communities of confidence in values, principles of social organization, orientations toward the other, self-understandings, and fundamental terms of organizing collective experience.

The increasing divergence between truth and trust, reason and empathy, justice and mercy—that is, between the claims of a moral community and those of justice—is one of the most challenging of all boundary issues facing us today. The right side of our chart—representing confidence, security, and abstract justice, with the other assumed to be dangerous—is one of individual rights bearers, whose boundaries are sheer and absolute with but the thinnest of margins. The left side of our chart, on the other hand—defined by trust and moral credit, where peace is the supreme value—is to a large extent a social space constituting wide margins and thick boundaries, where a good deal of discomfort, occasioned by actions of the boundary of the community, is "tolerated" precisely because individuals are seen as essentially part and parcel of one's own ideas of self. Think here of a family—even an extended family, or members of one's church, synagogue, temple, or mosque—to get a sense of such broad boundaries that encompass both self and multiple others.

It may be useful to conceptualize these worlds, which are really worlds of shared belonging, in terms taken from the legal theorist Robert Cover. Cover emphasized the importance of shared narrative—that is, shared stories—to the making of community, irrespective of the shared legal order that binds different communities into one society. In his writing, Cover shows how legal orders themselves are positioned within much more extensive narrative frameworks of communal meaning and belonging that make up an embracing worldview (of which law is but one element). "No set of legal institutions or prescriptions exists apart from the narratives that locate it and give it a meaning. For every constitution there is an epic, for each Decalogue there is a scripture."[17] And we often know the stories much better than the intricacies of the law itself.

In today's world, however, the concepts of moral individualism and a secular public space, with their stories of liberal humanism and of citizens as autonomous moral decisors, are increasingly alien to many groups within civil society. Since these groups share different narrative universes, the establishment of trusting relations between such (religious) groups and the state and between such groups and more secular liberal groups and organizations becomes close to impossible. Consequently, social interaction between them rests solely on the legal order—that is, on a type of confidence guaranteed by the state. Trust, by contrast, is reserved for those within the communal boundaries who share epics and scriptures that are alien to the legal orders of the state. With time, the boundaries of these different universes become impenetrable, because we can no longer listen to the stories of others.

The problem with this bifurcation of our social world is not that we live in two universes. In truth, we live in many more. The real problem is that the first world, of trust and moral community, of mercy and "the gift," is predicated on sameness, familiarity, and our assumptions of knowledge of the "other"—who, of course, is no longer an other once she is known. The problem with this model is that sameness is always illusory—always partial, incomplete, and given to disruption. Nothing in the world is really "the same"; even snowflakes, we are told, are each different from one another in small ways.

If we predicate our moral community on sameness—even liberal sameness—we will always be disappointed. We will always find one group or another existing somewhere on the margins of this "sameness" whom we will see as traitors who violate our shared moral code and reveal their true colors of strangeness and difference, especially in times of trial and tribulation. We will always fall into Freud's "narcissism of the small difference" and so continually produce an other, against whom to define our own sameness.[18] At this point, the near other, he or she who is similar in so many ways but not in that one attribute, whatever it may be, achieves iconic standing as representing all that is different and threatening and therefore to be destroyed.

As long as trust is restricted to those who are the same, we will continually be patrolling the borders of this sameness to check for deviations and differences. The boundaries will be points of continual contention, fear, and opprobrium. In times of crisis (when the next bomb goes off on a London bus, or the next imam is arrested in Paris, or even, perhaps, when the economy slumps and I can no longer pay my mortgage), those who are a bit like us, but also a bit not like us, will come to take on a new aspect: not at all like us. The rise of political parties such as the Golden Dawn Party in Greece, Ataka in Bulgaria, Jobbik in Hungary, and the British National Party in the United Kingdom offer ample evidence of this phenomenon, illustrated by their very strong showing in the 2014 elections for the European Parliament. Those who are a bit different begin to be looked upon suspiciously, as possibly, perhaps even probably, dangerous; we will therefore invoke the laws of justice and the sanctions of the state and its security forces, rather than the moral credit of our shared communal experience. As we know, this was the experience of Jews in nineteenth- and twentieth-century Europe. In some ways, the pattern is repeating itself with Muslim citizens of European countries today.

The question thus becomes, how can we get beyond these models to build, or at least imagine, a new and creative way to live together differently? To do so, we will have to reinvent a space of interaction not predicated on liberal and modernist ideas of the self and of the boundaries between and interaction of different selves. We will need to have recourse to different foundations for mutuality, rooted in a recognition of "otherhood," and confront the problem of tolerating difference head on instead of attempting to define it away.

CENTERS AND DECENTERING

To return to this chapter's opening concerns, we must recognize that the margins, or boundaries, define the center. Beyond these margins the center no longer defines reality. This is true in multiple realms of human inquiry and practice—law, architecture, music, social science, literature, religion, medicine, physics—as well as, crucially, politics and society. It is true of ourselves as well. The center holds only as long as it organizes its margins. When the margins collapse, be they the margins of a discrete realm of knowledge, a building, species, metaphor, empire, or individual ego, the center's collapse will not be long in coming. The somewhat paradoxical result of this insight is that we are constituted on our boundaries, which means we are constituted on a plane that we do not fully control. Our boundaries are by definition the point of distinction, the point where self and other meet. They are the point still organized by the power of the center but also open to that which the center no longer controls: the other, which is beyond the organizing power of the center. Hence, their vulnerability; hence, too, the need to tolerate what is on and even beyond those margins, which are still defined by the center.

Boundaries both join and divide, bring together and distinguish. Even more important, they constitute the very existence of an object. As Martin Heidegger points out, "A boundary is not that at which something stops, but, as the Greeks recognized, the boundary is that from which something begins its presencing."[19] The problem of boundaries—their constitution, limiting structures, organizing power, and relation to what is beyond their purview—is one of the central challenges facing us in the contemporary world. While the analytic dimensions of this problem are as old as

humankind, the very proliferation of realms of knowledge and bits of information from these realms makes the problems ever more pressing. Yet we
must also remember that boundaries, precisely because of their inherent
complexity, also point to areas of creativity with the potential to restructure
relations between individuals and societies as well.

The importance of the margins in defining the center, and the challenges
to which this gives rise, is a truth that we know from both anthropology and
psychoanalysis. Marginal states and statuses become precisely those social
spaces where the identity of society is represented and the solidarity of the
group as a whole expressed.[20] In this role, the margins carry the potential to
provide an ongoing challenge to and critique of society and its received
knowledge, and become the live embodiment of that skeptical conscious-
ness which is necessary to a life meaningfully led with other people.

However, to have another patrol one's boundaries creates an inherently
unstable situation, one that requires a great expenditure of psychic energy to
maintain. As a result, there is often a tendency to do away with the other
who has such power over us—a tendency that is evinced all too often in the
fate of minorities within majority cultures. Doing away with the other,
either by elimination or incorporation into ourselves, thus allows us to patrol
our own boundaries. However, it also by definition means destroying the
other, who is necessary for the very constitution of self. It means, as the
nineteenth-century philosopher G. W. F. Hegel might have said, turning
the other into a slave from whom no recognition is possible or worthwhile.[21]
The move to incorporate the other may grant us safety and control, but not
recognition. Living with the reality of others' control thus leads to a situation of great fragility and uncertainty. The fact that our own boundaries are
in the hands of an other presents us with a frightening situation—namely,
less than total control over our very own constitutive terms of ordering,
meaning, and integration.

There is no final way out of this tension, and living with the uncertainty
of the other patrolling the boundaries of our own selves, whether collective
or individual, is no small burden to bear. Yet as Martin Buber observes,
"Every actual fulfillment of relations between men means acceptance of
otherness. . . . The strictness and depth of human individuation, the ele-
mental otherness of the other is . . . the necessary starting point. . . . The

individual is a fact of existence insofar as he steps into a living relation with other individuals. . . . The fundamental fact of human existence is man with man."[22]

Tragically, all attempts to overcome this type of mutuality have all been disastrous in their consequences. Not surprisingly, following World War I, Buber saw the breakdown of dialogue as the greatest threat to human existence, which he viewed in turn as dependent on "the rebirth of dialogue."[23] Preserving the realm of what he termed "betweenness," what we are calling the boundary or margin, is the precondition for living with the other—that is, living with difference

We will always remain dependent on that other who posits our own boundaries, even as we bridle at that very dependence. We are condemned to coexist in the mutual tensions of these relationships. To accept this fundamental truth of human life, the power of the other to constitute the core of our own existence on the personal level, is what psychoanalysts would term ego-maturity, a rejection of infant narcissism. To accept it on the collective level is what we would call tolerance, a rejection of group certainty, whether religious or secular. Engaging with it intentionally may well be the therapeutic action best suited to our present situation—an ethic of responsibility and not, as Max Weber warned against, of "ultimate ends."[24]

The question is, how do we manage this boundary work, this straddling of the margins, without demanding conformity to our own center of meaning or community of belonging? One possible mode of such engagement, advocated in CEDAR programs, is to implement a notion of shared usage rather than shared meanings. We can attempt to instigate a practice of shared usage as a way to reconstruct the space we share with our others, concept by concept, place by place, artifice by artifice. Such a practice would allow us to rethink our mutual world from scratch and to recognize the boundaries between what can be shared (usage) and what cannot (meanings).

In fact, and often enough, what we share is not so much meaning but a common use of words. We do not share a meaning with others "all the way down" (see the discussion on the limits of shared meaning in chapter 1) so much as agree on a common use of our words. Thus, I may, lacking a hammer, use a handy rock to knock a nail into the wood of my porch; after I get tired, you will help me, taking the rock up and using it in a similar manner. You have not at this point rejected your preexisting definitions of rocks and hammers, but you have agreed to work with me to solve this problem of getting the nail into the wood with no hammer in sight by using the rock in this manner. This is what we do with words. We share usage, not necessarily meanings, or always, only, partial meanings.

That we share usage rather than meaning is a significant point. Often, entering into situations of dialogue, we feel we have to arrive at shared or common meanings. This aim, however, is often illusory, frustrating, and ultimately destructive of one set of meanings, resonances, identities, and symbols. It simply does not make sense to wish a Muslim and a Catholic from Mostar to arrive at the same associative meanings on viewing a cross. It is also, at the end of the day, deeply disrespectful of differences. If the meaning is shared, then in some sense one of the meanings is promulgated and accepted by all parties. What is lost is the difference in meanings, symbols, resonances, and so on. Shared usage, however, does not compromise the different meanings, and its potentialities for mutuality are therefore correspondingly greater.

Needless to say, in some cases this whole problem does not even arise. When we discuss parts for the lawn mower with the mechanic, the overlap of meaning is probably close to 100 percent. Usage and meaning coincide, and little potential for misunderstandings exists.

This overlap, however, is not a state that we should generally strive for beyond the realm of spark plugs or the gasoline/oil ratio in a chainsaw. It is certainly not desirable when discussing matters with which each of us identifies most intimately, and which represent for each of us the core of truth, belonging, and meaning in life. To attempt to enforce such shared meanings destroys what it is we each seek to preserve, and through which our own selfhood and unique way of being in the world is made manifest and meaningful.

Moreover, as already noted, the illusion of so-called shared meanings often only hides a deeply discordant reality in which meanings are not shared at all, even though we act as if they were. However, this understanding can hold only so far. When pushed, the "as if" is broken, and one falls back into quite exclusivist understandings of a reality that is no longer shared at all. The story about the cross in Mostar is one example; another is the Palestinian Authority official who did not come to the meeting. In fact, in the latter case, after it was clear why the official was not there to meet us, it was fascinating to hear the Palestinian participants voice their opinions that the real explanation for our failure to meet a Palestinian Authority official was the "Jewish money" that was behind the program. They were somewhat nonplussed when it was pointed out to them that all sources of funds were listed on the program, that only a small percentage of the funds originated with Jews, and that the person in charge of funding was Seligman. They were even more confounded because Seligman had been clearly identified as pro-Palestinian in the context of the national struggle between Israel and Palestine; in fact, earlier in the school, he had pointed those very questioners in the direction of texts about the 1948 war that gave a good description of the destruction of Palestinian national culture and homelands at that time, texts with which they were unfamiliar.

If we can shift our orientation to that of shared usage, rather than demanding shared meaning, we might simultaneously transpose the whole problem of boundaries of self and other to a new plane of mutuality. The boundary of self and other would then no longer be the absolute boundary of different meanings, for which the only solution is either (a) destruction (physical or symbolic) of the other or (b) the ultimately hypocritical positing of "shared" meanings (which is in fact also a form of destruction of the other). A realm of shared usage could overlap with that of shared meaning, but it would not have to do so. It could have its own set of (pragmatically defined) practices, allowing interaction, collective action, shared orientation to goals, and so on without demanding either the reduction of all shared action to (a) shared interests or (b) shared meanings.

Shared usage would minimize the need for shared meanings or would, at least, allow us to construct a shared world in which the "shared" aspect of the meanings was not absolutely necessary to constitute our interaction. It would even allow us to admit this to ourselves and others. Quite consciously, we would from the start set out a circumscribed understanding of what is shared. As pointed out earlier, we do this all the time, mostly when involved in economic transactions—that is, in our market interactions. In our churches, synagogues, mosques, and schools, however, be they public or parochial, the assumption is that we share meanings "all the way down." Hence we conduct debates over school curricula, the presentation of gay lifestyles therein, gay priests in the Anglican communion, and so on. In point of fact, however, the assumption that the person sitting next to me in the pew is experiencing the same meanings of the prayer as we recite or chant the same liturgy is probably false—and certainly not verifiable.

There is a certain hesitancy to admit that we often share usages, or could conceivably share only usages, without necessarily sharing meanings— though we could share these as well, if only we could agree on them. The point, though, is that we could live together without such shared meaning as long as we agreed to share usages. All too often our demand for shared meaning gets in the way. If we could bracket out—even temporarily—the need for shared meaning, we could perhaps begin a process of questioning, playing with, reframing, and reshaping boundaries that would only resound to our credit and make our life with other people less filled with feelings of friction, betrayal, and mistrust. This is what we attempt to do in CEDAR programs through the pedagogy outlined in our previous chapters.

When successful, such a process can lead to the challenging of existing categories of thought, at which point new ways of arranging or framing reality appear that either define anew the work done on what are now newly constituted boundaries or are defined around a different vision of boundaries. We saw this happen in the 2005 CEDAR program in the Israeli military cemetery at Kiryat Anavim, where the citizen soldiers of the nascent Israeli army who fell in the struggle over the Jerusalem corridor in the 1948 War of Independence (what for the Palestinians is the *nakba*) were buried. At that moment, and one cannot extrapolate beyond that moment, the Palestinian Israeli fellows could not, according to their own testimony, look at the Israelis only as oppressors and conquerors; they saw them also as young, fallen men and boys.

An American Muslim woman experienced a similar reframing of her taken-for-granted assumptions about the world in 2006. She was surprised that her Muslim hosts in Stolac were warmer and friendlier toward, and identified more with, the Palestinian Christian fellow whom they were also hosting. In this case their identification with the Palestinian as fellow sufferer clearly trumped the American's status as a coreligionist. In these and similar cases, the taken-for-granted reality that was questioned was not so much a specific, discrete event within the context of the school (the failure of a Palestinian official to show up to a meeting, feelings of voicelessness, etc., as discussed earlier) but rather a more general orientation or disposition toward the other that the participant had to recalibrate in the wake of the CEDAR experience. In all cases, experience—in the face of and together with other fundamentally confounded meanings—forces the individuals involved to recalibrate boundaries and reimagine the relationship between themselves, their community, and the community and boundaries of others.

These examples and others discussed throughout our study present the possibility of change, of reframing and reconstituting boundaries and the frames of experience. It is precisely this potential on which we all must draw to develop new educational models that make use of a "decentered" self as part of the moral and character development of younger (and older) adults. After all, if educational institutions in general, and universities in particular, are to support the moral development of the individual, they must develop the wherewithal to provide for social and emotional, and not just intellectual, skills—what are called in early childhood education "noncognitive abilities" (the need for which, however, does not cease at middle school). To be effective citizens in the twenty-first century, students (in the Aristotelian sense) must develop certain capacities, particular sets of personal, emotional, intellectual, and social skills that include the ability to accept ambiguity, to live with discomfort and make decisions in situations of less than full knowledge, and to be reflective on such decisions and judgments. These are all capacities developed in CEDAR programs, together with new understandings of the nature of knowledge, its social components and inherent limitations, and the difference between *knowledge of* and *knowledge for*, all of which, as we have argued throughout, are essential to learning to live with difference.

Conclusion

Ultimately there are really only two ways to increase our tolerance to what is different. One is, in fact, to erase or minimize the difference. This entails reframing our terms of sameness and difference so as to diminish or trivialize the differences. In the context of the Protestant Reformation of the sixteenth century, this was known, among Christians (Protestants and Catholics), as irenicism, most often associated with the name of the great humanist scholar Erasmus. The idea here was that what united Catholics and Protestants, and hence all believing Christians in the West, was much more important than what divided them; they should therefore focus on what was common rather than what was contested. As we know from the religious wars of the next hundred years, this approach was not a huge success.

In many ways, however, it is the approach that most of us continue to adopt when engaging with difference. We seek "common ground," or what we share with the other, rather than "harping" on what is different. In today's world, our common or shared humanity is often the trump card in any argument over accommodating difference. The contemporary, post–World War II ideology of human rights is perhaps the best example of this type of approach. We are all human; we all have rights; and these rights trump other, more particular concerns or obligations and so must be respected above all else. When these rights come up against other, ingrained communal dictates and traditions (such as infant circumcision) a huge conflict of values ensues. As discussed in the introduction, the extension of the notion of rights to all sentient beings, including animals, has resulted in similarly irreconcilable conflicts over different types of religious slaughter. Divergent views concerning the place of women and minors in different religious communities revolve around similar issues.

In all cases the core problem is that certain groups are less amenable than others to dissolving their sense of group belonging in favor of notions of a universal humanity. The thrust of the modern world, first within the nation-state over the course of the eighteenth and nineteenth centuries, and now on a global scale, is after all to transform all particular identities and loyalties, in all regional communities, into a more overarching sense of identity and common values. As we discussed in chapter 6, however, this orientation has often failed to provide people with a sense of belonging and meaningful connection and is at present being challenged by communities with religious, ethno-religious, or often just plain nationalist identities and commitments, across Europe, Africa, Asia, and elsewhere.

In fact, we seem to have gone as far as we can go in the move to dissolve particular commitments and identities, to shorten the distance between self and other, or to render the gap meaningless in our new globalized consumer culture. A reaction is setting in, and neoliberal accolades for globalization are not going to reverse the trend. More of the same is not a solution. Attempts to deal with difference by denying it, further dismantling those group identities that make difference meaningful, or understanding difference solely in terms of individual acts or behaviors (or beliefs), are simply not going to work.

We come thus to the second approach to living with difference, which has been argued throughout this book. This approach is not about denying difference, or refusing to admit the saliency and importance of the ways people are different, but rather about modifying people's attitudes toward what is different and what they find objectionable. In essence, then, we advocate that all of us learn to judge our judgments in a new way and develop certain capacities for what has been termed "second-order" thinking, or thinking about thinking.[1] This goal can be accomplished only in the crucible of experience, where thinking is not an abstract activity but must continually be measured against practical experience—in this case, practical experience of individuals who are different, even if that difference is somewhat uncomfortable, or threatening.

The anthropological work of Mary Douglas has made famous the insights of the sociolinguist Basil Bernstein concerning two critical variables of culture: group and grid.[2] *Group* refers to the axis of group membership and belonging, and the group's social controls may be tight and rigid (say, a combat unit in the armed forces) or relatively lax (a graduate student cohort in a university humanities department, for instance)—or of course something in between (a sports team). As developed by Mary Douglas, the other axis of culture, grid, is that culture's classification system: the grid, or matrix, through which we make sense of the world. In Bernstein's original work this grid was understood as being highly context-dependent, as opposed to relatively abstract. A context-dependent grid of meaning would be used by, say, a family firm that has worked in the same building for three generations—deciding to whom to grant credit, for example. A more abstract grid would be one used by a multinational corporation that would not know its customers but would use an algorithm prepared by yet another multinational corporation to make policy decisions.[3]

However, we can use these two axes to help clarify our argument. Thus, the original diagram would look something like this:

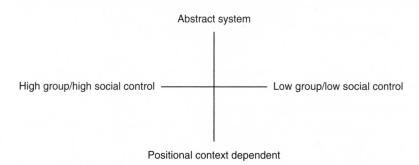

We can in fact see the general thrust of modernity as one that has eviscerated the axis of group membership and belonging as far as possible. It has advanced the agenda of difference by simply denying group belonging and thus making difference a purely individual attribute, a move we can represent visually as follows:

However, our contemporary world is characterized by identity politics and demands for recognition put forward by many different groups—religious, ethnic, and tribal, as well as those organized around sexual preference—the emergence of which has revealed the limits of the modern approach and the need, whether we like it or not, to accommodate group belonging and identity in the shared sphere of our public culture.

What this suggests is that this new reality requires a drastically different approach, using the vertical axis of classification systems instead of the horizontal axis of group membership. We must henceforth produce our social classifications of the other within the crucible of particular experience, rather than through the abstract schema of different ideological systems (regardless of how liberal they may be).

In effect we must return to a more particular, positional, and less abstract set of classification schema and continually refer back to (as well as judge) the "to do" that is at the basis of our schema. The very stress on *knowledge for* rather than *knowledge of*, discussed throughout this book, focuses the mind on the concrete and experienced rather than the abstract and the generalizable. Again, to present the argument visually, we must adopt behaviors that move us in the following direction:

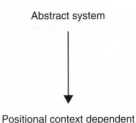

Abstract system

Positional context dependent

In a sense we are arguing for a shared, even if dissimilar, way of life rather than common legal norms as the basis for a life with difference. This argument curiously resonates with ancient Confucian political thought, which makes its own distinctions between *li* (the power of ritual) and *fa* (the power of law). *Fa*, which is essentially words, is of limited efficacy in establishing social harmony, because any word, any claim, can be disputed. Words—and all commands, all laws are words—immediately call forth their contraries. Any argument calls up the possibilities of a counterargument, just as any command and any truth claim can invoke its counterfactual. For these reasons the Confucians preferred *li* (ritual) as the basis of a shared life. Having no verbal or denotative dimension, rituals could not be argued, refuted, or opposed.[4] They simply were. As acts, they had no contraries. This argument is similar to that made by the anthropologist Roy Rappaport on the critical role of ritual in establishing and maintaining social order, given the indeterminacy of language and even its downright propensity to lie that is inherent in our use of symbols.[5]

While we, the authors, do not advocate shared rituals—indeed we are skeptical of such a notion, because different communities each have their own—we do strongly advocate shared experience. And this is where the notion of shared, albeit dissimilar, needs to be explicated and parsed. We recognize that such experience may sometimes be uncomfortable. You may be the only observant Jew—wearing a *kippah*, no less—in a sea of Irish faces at a wake; or you may be the only Irish Catholic family attending a *shiva* (seven days of Jewish mourning rites, carried out in the home of the mourner). In both cases you will probably be clueless about the etiquette. But that is OK. An experience is being shared, and a common habitus constructed—even as each group maintains its own loyalties and commitments and can participate only at the boundaries of the other's ritual world, and even as all feel somewhat uncomfortable in the interaction. Comfort is not the point; sharing is. Boundaries, after all, are exciting places, as we discussed in chapter 6. They separate but also connect. Our property line divides us from our neighbors, even as we can reach across it and share the time of day or a cup of tea.

For centuries, within the Ottoman Empire, Jews and Muslims in North Africa and the Arab lands shared sacred shrines, as did Christians and Muslims in countries such as Cyprus, Greece, Bulgaria, Macedonia, and other Balkan lands. Only with the destruction of the empire and emergence of ethnically and religiously homogeneous nation-states did this practice end, with different saints becoming firmly identified with one or another ethno-religious community. To be sure, in Morocco to this day such sharing can be found at the level of folk religion, as can the practice of Muslims bringing the Jewish communities the first baked bread at the end of Passover (the custom termed *mimouna*, reciprocated in past times by Jews bringing Muslims the first bread eaten at the end of the days of Ramadan). Here too, then, a shared life, a common culture built around *different* ritual obligations, nevertheless served to bind *different* communities together. A shared shrine is not a common religion; but one space shared and reserved for dissimilar practices is a strong marker of the ability to live in close proximity to the other in a common, though dissimilar, culture. The reactions of many of the CEDAR fellows to the documentary film on such a shrine in Macedonia shows how far we have come from that world, which has been largely replaced by the limiting conditions of law and the abstract notational systems separating individuals and groups into different places and separate spaces.

Today, the most common arguments for how diverse peoples can share a world are predicated on human rights—that is, on law par excellence. Recent in origin (gaining real traction only in the 1970s), the human rights argument has come to be seen by many as the panacea for almost all social ills, from the evils of social exclusion to different forms of prejudice, oppression, and the refusal to recognize or respect the other.[6] In fact, according to Michael Ignatieff, human rights can even be seen in some contexts as a form of idolatry—putting human needs and aspirations on a pedestal that ultimately cannot be defended philosophically.[7] Others see the whole discourse of human rights as rooted in a religious sensibility.[8] Shorn of any political context, or indeed of any notion of human beings as existing within communities, the ideology of human rights is one of a universal individualism that at least one social thinker, Samuel Moyn, sees as a contemporary utopia. Significantly, human rights have never been tied to social rights or social democratic commitments, precisely the "positive liberties" or entitlements that humans can enjoy only within community.[9]

Hannah Arendt offered one of the most salient critiques of the idea of free-floating rights when she pointed out that rights, as understood in the eighteenth and nineteenth centuries, were all functions of men's and women's positions within political communities; divorced from these communities, rights simply made no sense.[10] Where, she asked, would the "right" to have rights come from, if not from membership within a community and all that that entailed?

However we view the case, and whatever one's assessment, the fact remains that a rights discourse suffers from the weaknesses of all other forms of *fa*, or legal notation: their very articulation invites contraries. As soon as human rights are invoked, so are opposing demands for a discourse of "Asian values" or the idea of an "Islamic Declaration of Human Rights" (which was suggested in 1947, contesting the proposed UN declaration that was ratified the following year). Indeed, the challenge of squaring a global, rights-based civilizational discourse with local cultural reasoning, whether predicated on Islamic sharia law or Jewish halacha, is proving a formidable challenge to those involved.[11] As the foreign minister of the Taliban in Afghanistan reportedly said, "We believe we are actually here to serve human rights, but there is a slight difference on the definition of these rights. We believe in rights according to Islam, and if anybody is trying to impose their definition of the human rights on us, they will be sadly mistaken, because this world is not a world of one culture or one religion."[12] While we may easily condemn the Taliban and detest their actions, it is more difficult to critique the point. A brief example will illustrate.

In October 2013, the Council of Europe overwhelmingly passed a resolution condemning infant circumcision as a "violation of the physical integrity of children."[13] The pan-European intergovernmental organization called on member states to both initiate public debate over the issue to protect the rights of children against human rights violations, and adopt legal provisions to ensure certain "practices will not be carried out before a child is old enough to be consulted." At the same time, the Nordic Ombudsman for Children has also argued that religious circumcision without the child's consent contravenes the basic rights of boys, and that it should be banned.[14]

This followed a series of rulings in German courts, first in Cologne in May 2012 and then in Hamm in September 2013. The first ruled that circumcision caused grievous bodily harm and so was made an illegal act; the second demanded that circumcision be discussed with the child and be performed only with his consent (Jewish male infants are circumcised when eight days old).[15] In December 2012, in response to widespread protests, Germany passed a law (1631d) declaring circumcision legal when performed by a trained practitioner. This law, however, has done little to calm the waters or solve the irreconcilable conflict at the heart of this controversy. From the perspective of absolute individualism, ensconced in an ideology of abstract human rights, it is in fact difficult to defend cutting off a male infant's foreskin if there is no medical reason for doing so. (Note, moreover, that it is only in the United States that medical reasons for circumcision are regularly advanced and accepted; this is decidedly not the case in other countries. The rate of circumcision in the United States is the highest by far of any non-Muslim and non-Jewish country.) How, then, should we address difference? How should we accommodate particular communities claiming adherence to the authority of a revealed (and hence nonrational) text and set of obligations that are outside the rational discourse of individual and abstract rights? Indeed, if we recall the current attempts in Europe to ban kosher and halal slaughter on the basis of protecting animal rights, mentioned in the introduction, we arrive at a most paradoxical situation. We end up with a set of rules that, if fully implemented, would make it impossible for Jews or Muslims to live in Europe. They would not be able to eat, nor would they be able to induct their male children into their communities. Under the rubric of a purely abstract and certainly reasonable set of strictures, we would end up effectively ridding Europe of communities that in some cases have lived there for millennia. A liberal, rights-based approach would thus accomplish by law what Hitler failed to do by force. Surely there must be another way.

This problem, in fact, takes us right back to the issues we dealt with in chapter 6: communities of trust and confidence, membership in and belonging to a moral community, and how the values and defining terms of such a community are markedly different from those of a community based on abstract rights guaranteed by law alone. A propos, American readers will remember well just how easily long-established liberties were challenged by the Patriot Act following the September 11, 2001, terrorist attacks. Yet once we accept the communal aspect of our lives, we are immediately faced with the inherently exclusionary character of such communities and the ensuing challenges posed by that exclusion. How do we ultimately live with difference and share civic space with individuals and groups who embrace a radically different view of the good life, the meaning of divine commands, and the social definitions of communal membership?

This whole book has been an attempt to explore an alternative to abstract rights, legal formulations, and definitions of human beings as essentially individual agents devoid of collective or communal obligations, commitments, and understandings of self. Indeed, as noted in chapter 5, bringing CEDAR pedagogy and practices into this highly abstract and mediated realm of legal rights and entitlements would be a significant contribution to how we address social crises that are now understood solely in terms of a "rights deficiency." We need, rather, to review our often less than critical acceptance of the "ideology" of human rights in any and all circumstances without attending to the differences and of each and every particular case. There are no "best practices" that are applicable globally. There are only the solutions that emerge from within local environments and constraints. Trying child soldiers from northern Uganda at the International Criminal Court may not, at the end of the day, be the most effective way to reestablish social life in a war-ravaged region. Imposing European notions of personhood and gender on the refugee populations of Africa may, similarly, be less than respectful of people's agency and real needs for self-determination. We must learn to see and respect difference, not simply as producing variants of who "we are," but as constitutive of real, lived differences in individuals and societies—differences that must be factored into our political solutions to social crises.

Bringing these understandings into the institutional arena of law, we can say that not only human rights law is of great importance to generalizing the practices and perspectives developed in CEDAR programs. We do well to recall that the principle of difference is inherent to the workings of our legal system. After all, the notion of differently situated individuals who must be treated differently in order to be treated equally (i.e., substantive equality) is the very heart of equality jurisprudence. If the law cares about equality, what does it mean, we must ask, to treat differently situated people equally? This problem is of major importance in all religious freedom jurisprudence and appears continually in cases involving sexual orientation and child welfare, and indeed in all arenas where the indeterminacy of difference makes itself felt.[16] While the problem goes back to Aristotle and his ruminations on equity in the Nicomachean Ethics, it is of great and continuing contemporary relevance, both in all issues of legal pluralism and, in the U.S. and European courts, in all cases involving multicultural jurisprudence.[17]

Not surprisingly, CEDAR's pedagogy has found most resonance with people who already share an understanding of who we are and how we live in the world and so recognize the need to use CEDAR techniques and approaches in their own communities. The real challenge is bringing these practices and pedagogic perspectives to bear on wider institutional realms in society—law, refugee resettlement, education, and so on. As we have seen from the case of Uganda, this can be achieved, slowly, carefully, from the ground up, and always with attention to the particular case at hand.

To no small extent, CEDAR programs are devoted to the creation of a third space, that "potential space" that the developmental psychiatrist D. W. Winnicott discusses as central both to the development of the individual ego and to the ego's ability to relate to an alter, or other. For Winnicott, the third space of "transitional objects," like an infant's teddy bear, which occupies a space that is neither the baby nor the mother, allows the infant over time to perceive himself (and so mother) as a separate entity and hence establish a relationship to the world beyond based on what he or she contains within.[18]

This ability to reach across the boundary between self and other, to grasp one's own feelings through the imaginative leap toward the other, is the heart of empathy. Empathy rests on some elision of self. It requires some renunciation, however fleeting, of the ego's central place in its own symbolic universe. It is contingent on some blurring of boundaries and of one's taken-for-granted assumptions about the world. This decentering of self and one's collective assumptions is the different pedagogy that we have attempted to put into practice at CEDAR and that we have been advocating throughout this book.

A shared culture requires at least some degree of empathy, whether understood as trust, solidarity, or what Emile Durkheim understood as membership within a "moral community."[19] We can see this place in the different stories told here, which illustrate the changing perceptions of CEDAR fellows toward the other, and their redefinition of themselves with respect to those others. The space of the program allows for the spanning of self and other in a repositioning of the boundary line between them, as reframed through the experience of CEDAR pedagogy. However, and as we, the authors, have attempted to indicate throughout, this spanning of self and other can be translated into concrete organization activities with significant impact in society.

The psychoanalyst Thomas Ogden defines empathy as "a psychological process . . . that occurs within the context of a dialectic of being and not-being the other. Within this context, one plays with the idea of being the other while knowing that one is not. It is possible to try on for size one identification and then another (i.e., to play with the feeling of being the other in different ways), because the opposite pole of the dialectic diminishes the danger of being trapped in the other and ultimately of losing oneself in the other."[20] This "trying on for size" of the other, being and not-being the self and other at the same time, is the core of our projective identification with the other and the origins of empathy. Through such fellow-feeling, it is the source of world creation as well.

Creation, or at least all creation after God's initial creation *ab nihilo*, takes place in the spaces in between. Only in those in-between spaces is the place for the emergence of the new, or other. It is this very space that opens up the potential for something new—not previously represented, symbolized, or imbued with meaning—to be truly created. As we have tried to show in this book, CEDAR pedagogy is about creating such spaces.

Signposts for Organizers

INTRODUCTION: ON THE ETHICS OF ORGANIZING

Organizers and hosts must have a clear idea of why they are organizing the school and what they wish to achieve. They must make this clear to the fellows from the beginning of the program, both in their first, digital communication with potential fellows and when all meet for the first time. The amount of work that is demanded from everyone in the school—fellows, staff, organizers, and others—is immense and, for most, totally unexpected.

Precisely because it challenges people to change the frames of their knowledge, not just to add bits and pieces to already constituted frames of understanding, the school must be a place of utmost integrity. Not only must the organizers demand of themselves ten times more than they demand of the fellows, during the working of the school they must also be willing to set aside other goods and goals. The authority of the organizers rests, at the end of the day, not just on the work they invest but also on the integrity of the process: no integrity, no authority—and for that matter no community, just a site of contract and exchange. This position is not in itself illegitimate, but it is inimical to the realization of the school's goals and will ultimately defeat its purpose.

The school seeks to move people to a new understanding of difference and the possibilities of solidarity between people who are, nonetheless, irredeemably different. There is nothing we can do about difference—it is essential to who we are—and we should thus seek the solution to the challenge of living together not in overcoming difference but in living with it. This is the hard work of the school, the rough ground of its pedagogy. And it can be achieved only through maintaining the integrity of the process at all levels of planning and programming.

Not everyone working with and in the school need be so devoted to the school's aims. Lecturers who come for one or two or three days clearly cannot have this level of commitment to (or for that matter, understanding of) the school's goals. Administrative personnel who help local organizers also need not have this type of relationship to the school. But the directors, organizers, and staff—those who set the tone and who are, ultimately, invested with the authority and responsibility for the program—must understand what is demanded of them so that they in turn can, reasonably and ethically, make the demands they will inevitably make of others in order to run the school successfully.

PLANNING THE SCHOOL: DEVELOPING A THEME, GETTING THE WORD OUT, CHOOSING FELLOWS

The schedule is the heart of the school. It takes a whole year to build a schedule.

The cornerstone of the schedule is the Call to Fellows, which should go out nine months before the school takes place. Dissemination of the call can take many forms, but it is usually done through listservs, affiliated websites, and similar forums. The call includes the title for that year's school and two or three paragraphs on what it will explore. This task is much harder than it seems, for what is needed is something very different from academic conference titles. A school's theme must be practical, concrete, and particular. It must refer to a local reality, but it must also be generalizable and transferable to other realities beyond that year's locale. Titles dealing with neighborhoods or comparing cities have been used in the past and work well. For example, the 2011 CEDAR title, "A Mosaic of Margins," was good for Bulgaria but is also evocative of other places and other realities. The title of the December 2012 EPA in Uganda, "Whose Community? Memory, Conflict and Tradition," was relevant both to African realities and those in the many other parts of the world from which fellows were coming. After the title is chosen, it must then be "unpacked" in two paragraphs explaining what the school will explore and how this flows from the given title. Here, too, the concrete aspects must be given primacy, but in such a way that people from a broad range of different experiences and places can relate to it, even as it retains its local specificity and relevance.

The Call to Fellows ends with a website address where prospective fellows can fill out application forms and send their CVs and five-page essays on why exploring difference is important to their work or life experiences. This is important because it encourages applicants to actively think about how the goals of the program relate to the context in which they live and work. Ideally, fellows range in age from their late twenties to early sixties (younger fellows are usually not mature enough, and for older fellows the program can be too demanding). The maximum number of fellows is thirty, and optimally there should be a broad spread of different professions and occupational groupings among them (clergy, leaders of nongovernmental organizations, civil servants, graduate students, journalists, etc.). Gender parity is desirable, as is the greatest possible religious, racial, ethnic, national, and professional diversity. Since the goal of the school is to confront difference, organizers must ensure that there is as much difference as possible among the fellows. A number of spots (around 20 percent) should be reserved for applicants from the host country. The program provides need-based scholarships for all fellows; otherwise, attendance would be limited to fellows with financial means or access to such, restricting the group to a certain international elite and thereby defeating the purpose of the program.

BUILDING THE SCHEDULE
In principle, building the schedule is easy. In practice, however, it is challenging. There are three major components of the program: lectures, site visits, and facilitation (see the section "What Needs to Happen"). Usually, in addition to day trips in the city or region, at least one site visit involves a night or more away from the major site of the school. We show films and hold discussions about them, both of which are powerful learning tools in the environment of the group.

In addition, communal lunches and dinners must be scheduled, as these meals are always shared, along with some daily, low-intensity physical activity (dance, yoga, stretches, etc.). Time must be found for all. Every day should begin with a fifteen-minute "housekeeping" session to go over the daily program, review problems, and address last-minute changes and complications. Ideally, half an hour of deconstruction should follow, in which the events of the previous day are reviewed and assessed for their importance to the learning experience.

The key to the schedule, however, is to see to it that the pieces fit together. Every decision must be queried: why we are giving this lecture, why we are going to this place and not that one (presumably because it is connected to the program in some way, not just because it is a tourist attraction—explain why and how). There must be thick contextualization of site visits, explanations, and discussions of how the sites relate to the theme of the program. Ideally, of course, lectures and site visits should be linked chronologically, though we must also realize that logistically this is not always possible.

The first day's activity should always be a get-together and general introduction, and the final day should always include a final evaluation and ceremony, which means that there are actually twelve working days. Typically, weekends are workdays. Days are typically twelve hours long, from around 8:30 A.M. to 8:30 P.M. (with breakfast at 7:30 A.M.).

Similarly, care must be taken to strike a balance between international lecturers and local ones. Just as we need international fellows, so too we need international lecturers. Both give the necessary perspective and can provide a broader frame than simply local views. These lectures too must be coordinated.

It is important to arrange an initial overview lecture and a walkabout in the locale where the school takes place to see the problems fellows will be confronting and sense the contextual, experiential, and lived, rather than the abstract, general, and intellectual.

The real trick of building a schedule is striking a balance between the desire for openness and flow and the need for structure. Without planning and structure, there can be no school. On the other hand, if everything is set up far in advance without due attention to context and changing circumstances, the school cannot work properly. For a July or August program, the schedule can be roughed out in January or February to provide some idea of how the days will look and what we will do when. Deciding the dates of the field trips is of great importance. April is, then, the time to begin to go over the program day by day to see how each day is shaping up, what we know, what we still need to find out, which ideas can be realized, and which must be sent to the scrap heap. For a summer school, this period of late spring is the most intense and difficult in terms of planning. It is important for someone in an administrative position to visit every site, restaurant, and so on and find out what to expect and whether our plans for the place are going to work (the restaurant may be great but, for example, unable to handle forty-five people). The trick, of course, is to be able to see clearly what a situation is going to look like six months down the road. (Example: failure to take into consideration in April that the swimming pool in Velingrad, Bulgaria, would be packed with locals on a Sunday in July, leaving no room for fellows, resulted in awkward moments and lost time.)

Time must be left for staff meetings each morning; these can take place over breakfast if need be.

Reasonable time between meals must be programmed.

Meals in restaurants usually take a bit more than an hour.

RUNNING THE SCHOOL: DAILY CONCERNS

The school is a vast enterprise that requires coordination of people, programming, and provision for people's material needs (food and lodging), as well as leaving room to have some fun and give people a little (not too much) free time. Any change in the schedule generally necessitates changes throughout. If some lecturer writes a month before the school begins to say she cannot come on the date set but is available two days later, it involves redoing the whole schedule and contacting numerous other people to see if they can accommodate the change.

That is perhaps obvious; less obvious is the fact that not everything can be thought of and planned in advance. One can plan for, say, how long it will take to get from the breakfast location to the first activity, but it must first occur to someone that this planning needs be done. Equally, one can calculate how long it will take to get from the day's last activity to dinner, but one cannot always plan for how long a trip will take, or how the day will flow during such a day or overnight trip. Trips to houses of worship, or to nongovernmental organizations, or to offices of other social actors are by their nature open affairs. We schedule a time, but it is never certain that we can keep to the schedule, especially if we are guests in another's house. Thus, some wiggle room must always be allowed, especially on trips.

More critically, and to ensure the best possible operation of the school and that the evaluator's feedback is assimilated by staff and organizers, daily staff meetings (mornings work better than evenings) before programming begins are essential to assess how the program is developing, check up on emerging problems, and coordinate planning. All staff need to be on the same page and similarly informed of developments.

Aside from the huge number of logistics that must be tackled before the school takes place—arranging flights for international fellows, hotels and food provisions, the always difficult issues of visa requirements—one of the greatest challenges of this period is imagining how the programming will appear in reality. This is both impossible and necessary. Each and every event facilitation—day and overnight trips, meals, etc.—involves a mass of details, which should be thought through as much as possible during the planning stage. Moving forty people around a town or in and out of buses in the heat of summer is no easy task and demands both planning and flexibility. (Is there water for everyone? Where can we make a bathroom stop? Are we on time for all planned activities? What do we do with Henry, who got left behind because he was sick and had to see a doctor?)

Moreover, each and every such visit or meeting with local churches, mosques, nongovernmental-organization activists, journalist associations, and so on must be "deconstructed" after the fact, contextualized, and analyzed, because the vision of reality presented by local actors such as these is always one of many, and it is highly influenced by their own political agenda and view of society and by the social forces at work in their environment. It always represents only partial knowledge and highly inflected knowledge (though presented, as often as not, as hewing to universal standards of validity), and so the schedule must accommodate some sort of reflection on such visits. (Of course, one cannot allot time to reflect on each and every site visit or meeting, and it is usually precisely the ones not scheduled for reflection that end up being the most "charged.") Here, too, staff must think on their feet to accommodate situations that arise, which probably means making slight changes to the daily schedule, which in turn means delving into and rearranging a mass of details.

One particularly difficult issue that continually arises, and which was discussed in chapter 4, is that of food and of providing for the dietary needs of all school participants. One possible guiding principle is to see "who is at the table" and develop one's strategy accordingly. That is to say, rather than developing any abstract principles about what to do (other than to try to accommodate everyone), see who is actually coming, determine what their needs are, and work from there. While this approach is good in theory, in practice it does not always work. For one thing, a number of people may use the terms *kosher* and *halal* but mean very different things by them. When Muslims say they do not eat pork or eat only halal meat, they may or may not eat fish cooked on the same grill as pork (and people coming from Muslim countries to Europe may not realize that this is a problem until it is too late). Jews too have almost as many levels of observance as there are individuals, and it is exceedingly difficult to provide for the religion's most stringent adherents (Jews with a certain standard of observance will demand separate dishes and silverware for meat and milk and require all food to be approved by a rabbinic authority).

Just to note the obvious, the school can only work with set meals. We cannot enter a restaurant and have forty different orders. This would be much too costly and take far too much time. Restaurants or cafeterias must know ahead of time how many people are coming, when they will arrive, and what they will eat. In this matter, buffet service is absolutely the best solution; it is the only way to restrict the mealtime to about one hour and to keep the price manageable.

It is important to note that people's eating needs are considered the school's concern. If we wish to build a safe space, one where people feel comfortable and can, at the end of the day, feel a sense of solidarity with people who are different from them, it is crucial that they be at ease at their table. Food is thus a public and not a private matter. Organizers must take the time and trouble to make everyone as comfortable as possible for the two weeks we are together. At a minimum, this means giving them food they can eat, whether they are religious Jews, Muslims, or Hindus or have other needs.

WHAT NEEDS TO HAPPEN: FORMING THE GROUP, FACILITATION, TOOLS OF PEDAGOGY, AND REFLECTIVE PRACTICE

Forming the group is one of the most important processes that happen over the course of the program. While there is always an introductory ice breaker, the real process takes place slowly over the first week.

Different types of activities go into group formation: bus rides, shared sports, dancing or yoga, cooking together (if that is possible), and of course facilitation. As noted earlier, the group is divided into small units of five members each (so six units for thirty fellows) that remain together for the duration of the program. They typically meet for an hour and a half every second day and share among themselves personal reflections on a theme that staff present to them. (The staff decide the theme during staff meetings). The theme is linked to that day's activities. Thus if a day's theme (and site visit) is focused on visiting a gay and lesbian church, the reflection could be: "Reflect on a situation when you felt you were judged by what you are rather than who you are." These reflections are personal, without being intimate, and remain within the small group. Only the fellows participate in these groups, and each fellow must speak without being interrupted by others; a timekeeper may be appointed to designate the time for each speaker in the ninety-minute session, with two rounds of speaking allowed.

It is important to encourage fellows to mix, sit down to eat, or ride on the bus with people not from their own country or linguistic community, and to *do* things with as many others as they can.

In the broadest of terms, the major pedagogical tool is the group itself. The combination of intellectual work in the lectures, experience in the practicums, and more personal reflection in the facilitation make the inter-relations between each fellow and the group the real nexus of learning. The forum in which this is most manifest is the deconstruction sessions in which the different pieces are tied together, but it is a process that goes on through-out the whole school.

Another component of this process is to continually make the connec-tion between the more personal or private encounters or interactions and the broader public and political issues. This step can be taken in the group dur-ing deconstruction or during different lectures, in the question-and-answer period. It can also happen in private discussions with fellows one on one. While not having the same impact as the larger, group discussion, this too is a very important tool of learning and teaching that staff must be aware of and use (to the extent that they feel comfortable doing so).

Again and again, fellows need to be reminded that they came to listen and to learn, and that this goal implies holding judgment in abeyance and rejecting final truth claims for much more modest aims and tentative understandings. Learning to listen and to reserve judgment are themselves important pedagogical tools.

The real tools of pedagogy in the school, however, are not the obvious ones. Of course the lectures are essential to imparting crucial bits of information about more general and more particular aspects of the school's problematique. And of course the site visits are central to an embodied experience of learning and understanding with more than one's mind and cognitive processes. These are the more obvious tools, and without them there would be, could be, no school. But the real learning takes place in the interstices between the different programmatic elements, in the juxtaposition of different forms of learning, in the relation of the group processes to the more academic lectures as well as to the site visits. The role of school directors and staff is to orchestrate this development in the subtlest of ways, to gently move this open-ended process along the lines of learning and understanding. Each, no doubt, will do so differently.

Reflection is built into the structure of all we do. Because the idea of the school is to query the assumptions we take for granted about the world and the other, we have built a reflective moment into the internal workings of the school.

In fact, the role of the internal evaluator, which is of major importance in the school, is to provide just this reflective practice (see appendix B, "Guide for Evaluators").

At a very different level, we have incorporated the practice of what we call "deconstruction" into the (almost) daily workings of the school. During this brief period in the morning before classes begin, we reflect together on some salient elements of what we experienced or learned the previous day (or days). Deconstruction is a critical part of the school; it is a time when the group as a whole can reflect together on the connection of the more intellectual and more personal aspects of the program. Integrative and reflective at the same time, it is the practice that moves the cognitive and intellectual work to a deeper level and, we hope, brings people to recognize the "stakes" of the different intellectual or political positions being espoused.

What deconstruction is for the group as a whole, staff meetings are intended to be for the staff. Staff meetings take place every morning and, ideally, permit staff to review what happened the day before and make any necessary adjustments to the schedule. Given restrictions of time, it is difficult to find the balance of logistical and substantive issues to be dealt with at these meetings. The whole time could easily be spent just on logistical matters; but this would be a huge mistake, because staff must have time to discuss issues arising during the school, whether related to particular individuals or to the group as a whole. Moreover, the staff meeting plays a very important role in keeping the staff together with a more or less shared and common vision of how the school should work.

The final reflective moment in the school is facilitation. The principle of small groups seems very good, as are the somewhat rigid structure (each person speaks for six minutes without interruption, with a second round of three minutes each before open discussion) and the absence of all authority figures from these groups. What must remain open for discussion and development in the course of any program, however, are the questions, which all staff participate in framing. As with any other component of the program, the challenge is always to see how the part fits in with the whole and how the questions posed to the groups encourage participants to reflect on the events of the day (or previous days).

Guide for Evaluators

Evaluation is reflection. In the context of intercultural programs it is critical to ensure that our actions and designs (at least the major ones) are thought through. We want our actions to stem from a careful thought process, based on evidence that connects the doing to a reason why we do what we do. While we are not always aware of all the motives and hidden goals behind our acts, we believe that through a process of reflection and evaluation we can in fact discover them (or most of them). We also want to have a way to track and understand our actions. Once we make sense of our actions and their impact on the program, we can change course midway if needed. We plan and design a program with our mission and values in mind. We design and reflect on the impact of the design on our goals and change course if needed. Any innovative program must emerge through the "doing." Goals are discovered and named as we reflect.

Here are some important assumptions about reflection itself:

Data is important. Meaning arises from the minutiae of the data collected. As reality is constructed in a group, the evaluators become part of the group and so may also buy into a vision, which might not be the fullest or the closest to what has in fact happened. Evaluators need the collected data to make informed judgments and reassess positions.

Immersion provides access to data. Because programs last for two weeks and encompass a small group (generally between thirty and forty people), qualitative methods are the best tools. There are many such tools, among them open-ended questionnaires, but the most important one is permanent participant observation. Through a stance of intense curiosity and personal experience, it becomes possible to formulate questions and so understand how participants see the experience.

Meaning emerges from data. We all need to make meaning. The goal of the evaluation is to be useful to and used by staff to understand the impact of their actions on the fellows and on the program. Every year a different "story" can be found, and it is crucial to capture that story, which will present the experience from as many points of view as possible.

Data is important to assess impact. We want the program to have an impact and to allow fellows to learn from our designs. Grand designs, however, may not be useful for the participants. We need to check and assess the consequences of our design. We need to ask participants and gauge the experience from their point of view. We need to see the program from the point of view of all stakeholders.

Methods of inquiry emerge from the questions posed. Different evaluators have different styles of evaluation. Each methodological choice is made according to what it is that we wish to learn. We may need to change our methods of inquiry as the program develops. Questionnaires will change from year to year, and they should be circulated among staff before the program starts, to make sure that they are not missing something that someone wants to learn and assess.

Mental agility is required. Speaking face to face is one of the most important tools for learning about the other's experience. We would like to understand every one of the fellows' experiences, but we cannot interview all of them in depth face to face, so we interview a few (it does not seem feasible to interview more than four in the course of a two-week program). Evaluators should craft a questionnaire that will capture their experience. They must observe and follow the program during its two weeks and not assume that the interviews or the survey alone will capture the experience.

What are the purposes of the evaluation?

+ To improve the program so that it can be the best it can be.
+ To describe what happens.
+ To establish organizational memory.

These objectives can be accomplished by focusing on the following:

+ What the experience was like from the point of view of each of the stakeholders, fellow organizers, and other participants.

+ What the story of this year's program was.

+ Which part(s) of the program went well from an organizational point of view and which did not (organizational and system assessment).

+ What part of the design needs improvement or change.

+ How to see criticisms not as personal attacks but rather as learning experiences (ask for clarifications rather than being judgmental).

Remember that the evaluator is in a difficult position. She needs to create the right distance from her fellow staff members as she joins in as one of the team. The evaluator's challenge is to keep the process independent, reliable, and friendly to all. She needs to work together with the staff for the good of the program as a whole. This "right distance" is essential for the evaluation process and the good of the program.

THE EVALUATION PROCESS

1. Before the Program Starts

+ Send three questions to fellows about the program and their expectations.

+ Follow and track developments with the organizers. For example, check in by phone or by email every two weeks or month before the school. Be a compulsive note taker; it will help reinforce or debunk some of your own views. Because the evaluator is part of the group, she or he tends to buy into the group construction of reality; but notes are important counterfactual data. They provide necessary evidence to pass judgment about any action.

+ Speak with everyone on staff to find out if they are aligned with the overall goals. Also make sure to ask about their specific roles and their own personal goals.

+ Work as a team; help organizers and staff reflect on actions.

- + Prepare an end-of-program, semiopen questionnaire (align your questions to the needs of the program of that particular year).
- + Prepare the last evaluation session (generally just before the closing ceremony).

2. During School

- + Keep a journal of what is going on when; make sure to date everything carefully; write your impressions down all the time; trust your feelings; and speak with your co-organizers and write down what they say.
- + Keep a log of all activities (make sure you have a copy of the schedule and any other material that fellows have access to).
- + Keep a log of who speaks when.
- + Keep a log of the most important discussions and debates.
- + Keep charts of seating arrangements during lectures and meals.
- + Pay attention to the groupings and subgroupings while traveling and in informal settings such as eating.
- + Speak informally with everyone; above all speak with the person(s) you feel you do not want to speak to.
- + Keep your finger on the pulse of the group.
- + Attend staff meetings and take notes of the debates or issues.
- + Debrief with staff as the program develops.
- + Interview four fellows in depth.

Everything is data during the two weeks of the program. Once you have written it down, it is data. Decide with other staff what they want to know; this is also data for you, and you can learn about the hidden assumptions of your fellow staff by asking and listening. Meanings come out of details. Do not consider your memory foolproof. You will buy into the construction of reality of the staff and organizers, and your collected data will help you decide if you are right to do so or if you need to reassess.

3. Last Evaluation Session

During this hour and a half, fellows reflect together on the program without the presence of staff members. It is designed as a two-step session. Give an introduction about the role of evaluation for the school, review what you did, and explain the anonymity rule (no name will appear in the final report). Divide the fellows into three small groups, with an assigned note taker in each, and explain that she or he will collect these sheets. Then give the following prompt: "Brainstorm and come up with at least three things that you would definitively keep and three things that you would change." Make sure that the note taker writes down names of speakers and how many times the issue is raised in the small group. After forty to fifty minutes, have the groups come together and share between them. The goal of this exercise is to leave with the feeling that no major issue has escaped you. Issues will invariably come up, and people will discuss them. This is their chance to tell each other and the program how they feel about the experience.

4. After School Is Over

+ Debrief with all staff (international and local) before everyone disperses. Make sure to schedule time for this. Write notes. This is a very important step in determining the story of the school that seems to be emerging.

+ Take a vacation!

+ Analyze the data—immerse yourself in it. One way to do this is by typing people's answers to the questionnaire. Read the data over and over again, and use sticky notes to come up with the coding. (Coding: To create a story, you need to reflect on what people experienced and will need to substantiate your claims with quotations. Quotations are really very important to this process. Coding is basically organizing the data according to categories that make sense to you. It is quite a process.)

+ Write your report.

5. The Report

This will become the "official" memory, so be careful what is included and what is not. What questions should you ask yourself as you write your report?

These always depend on the particular goals for the program for the year. The program has overall goals, but also very specific goals for the particular school. Make sure you differentiate between them. Though the evaluation is based on the minutiae of your collected data, trust your gut feelings. However, make sure your intuition and your gut feelings are substantiated by the data. Making meaning is a dance between your intuition and the details of the data collected.

Ask yourself what happened: what was successful from whose point of view; and what was not, from whose point of view. Create a narrative, a story of what happened during the program. You can ask yourself how to improve and make your suggestions known. Present the program from the point of view of the fellows, and note whether staff saw it differently. How did stakeholders (staff and organizers, visitors and fellows) experience the activities, the classes, the facilitations, the informal aspects of the program, and so on?

Describe the program: activities, experiential components, goals, fellows, and staff responsibilities. Be careful not to identify anyone by name or by any other means; never quote anyone by name. Reflect on whether the organization worked. Be polite and do not blame your coworkers for missteps (though there will be many). If possible, write your comments and suggestions from the point of view of the structure. Make sure you know who your audience is, and think of them as you write the report.

Make sure you praise what was well done, what worked well. Do not focus only on the negative; staff also need to hear what they did right. If you want to improve something, point to what has worked well and turn that into a model.

Always check with your organizer before publishing the report. The report is an internal learning document, and if possible people should feel good about it, though this may not always be possible. You want them to be open to learning from it so that they can improve, change, and refine the program.

Study Questions for Discussion

CHAPTER 1

1. Why do many of us find it difficult to live with difference?

2. What is a community of difference, and why is such a community central to the practices and methods laid out in this book?

3. What can be achieved when we allow experience to precede judgment?

4. What types of orientations are necessary for this to happen?

CHAPTER 2

1. What are some common scenarios of nonengagement with the problem of difference in the contemporary world?

2. What is lost when we conflate experience of a particular reality with cognitive knowledge of it?

3. How can "moral credit" be a force that allows tolerance? How can we start giving moral credit to our others?

4. What is *knowledge of?* And how does *knowledge for* help us grant moral credit across boundaries of belonging?

5. How can the principles of shared practice allow for preserving difference while at the same time engaging with what is different?

CHAPTER 3

1. How can discomfort become a tool for learning?
2. What tools do we have to help uncover our taken-for-granted assumptions regarding our own group of belonging?
3. Why is it so difficult to act rather than *react* when we meet others?

CHAPTER 4

1. What is common to the three vignettes with which we opened this chapter?
2. Discuss the impact of emotions such as discomfort on experience and learning?
3. What would your experience of difference add to your understanding of difference?

CHAPTER 5

1. What is the role of power in politicizing cultural differences?
2. What attitudes should civic leaders take toward difference in their communities?
3. How is it that any difference can be made socially significant?

CHAPTER 6

1. How is the core of our identities defined by those who sit on our boundaries?
2. What are your own core identities and boundaries?
3. Do you have one core identity, or are we all eclectic beings?

CONCLUSION

1. How do human rights contradict the practice of living with difference?

Further Readings

Living with Difference is based upon more than a decade of developing the CEDAR pedagogy. During this time, there have been a number of sources to which we have turned in evolving the theoretical framework of our pedagogy, and most formative in that respect has been the work of John Dewey (1954, 1980, 1991, 1997) and Donald Schön (1983, 1990). We have found insights from a wide range of literatures—anthropology, sociology, religious studies, psychology, education, philosophy, international relations, literature, and poetry, among others—and most important, from a wide range of experiences with CEDAR communities of difference. Nonetheless, academic conventions require one to situate a text within a certain literature. While we maintain that the value of *Living with Difference* is best understood in the everyday of social life—and that this work is an example of publicly engaged anthropology (or publicly engaged religious studies) that is relevant to the theoretical projects of an array of academic disciplines—we recognize that many will see the challenge of living with difference as innately connected to issues of conflict and peace.

Conflict and peace are, of course, at the heart of *Living with Difference*, and our contention is that the key to keeping social relations from devolving into violence is engagement with others that encourages ethnographic self-reflection of taken-for-granted assumptions, epistemological humility, and shared experiences across lines of difference, therein seeding opportunities for relationships to develop. One of the most successful books on peace-building has been John Paul Lederach's *The Moral Imagination: The Art and Soul of Building Peace* (2005), and much of the appeal of Lederach's work is that he gives a context in which the individual can contextualize his or her peace-building efforts. *Living with Difference* applies Lederach's insights writ large by showing how morally engaged and civically responsible communities can be built. We do this largely by rejecting the dominant paradigm in peace-building—that difference should be privatized—and suggesting instead a way of living together by respecting difference, rather than aspiring to sameness. In a sense, we take very seriously Lederach's argument that the moral imagination is imagining oneself in relationship with another, and give an example of how we have put this into practice: the operationalization of the moral imagination is experiencing oneself in relationship with another who is different yet who can still be part of a shared community.

Community is an ongoing process, and *Living with Difference* draws upon classic works that show the impact of social restructuring on group relations (Lynd and Lynd 1959; 1982; Riesman, Glazer, and Denney 2001; Bellah 1970; Bellah et al. 1996; and Putnam 2000). As such, group development is central to the CEDAR pedagogy and influenced by work in education (Freire 1998a; 1998b; 2000; hooks 2003) and community organizing (Alinsky 1971; Warren and Mapp 2011). For it is through engagement and sustained dialogue (Saunders 1999) with others that transformation of relationships can emerge.

Such transformations are essential to peacebuilding, and there are many literatures that address issues similar to ours, contributing to the under-standing of conflict, violence, peacebuilding, and development, albeit from different approaches. One such body of literature focuses on religion and peacemaking. This includes works like Appleby's *The Ambivalence of the Sacred: Religion, Violence, and Reconciliation* (2000) and Gopin's *Between Eden and Armageddon: The Future of World Religions, Violence, and Peacemaking* (2000) that have been seen as setting the foundation for the field of religious peacebuilding. In *The Complex Reality of Religious Peacebuilding: Conceptual Contributions and Critical Analysis* (2010), Hertog roots her argument in the work of Appleby and Gopin and gives an overview of the field of religious peacebuilding. While she argues for religion as a resource in peacebuilding and seeks to provide a framework for analyzing those potential resources within a particular religion, her book looks largely to religious elite as the resource. As well, it suggests taking the good of religion and using that as a tool for peacebuilding. The problem with this is that in functionalizing religion she largely ignores the fact that religious convictions are often part of a worldview filled with prejudices. As well, in focusing largely on the tools elites use, she overlooks the contribution of religious lives to everyday understandings of community. In our book, we begin with the everyday of the community and argue that religious peacebuilding does not have to be about religion per se but rather can be about the place of difference in public or private lives. Most works that deal with religious peacebuilding assume religion as a tool but state that, for the sake of peace, religious belief should be privatized and kept private. In our efforts to take religion seriously, we see it not as something that is only private but rather as part of the public sphere that thus pushes us to respect the meaning of religion to those for whom it is a lived category and to appreciate the challenge of difference. As such, we approach religious peacebuilding—and peacebuilding in general—not as a component of religion itself but rather as an aspect of public life. This approach is akin to, inspired by, and in dialogue with the books of a number of thinkers, perhaps most prominent of which is Rabbi Jonathan Sacks's *The Dignity of Difference* (2002).

Not surprisingly there is a good deal of literature in history and in the history of ideas that deals with the intersection of religion, public life, and the challenge of sharing collective life with the religiously defined other. We often assign selections from this literature in our programs and use it together with our more experiential pedagogy to highlight a very different place of religion in the construction of a shared world (Elukin 2007; Laursen and Nederman 1997; Nederman 2000; Remer 1996; and Kamen 1967 are all excellent entry points to this literature). An important complement to this literature is a now growing corpus of work on tolerance and toleration as a concept in philosophy, sociology, religious studies, and history. The problems of tolerance are, as we discussed in chapter 2, of a set with the type of challenges fellows must face during the program. Much useful work on tolerance can be found in edited collections by Heyd (1996) and Mendus (1988), as well as in the works of Walzer (1997) and Seligman (2004). Further works, such as by Stanton and Stroumsa (1998), Sachedina (2001), Soroush (2000), and Zagorin (2003), explore the place of toleration in different religious traditions.

It is around issues of tolerance and coexistence that human rights are put forth as a means for assuring proper treatment of others. The vast literature on human rights ranges from their historical emergence (Hunt 2008; Ishay 2008) and applicability (Shute and Hurley 1993; Ignatieff 2001; Robertson 2013) to their universality (Donnelly 2012; 2013; Goodhart 2013) and relationship with religion (Kelsay and Twiss 1994; Banchoff and Wuthnow 2011; Perry 1998; Witte and Green 2012). Because human rights are predicated on individual rights, they can at times be found to be in conflict with the worldviews of some collectivities that do not prioritize individual interests over group interests. The cultural discourse around the applicability of human rights (Cowan et. al. 2001; Goodale 2009; Ignatieff 2001; Moyn 2010) shows that they are not the necessary precursor to tolerance and coexistence but rather a vision—or at least a set of guidelines—of how some wish the world to be.

Yet another literature concerns itself with this disjuncture between how the world could be and how the world is by giving an ethnographic face to conflict. A few examples include Bolten's *I Did It to Save My Life: Love and Survival in Sierra Leone* (2012); Neofotistos's *The Risk of War: Everyday Sociality in the Republic of Macedonia* (2012); Nordstrom's *Shadows of War: Violence, Power, and International Profiteering in the Twenty-First Century* (2004); and Ring's *Zenana: Everyday Peace in a Karachi Apartment Building* (2006). The strength of these works is that they convey the complications of violence and peace through their ethnographic stories and help us understand the environment in which a certain population toils. As discussed in detail, we ethnographically explore the problem of living with difference and building community in various locales where people from around the world all experience what it means to be outsiders and insiders. Various bits of the stories Bolten, Neofotistos, Nordstrom, and Ring tell are shared by CEDAR participants and get negotiated as they strive to form a community of difference. *Living with Difference* synthesizes the struggles people endure with a prescription for developing communities through a pedagogy of practice.

Again, our approach is markedly different from the many contemporary texts on conflict and peacebuilding (Barash 2010; Barash and Webel 2009; Crocker, Hampson, and Aall 2007; Darby 2001; Darby and MacGinty 2008; Fox 2014; Francis 2010; Fry 2007; Lederach and Jenner 2002; Murithi 2009;

Nye 2000; Philpott and Powers 2010; Richmond 2010; Zartman 2007) and even those focusing on peacebuilding and religion (Abu-Nimer 2003; Appleby 2000; Gopin 2000, 2002; Heft 2004; Hertog 2010; Johnston and Sampson 1994; Smock 2002). The implication of the vast majority of texts on conflict and peacebuilding is that the reader knows how to put theory into practice, and thus that the many hours of preparation studying theory and past conflict will translate into a more peaceful world. It is undoubtedly important to understand the nature of conflict and peacebuilding, but we argue that above all we need to move from *knowledge of* to *knowledge for;* and through our case study of the CEDAR programs we further highlight some of the limits of the approach of existing scholarship on peacebuilding, engaging with the theory through stories of group development. To do this, we make use of anthropology's humanizing insights into conflict (such as Bolten 2012; Chew 2001; Hinton 2002; Nordstrom 2004, 2007; Scheper-Hughes and Bourgois 2004; Tate 2007; Tishkov 2004) and apply them to the programs we create. Thus, *Living with Difference* advocates taking learning out of the classroom and into the world and seeing within the ethnography of a problem an example of how to turn theory into practice.

INTRODUCTION

1. Eugene Weber, 1976, *From Peasants to Frenchmen: The Modernization of Real France, 1870–1914* (Stanford, CA: Stanford University Press).

2. See Jay Bercovitz, 1986, *The Shaping of Jewish Identity in Nineteenth Century France* (Detroit, MI: Wayne State University Press), 44.

3. Quoted in ibid., 71.

4. Adam Withnall, 2014, "Denmark Bans Kosher and Halal Slaughter as Minister Says 'Animal Rights Come before Religion,'" *The Independent*, February 18.

5. Steven Erlanger, 2014, "As Hate Crimes Rise, British Muslims Say They're Becoming More Insular," *New York Times*, February 13.

6. Michael Paulson and Fernanda Santos, 2014, "Religious Right in Arizona Cheers Bill Allowing Businesses to Refuse to Serve Gays." *New York Times*, February 21.

7. Gregory Bateson, 1972, *Steps to an Ecology of Mind* (New York: Ballantine Books), 271, 272, 315.

8. David Cannadine, 2014, *The Undivided Past: Humanity beyond Our Differences* (New York: Vintage).

9. Lewis Carroll, 1973, *The Hunting of the Snark* (London: Chatto and Windus).

10. From 2003 to 2013, CEDAR operated under the name International Summer School on Religion and Public Life.

CHAPTER ONE. THE STORY OF PRACTICE

1. The first affiliate program, launched In December 2012 in Uganda and Rwanda, was organized by the Equator Peace Academy (housed in the Uganda

Martyrs University) and run by CEDAR alumni. Additional affiliate programs took place in the summer of 2013 in Canada (University of Toronto, Connaught Summer Institute on Islamic Studies) and Bulgaria (University of Plovdiv, Balkan Summer School on Religion and Public Life), both of which were organized by former hosts and lecturers of CEDAR programs. Additional programs are being planned in Zimbabwe, Guatemala, Botswana, Kyrgyzstan, and the United States—all similarly organized by CEDAR alumni and former staff.

2. All three stories are from Wasserfall's field notes.

3. See Martin Rein and Donald Schön, 1993, "Reframing Policy Discourse," in *The Argumentative Turn in Policy Analysis and Planning*, ed. Frank Fischer and John Forester (Durham, NC: Duke University Press), 145–166; Donald A. Schön, 1994, *Frame Reflection: Toward the Resolution of Intractable Policy Controversies* (New York: Basic Books).

4. John Dewey, 1916, "The Control of Ideas by Facts," in *Essays in Experimental Logic* (Chicago: University of Chicago Press), 239.

5. John Dewey, 1991, *How We Think* (New York: Prometheus Books), 13.

6. John Paul Lederach, 2005, *The Moral Imagination: The Art and Soul of Building Peace* (Oxford: Oxford University Press), 37.

7. On the concept of the "banking" model of education and the need to replace it with a "problem-posing" educational strategy, see Paulo Freire, 2000, *Pedagogy of the Oppressed*, trans. Myra Bergman Ramos (New York: Bloomsbury), 66–74.

8. On "being with" and what it entails, see Paulo Freire, 1998b, *Pedagogy of the Heart*, trans. Donald Macedo and Alexandre Oliveira (New York: Continuum), 29–30.

CHAPTER TWO. A PEDAGOGY OF COMMUNITY

1. Sigmund Freud, 1961, *Civilization and Its Discontents* (New York: Norton), 72.

2. The classic sociological study of this is Kai T. Erikson, 1966, *Wayward Puritans: A Study in the Sociology of Deviance* (New York: John Wiley).

3. John Paul Lederach, 2005, *The Moral Imagination: The Art and Soul of Building Peace* (Oxford: Oxford University Press), 5, 29.

4. John Dewey, 1980, *Art as Experience* (London: Penguin), 88.

5. John Dewey, 2004, *Democracy and Education: An Introduction to the Philosophy of Education* (New York: Dover); Joseph J. Schwab, 1969, *College Curriculum and Student Protest* (Chicago: University of Chicago Press).

6. Again, we refer to Lederach's work on peacemaking and the creative, and often serendipitous, moment that makes it possible. CEDAR, in fact, attempts to provide the container for such serendipitous moments in our meetings with the other.

7. Emile Durkheim, 1995, *The Elementary Forms of Religious Life*, trans. Karen E. Fields (New York: Free Press).

8. Francis Bacon, 1818, *Novum Organum Scientiarum* (London: Sherwood, Neely, and Jones), bk. 1, pp. 52, 53, 59.

9. This is the case worked out in the Jerusalem Talmud, Bava Metzia 8c, in the story of Simeon B. Shatah and returning a precious stone found on a mule that his students purchased from a gentile. The glorification of God's name as a reason for proper relations with gentiles (rather than purely prudential reasoning) can be found as well in Maimonides's Laws of Slavery (9:7–8) in his Mishna Torah, as well as in the Babylonian Talmud, Bava Kama 37b–38a. This last shows the great unease of the rabbis with laws ruling differential treatment of Jews and Gentiles. The Babylonian Talmud, Tractate Yoma 86a, shows just how serious an offense is the profanation of God's name, which Simeon B. Shatah said would result from not returning lost property to a gentile. These points are dealt with in Menachem Fisch, 2014, "Judaism and the Religious Value of Diversity and Dialogue," in *Diversitat-Differenz-Dialogoizitat: Religion in Pluralen Kontexten*, ed. S. Alkier, M. Schneider, and Ch. Weise (Berlin: De Gruyter).

10. Wilfred Cantwell Smith, 1991, *The Meaning and End of Religion* (Minneapolis, MN: Fortress Press).

11. Dewey, *Democracy and Education*, 134.

12. Ibid., 137.

13. Term taken from Marion Milner, 1952, "Acts of Symbolism in Comprehension of the Not-Self," *International Journal of Psychoanalysis* 33 (2): 189.

14. Massimo Rossati, 2015, *The Making of a Postsecular Society: A Durkheimian Approach to Memory, Pluralism and Religion in Turkey* (Aldershot, U.K.: Ashgate).

15. John Dewey, 1991, *How We Think* (New York: Prometheus Books), 109.

16. Ibid., 105–106.

CHAPTER THREE. A COMMUNITY OF PEDAGOGY

1. Paulo Freire, 2000, *Pedagogy of the Oppressed*, trans. Myra Bergman Ramos (New York: Bloomsbury), 110–118.

2. Deconstruction, one of the aspects of the reflective practice in our program, is discussed later in the chapter.

3. The Equator Peace Academy, created by CEDAR alumni, is modeled on the CEDAR methodology; it held its inaugural program in December 2012 in Uganda and Rwanda.

4. Islam is said to have doubled the number of its adherents in Rwanda since 1994, when the safest places during the genocide were Muslim neighborhoods and mosques. Muslims did not participate in the rampage and saved the lives of

Muslim as well as non-Muslim Hutus. See Marc Lacey, 2004, "Since '94 Horror, Rwandans Turn toward Islam." *New York Times*, April 7.

5. All stories are from Rahel Wasserfall's field notes.

6. Donald A. Schön, 1983, *The Reflective Practitioner: How Professionals Think in Action* (New York: Basic Books), 268.

7. Ibid., 280.

8. See for example, Renee Tipton Clift, Robert W. Houston, and Marleen C. Pugach, eds., 1990, *Encouraging Reflective Practice in Education: An Analysis of Issues and Programs* (New York: Teachers College Press); Paul R. Dokecki, 1992, "On Knowing the Community of Caring Persons: A Methodological Basis for the Reflective-Generative Practice of Community Psychology," *Journal of Community Psychology* 20 (1): 26–35; Julie S. Byrd Clark and Fred Dervin, eds., 2014, *Reflexivity in Language and Intercultural Education: Rethinking Multilingualism and Interculturality* (London: Routledge); Sharon Brisolara, Denise Seigart, and Saumitra SenGupta, eds., 2014, *Feminist Evaluation and Research: Theory and Practice* (New York: Gilford Press).

9. John Paul Lederach, 2005, *The Moral Imagination: The Art and Soul of Building Peace* (Oxford: Oxford University Press), 2, 7.

10. Shulamit Reinharz, 1992, *Feminist Methods in Social Research* (New York: Oxford University Press); Rosanna Hertz, ed., 1997, *Reflexivity and Voice* (Thousand Oaks, CA: Sage Publications); Rahel Wasserfall, 1993, "Reflexivity, Feminism and Difference," *Qualitative Sociology* 16 (1): 23–41; Ann Oakley, 1981, "Interviewing Women: A Contradiction in Terms," in *Doing Feminist Research*, ed. H. Roberts (London: Routledge), 30–61.

11. In 1980 and 1990, armed conflict between the Turkish government and Kurdish separatists led to the destruction of many villages in this area. The conflict started with the armed rebellion of ethnic Kurds in the 1920s. This area has seen open warfare between guerrilla organizations and the Turkish army. See Susan Meiselas and Martin van Bruinessen, 2008, *Kurdistan: In the Shadow of History*, 2nd ed. (Chicago: University of Chicago Press).

12. From a fellow at the International Summer School on Religion and Public Life, 2007.

13. David A. Kolb, 1984, *Experiential Learning* (New York: Prentice-Hall), 21.

14. For the importance of the subjunctive in social relations, see Adam B. Seligman, Robert P. Weller, Michael J. Puett, and Bennett Simon, 2008, *Ritual and Its Consequences: An Essay on the Limits of Sincerity* (Oxford: Oxford University Press).

15. Here and earlier, in chapters 1 and 2, we have used the concept of "bracketing" in a way similar to that discussed by Linda Finlay, 2011, *Phenomenology for Therapists: Researching the Lived World* (Malden, MA: Wiley-Blackwell), 161.

16. Slavica Jakelić quoted in Omar Sacirbey, 2006, "Taking a Tough Road to Tolerance: BU Professor Brings People Together by Confronting Differences," *Boston Globe*, October 2.

17. B. K. S. Iyengar, 2005, *Light on Life: The Yoga Journey to Wholeness, Inner Peace, and Ultimate Freedom* (Emmaus, PA: Rodale Books).

18. Lukianoff quoted in Jennifer Medina, 2014, "Warning: The Literary Canon Could Make Students Squirm," *New York Times*, May 18.

19. Adam B. Seligman and Robert P. Weller, 2012, *Rethinking Pluralism: Ritual, Experience, and Ambiguity* (Oxford: Oxford University Press).

20. Václav Havel, 1990, *Disturbing the Peace: A Conversation with Karel Hvízdala*, trans. Paul Wilson (New York: Alfred A. Knopf), 181.

CHAPTER FOUR. ETHNOGRAPHIES OF DIFFERENCE

1. Barbara Coudenhove-Kalergi and Christian Seelos, 2012a, *Case Study: EVN in Bulgaria (B)—Engaging the Roma Community* (Stanford, CA: Stanford Community Center on Philanthropy and Civil Society, August).

2. See ibid.; Barbara Coudenhove-Kalergi and Christian Seelos, 2012b, *Case Study: EVN in Bulgaria (C)—Making It Work . . .* (Stanford, CA: Stanford Community Center on Philanthropy and Civil Society, August).

3. Mouvement International ATD Quart Monde (International Movement ATD Fourth World) seeks to eradicate extreme poverty. It partners with people in poverty to create public awareness about the challenges of extreme poverty, to influence policies addressing poverty, and to give dignity to the poor. See www .atd-fourthworld.org/en.html, last accessed July 17, 2014.

4. As noted earlier, the Equator Peace Academy, organized within the Uganda Martyrs University, was begun by 2010, 2011, and 2012 CEDAR fellows, who participated in programs that took place in Cyprus, Israel, Bulgaria, and Indonesia. They ran their first program in Uganda and Rwanda in December 2012 and their second program in Uganda, Rwanda, and the Democratic Republic of Congo in December 2014.

5. Prometra in Uganda is a member of Prometra International, an international nongovernmental organization whose "purpose is to preserve African traditional medicine, advocacy and practice." Founded in 1971, with twenty-seven international chapters, its headquarters are in Dakar, Senegal. Here, we talk about Prometra Uganda, but for more on Prometra International, see www .prometra.org/about us/, last accessed July 19, 2015.

6. A physical woman who acts like a man is a "tomboy" (this is the term Indonesians use in conversation). Some in Indonesia identify five separate genders. See Sharyn Graham Davies, 2011, *Gender Diversity in Indonesia: Sexuality, Islam and Queer Selves* (London: Routledge).

7. There is no choosing; people need to attend all activities. It is interesting to note that most people over the years have obeyed the rule. Some might be late, some may get sick, but they participate. This rule has a very positive impact on the proceedings.

8. As Claudio Fernández-Aráoz observes, "Pushing your high potentials straight up the ladder will not accelerate their growth—uncomfortable assignments will." Fernández-Aráoz, 2014, "21st-Century Talent Spotting," *Harvard Business Review* (June): 54.

9. John Dewey, 1980, *Art as Experience* (London: Penguin), 260, 110.

10. Ibid., 106.

11. John Dewey, 1936, *Experience and Nature* (New York: Dover Books), 85, 86.

12. Ibid., 87.

13. This phrase was put forth by the authors in the early years of CEDAR to characterize the self-reflective pedagogic aim of the program.

CHAPTER FIVE. LIVING WITH DIFFERENCE

1. Michael Paulson, 2014, "Colleges and Evangelicals Collide on Bias Policy," *New York Times*, June 10.

2. Ben Feller, 2009, "Beer Summit Begins: Obama Sits Down with Crowley, Gates," *Huffington Post*, August 30.

3. Much has been written on these events. A brief review can be found in the following news outlets: on the Crawford killing, see Jay Caspian Kang, 2014, "Off Target on Toy-Gun Regulation," *New York Times Magazine*, December 16; on the Dontre Hamilton killing, see Monica Davey, 2014, "Former Milwaukee Police Officer Won't Be Charged in Death of Black Man in Park," *New York Times*, December 23; on the killing of Michael Brown, see Nikole Hannah-Jones, 2014, "How School Segregation Divides Ferguson—and the United States," *New York Times*, December 21; on the Eric Garner killing, see Nick Wing, 2014, "A Grand Jury Did Indict One Person Involved in Eric Garner's Killing—the Man Who Filmed It," *Huffington Post*, December 3; on the Freddie Gray killing, see D. Watkins, 2015, "In Baltimore, We're All Freddie Gray: Commentary," *New York Times*, April 29; and Sheryl Gay Stolberg, 2015, "Crowds Scatter as Baltimore Curfew Takes Hold," *New York Times*, April 29.

4. Jill Leovy, 2015, *Ghettoside: A True Story of Murder in America* (New York: Spiegel and Grau).

5. Christopher Winship and Jenny Berrien, 1999, "Boston Cops and Black Churches," *Public Interest* 136 (Summer): 52–68.

6. Christopher Winship, 2004, "The End of a Miracle? Crime, Faith, and Partnership in Boston in the 1990's," in *Long March Ahead: African American Churches and Public Policy in Post-Civil Rights America: The Public Influences of African*

American Churches, ed. R.D. Smith (Durham, NC: Duke University Press), 2:171–192.

7. Since 1999, Winship has been writing at least one article a year on the Boston collaboration between police and black ministers. This material is available at Scholars at Harvard, http://scholar.harvard.edu/cwinship/publications.

8. Winship, "End of a Miracle?"

9. Christopher Winship, 1999, "How Can Bitter Enemies Become the Best of Allies?" (Unpublished paper, Harvard University, Department of Sociology), 3.

10. Ibid, 21.

11. Separated by Pennsylvania Avenue, these two neighborhoods have the same architecture, though the condition of the buildings is different. Property taxes are higher in Shadyside, and the percentage of home ownership is lower in Homewood.

12. Pittsburgh City Planning, n.d., "Census Data by Neighborhood—Shadyside," last accessed June 20, 2014, www.city.pittsburgh.pa.us/cp/assets/census /shadyside.pdf (site discontinued); Pittsburgh City Planning, n.d., "Census Data by Neighborhood—Homewood West," last accessed June 20, 2014, www.city .pittsburgh.pa.us/cp/assets/census/homewoodwest.pdf (site discontinued). It is important to note that while a significant portion of the black community in the neighborhood is below middle class, 94 percent black does not mean 94 percent poor.

13. This vignette is based on David Montgomery's fieldwork.

14. For more on the dynamics of migration and development in Pittsburgh, see Roy Lubove, 1996, *Twentieth Century Pittsburgh*, vol. 1: *Government, Business, and Environmental Change* (Pittsburgh, PA: University of Pittsburgh Press).

15. On the great migration, see Isabel Wilkerson, 2011, *The Warmth of Other Suns: The Epic Story of America's Great Migration* (New York: Vintage). Those migrating north joined an already established black community, but the influx was quite significant. See Joe W. Trotter and Jared N. Day, 2010, *Race and Renaissance: African Americans in Pittsburgh since World War II* (Pittsburgh: University of Pittsburgh Press).

16. Sally Kalson, 2003, "Cartoonist Draws, Fires a Blank with Pittsburgh Joke," *Pittsburgh Post-Gazette*, November 19.

17. Steven High, 2003, *Industrial Sunset: The Making of North America's Rust Belt, 1969–1984* (Toronto: University of Toronto Press).

18. This shift affected those at the lower end of the economy, those more at risk of remaining at the poverty level. The shift continues to affect black males like Jaylen directly, since working-class positions in this new economy privilege female workers over male workers. See João H. Costa Vargas, 2006, *Catching Hell*

in the City of Angels: Life and Meanings of Blackness in South Central Los Angeles (Minneapolis: University of Minnesota Press).

19. See, for example, KDKA, 2014, "Pittsburgh Most Livable City in Continental U.S.," *CBS Pittsburgh*, August 26.

20. City of Pittsburgh Bureau of Police, 2010, *Annual Report*, p. 51, www.pittsburghpa.gov/police/files/annual_reports/10_Police_Annual_Report.pdf.

21. City of Pittsburgh Bureau of Police, 2012, *Annual Report*, p. 80, http://apps.pittsburghpa.gov/pghbop/2012_Annual_Report_v2.pdf.

22. Danielle S. Allen, 2004, *Talking to Strangers: Anxieties of Citizenship since Brown v. Board of Education* (Chicago: University of Chicago Press); Elijah Anderson, 2012, *The Cosmopolitan Canopy: Race and Civility in Everyday Life* (New York: Norton).

23. For more on this project, see the American Anthropological Association's online project "RACE: Are We So Different?" 2011, www.understandingrace.org.

24. Some African immigrants to Pittsburgh, such as the Somali Bantu, have ended up in predominantly black neighborhoods, largely because homes there have been more affordable than elsewhere. As a result, ethnic differences between Somali Bantu and black Americans have emerged, especially in primary and secondary schools. Personal communication with Ryan Gayman, July 22, 2014.

25. Personal communication with Gabby Yearwood, July 19, 2014.

26. Katrin Bennhold, 2014, "Reading, Writing and Allegations: Muslim School at Center of Debate," *New York Times*, June 23.

27. Alissa J. Rubin, 2014, "Questions Rebels Use to Tell Sunni from Shiite," *New York Times*, June 25.

28. Interview with Irina Chongarova, a partner in the Balkan Summer School on Religion and Public Life collaborative, August 20, 2014, transcript held in the CEDAR archives in Newton, MA (hereafter CEDAR archives).

29. Borislava Petkova, Milena Katsarska, and Desislava Dimitrova are all located at the University of Plovdiv and form part of the core of the Balkan Summer School on Religion and Public Life, a CEDAR affiliate. John Eade of the University of Roehampton (U.K.) is a partner in the Balkan Summer School on Religion and Public Life collaborative. Interview conducted August 20, 2014, CEDAR archives.

30. All quotes were taken from an interview with Paul Gwese, April 6, 2014, CEDAR archives. Gwese was a participant in the 2011 International Summer School on Religion and Public Life and is active in planning CEDAR programs in Zimbabwe. The authors thank Sarah Ligget for her assistance in transcribing the interviews of Angucia, Emon, and Gwese.

31. All quotes were taken from an interview with Anver Emon, April 4, 2014, CEDAR archives. Emon was part of the International Summer School on Religion

and Public Life programs in 2011 and 2012 and began the Connaught Summer Institute on Islamic Studies in 2013.

32. Wendy Gillis, 2013, "Islamic Scholars Experience Diversity of Muslim Practices at U of T Summer Program," *The Star*, August 25.

33. Rahel Wasserfall and Shari Goldberg, 2013, "Evaluation Report of the 2013 Connaught Summer Institute of Islamic Studies," CEDAR archives.

34. All quotes were taken from an interview with Margaret Angucia, April 5, 2014, CEDAR archives. Angucia was a participant in the 2012 International Summer School on Religion and Public Life and an organizer of the EPA.

35. For a strong, recent critique of this aspect of higher education in America, see William Deresiewicz, 2014, *Excellent Sheep: The Miseducation of the American Elite* (New York: Simon and Schuster).

36. From remarks made in an interview conducted on August 20, 2014, CEDAR archives. Both Elizabeta Koneska and Yuri Stoyanov are active members of the Network on Religion and Difference in the Balkans. Koneska participated in the 2011 International Summer School on Religion and Public Life held in Bulgaria, and both she and Stoyanov were active in the 2013 Balkan Summer School on Religion and Public Life, hosted by the University of Plovdiv.

37. On the importance of epistemic humility or modesty, see Adam B. Seligman, 2004, *Modest Claims: Dialogues and Essays on Tolerance and Tradition* (Notre Dame, IN: University of Notre Dame Press).

CHAPTER SIX. ON BOUNDARIES, DIFFERENCE, AND SHARED WORLDS

1. Elizabeta Koneska, 2009, *Shared Shrines* (Skopje, Macedonia: Macedonian Center for Photography).

2. Hans Gadamer, 1989, *Truth and Method,* trans. Joel Weinsheimer and Donald Marshall, 2nd rev. ed. (New York: Crossroads).

3. The most famous study is that of Gordon W. Allport, 1954, *The Nature of Prejudice* (Boston: Perseus Books).

4. For a greater discussion of boundaries see Adam B. Seligman and Robert P. Weller, 2012, *Rethinking Pluralism: Ritual, Experience, and Ambiguity* (Oxford: Oxford University Press).

5. Mary Douglas, 2002, *Purity and Danger: An Analysis of Concepts of Pollution and Taboo* (London: Routledge).

6. On modernism in this context see Adam B. Seligman, Robert P. Weller, Michael J. Puett, and Bennett Simon, 2008, *Ritual and Its Consequences: An Essay on the Limits of Sincerity* (Oxford: Oxford University Press).

7. See Adam B. Seligman, 2003, "Tolerance, Tradition and Modernity," *Cardozo Law Review* 24 (4): 1645-1656.

8. István Bejcz, 1997, "Tolerantia: A Medieval Concept," *Journal of the History of Ideas* 58 (3): 365–384.

9. Quoted in Jay Bercovitz, 1989, *The Shaping of Jewish Identity in Nineteenth Century France* (Detroit, MI: Wayne State University Press), 71.

10. Much of the foregoing argument is taken from Adam B. Seligman, 2004, *Modest Claims: Dialogues and Essays on Tolerance and Tradition* (Notre Dame, IN: University of Notre Dame Press).

11. Much of the following argument is taken from Adam B. Seligman, 2009, "Living Together Differently," *Cardoza Law Review* 30 (6): 2881–2896.

12. Lincoln Steffens, 1931, *The Autobiography of Lincoln Steffens* (New York: Harcourt Brace), 618.

13. Robert Merton, 1967, *On Theoretical Sociology* (New York: Free Press).

14. Karl Marx, 1992, "A Contribution to the Critique of Hegel's Philosophy of Right," in *Early Writings*, trans. Rodney Livingstone and Gregor Benton (New York: Penguin), 243–244.

15. Emile Durkheim, 1995, *The Elementary Forms of Religious Life*, trans. Karen E. Fields (New York: Free Press), 44.

16. For a greater explication of these terms see Adam B. Seligman, 1997, *The Problem of Trust* (Princeton, NJ: Princeton University Press).

17. Robert Cover, 1992, "Nomos and Narrative," in *Narrative, Violence and the Law: The Essays of Robert Cover* (Ann Arbor: University of Michigan Press), 95–96.

18. Sigmund Freud, 1961, *Civilization and Its Discontents* (New York: Norton).

19. Martin Heidegger, 1971, *Poetry, Language, Thought* (New York: Harper & Row), 154.

20. A fascinating example of this, on the role of prostitutes on the Iberian Peninsula in the fourteenth century, is found in David Nirenberg, 1996, *Communities of Violence: Persecution of Minorities in the Middle Ages* (Princeton, NJ: Princeton University Press), 138–160.

21. G. W. F. Hegel, 1976, *Phenomenology of Spirit*, trans. A. V. Miller (New York: Oxford University Press).

22. Martin Buber, 1975, *The Way of Response: Martin Buber—Selections of His Writings* (New York: Schocken), 113.

23. Ibid., 109.

24. Max Weber, 1946, "Politics as a Vocation," in *From Max Weber: Essays in Sociology*, ed. H. H. Gerth and C. Wright Mills (New York: Oxford University Press), 77–128.

CONCLUSION

1. Charles Taylor, 1985, "What Is Human Agency?" in *Human Agency and Language* (Cambridge: Cambridge University Press), 18, 19.

2. Basil Bernstein, 1973, *Class, Codes and Control: Theoretical Studies towards a Sociology of Language* (London: Routledge and Kegan Paul); Mary Douglas, 1973, *Natural Symbols: Explorations in Cosmology* (New York: Random House).

3. Bernstein himself was interested in linguistic codes (local, or what he termed *positional*, among working-class families, as opposed to more abstract ones among middle-class families), the ways of thinking that these codes engendered within children, and how that thinking in turn affected their life chances in the job market. Mary Douglas took these concepts of group and grid in much broader directions, though the details of their respective analyses are not really our concern here.

4. J. G. A. Pocock, 1973, "Ritual, Language, Power: An Essay on the Apparent Political Meanings of Ancient Chinese Philosophy," in *Politics, Language and Time: Essays on Political Thought and History* (New York: Athenaeum), 42–79.

5. Roy A. Rappaport, 1999, *Ritual and Religion in the Making of Humanity* (Cambridge: Cambridge University Press).

6. Samuel Moyn, 2010, *The Last Utopia: Human Rights in History* (Cambridge, MA: Harvard University Press).

7. Michael Ignatieff, 2001, *Human Rights and Politics and Idolatry* (Princeton, NJ: Princeton University Press).

8. Michael Perry, 1998, *The Idea of Human Rights: Four Inquiries* (New York: Oxford University Press).

9. Moyn, *Last Utopia*, 222.

10. Hanna Arendt, 1960, *The Origins of Totalitarianism* (New York: Meridian Books), 300.

11. Tore Lindholm and Kari Vogt, 1993, *Islamic Law Reform and Human Rights* (Copenhagen: Nordic Human Rights Publication).

12. Barry Bearak, 2001, "Afghans Present Aid Team's Sins, Complete with Theology Lesson," *New York Times*, September 7.

13. Council of Europe, Parliamentary Assembly, 2013, *Concern about Violations of the Physical Integrity of Children*, October 1, www.assembly.coe.int/nw/xml/News/News-View-EN.asp?newsid=4663&lang=2&cat=8.

14. Anne Lindboe et al., 2013, *Let the Boys Decide on Circumcision: Joint Statement from the Nordic Ombudsmen for Children and Pediatric Experts*, Oslo, September 30, http://barneombudet.no/wp-content/uploads/2013/11/English-statement-.pdf.

15. Landgericht Köln 151 NS 169/11—May 7, 2012.

16. Urfan Khaliq, 2012, "Freedom of Religion and Belief in International Law: A Comparative Analysis," in *Islamic Law and International Human Rights Law: Searching for Common Ground?*, ed. A. M. Emon, M. S. Ellis, and B. Glahn (New York: Oxford University Press), 183–225; Anver M. Emon, 2013, "The Paradox of

Equality and the Politics of Difference: Gender Equality, Islamic Law and the Modern Muslim State," in *Gender and Equality in Muslim Family Law: Justice and Ethics in the Islamic Legal Tradition*, ed. Z. Mir-Hosseini, K. Vogt, L. Larsen, and C. Moe (London: I. B. Tauris), 237–258.

17. Marie-Claire Foblets and Alison Dundes Renteln, eds., 2009, *Multicultural Jurisprudence: Comparative Perspectives on the Cultural Defence* (Oxford: Hart Publishing).

18. D. W. Winnicott, 1971, *Playing and Reality* (New York: Routledge).

19. Emile Durkheim, 1995, *The Elementary Forms of Religious Life*, trans. Karen E. Fields (New York: Free Press), 47.

20. Thomas H. Ogden, 1986, *The Matrix of the Mind: Object Relations and the Psychoanalytic Dialogue* (Northvale, NJ: Aronson), 227–228.

Abu-Nimer, Mohammed. 2003. *Nonviolence and Peace Building in Islam: Theory and Practice*. Gainesville: University Press of Florida.

Alinsky, Saul D. 1971. *Rules for Radicals: A Pragmatic Primer for Realistic Radicals*. New York: Vintage Books.

Allen, Danielle S. 2004. *Talking to Strangers: Anxieties of Citizenship since Brown v. Board of Education*. Chicago: University of Chicago Press.

Allport, Gordon W. 1954. *The Nature of Prejudice*. Boston: Perseus Books.

American Anthropological Association. 2011. "Race: Are We So Different?" Available at www.understandingrace.org.

Anderson, Elijah. 2012. *The Cosmopolitan Canopy: Race and Civility in Everyday Life*. New York: Norton.

Appleby, R. Scott. 2000. *The Ambivalence of the Sacred: Religion, Violence, and Reconciliation*. Oxford: Rowman & Littlefield.

Arendt, Hanna. 1960. *The Origins of Totalitarianism*. New York: Meridian Books.

Bacon, Francis. 1818. *Novum Organum Scientiarum*. London: Sherwood, Neely, and Jones.

Banchoff, Thomas, and Robert Wuthnow, eds. 2011. *Religion and the Global Politics of Human Rights*. New York: Oxford University Press.

Barash, David P., ed. 2010. *Approaches to Peace: A Reader in Peace Studies*. 2nd ed. Oxford: Oxford University Press.

Barash, David P., and Charles P. Webel. 2009. *Peace and Conflict Studies*. 2nd ed. Thousand Oaks, CA: Sage.

Bateson, Gregory. 1972. *Steps to an Ecology of Mind*. New York: Ballantine Books.

Bearak, Barry. 2001. "Afghans Present Aid Team's Sins, Complete with Theology Lesson." *New York Times*, September 7.

Bejcz, István. 1997. "Tolerantia: A Medieval Concept." *Journal of the History of Ideas* 58 (3): 365–384.

Bellah, Robert N. 1970. *Beyond Belief: Essays on Religion in a Post-traditionalist World*. Berkeley: University of California Press.

Bellah, Robert N., Richard Madsen, William M. Sullivan, Ann Swidler, and Steven M. Tipton, eds. 1996. *Habits of the Heart: Individualism and Commitment in American Life*. Berkeley: University of California Press.

Bennhold, Katrin. 2014. "Reading, Writing and Allegations: Muslim School at Center of Debate." *New York Times*, June 23.

Bercovitz, Jay. 1986. *The Shaping of Jewish Identity in Nineteenth Century France*. Detroit, MI: Wayne State University Press.

Bernstein, Basil. 1973. *Class, Codes and Control: Theoretical Studies towards a Sociology of Language*. London: Routledge and Kegan Paul.

Bolten, Catherine E. 2012. *I Did It to Save My Life: Love and Survival in Sierra Leone*. Berkeley: University of California Press.

Brisolara, Sharon, Denise Seigart, and Saumitra SenGupta, eds. 2014. *Feminist Evaluation and Research: Theory and Practice*. New York: Gilford Press.

Buber, Martin. 1975. *The Way of Response: Martin Buber—Selections of His Writings*. New York: Schocken.

Cannadine, David. 2014. *The Undivided Past: Humanity beyond Our Differences*. New York: Vintage.

Carroll, Lewis. 1973. *The Hunting of the Snark*. London: Chatto and Windus.

Chew, Pat K., ed. 2001. *The Conflict and Culture Reader*. New York: New York University Press.

City of Pittsburgh Bureau of Police. 2010. *Annual Report*. Available at www.pittsburghpa.gov/police/files/annual_reports/10_Police_Annual_Report.pdf.

———. 2012. *Annual Report*. Available at http://apps.pittsburghpa.gov/pghbop/2012_Annual_Report_v2.pdf.

Clark, Julie S. Byrd, and Fred Dervin, eds. 2014. *Reflexivity in Language and Intercultural Education: Rethinking Multilingualism and Interculturality*. London: Routledge.

Clift, Renee Tipton, Robert W. Houston, and Marleen C. Pugach, eds. 1990. *Encouraging Reflective Practice in Education: An Analysis of Issues and Programs*. New York: Teachers College Press.

Coudenhove-Kalergi, Barbara, and Christian Seelos. 2012a. *Case Study: EVN in Bulgaria (B)—Engaging the Roma Community*. Stanford, CA: Stanford Community Center on Philanthropy and Civil Society, August. Available at http://pacscenter.stanford.edu/sites/all/files/EVN%20in%20Bulgaria%20B_Engaging%20with%20the%20Roma%20community_2012.pdf.

———. 2012b. *Case Study: EVN in Bulgaria (C)—Making It Work . . .* Stanford, CA: Stanford Community Center on Philanthropy and Civil Society, August.

Available at http://pacscenter.stanford.edu/sites/all/files/EVN%20in%20 Bulgaria%20C_Making%20it%20work.pdf.

Council on Europe, Parliamentary Assembly. 2013. *Concern about Violations of the Physical Integrity of Children*. October 1. Available at www.assembly.coe.int /nw/xml/News/News-View-EN.asp?newsid=4663&lang=2&cat=8.

Cover, Robert. 1992. "Nomos and Narrative." In *Narrative, Violence and the Law: The Essays of Robert Cover*. Ann Arbor: University of Michigan Press.

Cowan, Jane K., Marie-Bénédicte Dembour, and Richard A. Wilson, eds. 2001. *Culture and Rights: Anthropological Perspectives*. Cambridge: Cambridge University Press.

Crocker, Chester A., Fen Osler Hampson, and Pamela Aall, eds. 2007. *Leashing the Dogs of War: Conflict Management in a Divided World*. Washington, DC: United States Institute of Peace Press.

Darby, John. 2001. *The Effects of Violence on Peace Processes*. Washington, DC: United States Institute of Peace Press.

Darby, John, and Roger MacGinty, eds. 2008. *Contemporary Peacemaking: Conflict, Peace Processes and Post-war Reconstruction*. New York: Palgrave Macmillan.

Davey, Monica. 2014. "Former Milwaukee Police Officer Won't Be Charged in Death of Black Man in Park." *New York Times*, December 23.

Davies, Sharyn Graham. 2011. *Gender Diversity in Indonesia: Sexuality, Islam and Queer Selves*. London: Routledge.

Deresiewicz, William. 2014. *Excellent Sheep: The Miseducation of the American Elite*. New York: Simon and Schuster.

Dewey, John. 1916. "The Control of Ideas by Facts." In *Essays in Experimental Logic*. Chicago: University of Chicago Press.

———. 1936. *Experience and Nature*. New York: Dover Books.

———. 1954. *The Public and Its Problems*. Athens: Swallow Press.

———. 1980. *Art as Experience*. London: Penguin.

———. 1991. *How We Think*. New York: Prometheus Books.

———. 1997. *Democracy and Education*. New York: Free Press.

———. 2004. *Democracy and Education: An Introduction to the Philosophy of Education*. New York: Dover.

Dokecki, Paul R. 1992. "On Knowing the Community of Caring Persons: A Methodological Basis for the Reflective-Generative Practice of Community Psychology." *Journal of Community Psychology* 20 (1): 26–35.

Donnelly, Jack. 2012. *International Human Rights*. 4th ed. Boulder, CO: Westview Press.

———. 2013. *Universal Human Rights in Theory and Practice*. 3rd ed. Ithaca, NY: Cornell University Press.

Douglas, Mary. 1973. *Natural Symbols: Explorations in Cosmology*. New York: Random House.

———. 2002. *Purity and Danger: An Analysis of Concepts of Pollution and Taboo*. London: Routledge.

Durkheim, Emile. 1995. *The Elementary Forms of Religious Life*. Translated by Karen E. Fields. New York: Free Press.

Elukin, Jonathan. 2007. *Living Together, Living Apart*. Princeton, NJ: Princeton University Press.

Emon, Anver M. 2013. "The Paradox of Equality and the Politics of Difference: Gender Equality, Islamic Law and the Modern Muslim State." In *Gender and Equality in Muslim Family Law: Justice and Ethics in the Islamic Legal Tradition*, edited by Z. Mir-Hosseini, K. Vogt, L. Larsen, and C. Moe, 237–258. London: I. B. Tauris.

Erikson, Kai T. 1966. *Wayward Puritans: A Study in the Sociology of Deviance*. New York: John Wiley.

Erlanger, Steven. 2014. "As Hate Crimes Rise, British Muslims Say They're Becoming More Insular." *New York Times*, February 13. Available at www.nytimes.com/2014/02/14/world/europe/as-hate-crimes-rise-british-muslims-say-theyre-becoming-more-insular.html.

Feller, Ben. 2009. "Beer Summit Begins: Obama Sits Down with Crowley, Gates." *Huffington Post*, August 30. Available at www.huffingtonpost.com/2009/07/30/beer-summit-begins-obama-_n_248254.html.

Fernández-Aráoz, Claudio. 2014. "21st-Century Talent Spotting." *Harvard Business Review*. June. Available at https://hbr.org/2014/06/21st-century-talent-spotting.

Finlay, Linda. 2011. *Phenomenology for Therapists: Researching the Lived World*. Malden, MA: Wiley-Blackwell.

Fisch, Menachem. 2014. "Judaism and the Religious Value of Diversity and Dialogue." In *Diversitat-Differenz-Dialogoizitat: Religion in Pluralen Kontexten*, edited by S. Alkier, M. Schneider, and Ch. Weise. Berlin: De Gruyter.

Foblets, Marie-Claire, and Alison Dundes Renteln, eds. 2009. *Multicultural Jurisprudence: Comparative Perspectives on the Cultural Defence*. Oxford: Hart Publishing.

Fox, Michael Allen. 2014. *Understanding Peace: A Comprehensive Introduction*. New York: Routledge.

Francis, Diana. 2010. *From Pacification to Peacebuilding: A Call to Global Transformation*. London: Pluto Press.

Freire, Paulo. 1998a. *Pedagogy of Freedom: Ethics, Democracy, and Civic Courage*. Translated by Patrick Clarke. Lanham, MD: Rowman & Littlefield.

———. 1998b. *Pedagogy of the Heart*. Translated by Donald Macedo and Alexandre Oliveira. New York: Continuum.

———. 2000. *Pedagogy of the Oppressed*. Translated by Myra Bergman Ramos. New York: Bloomsbury.

Freud, Sigmund. 1961. *Civilization and Its Discontents*. New York: Norton.

Fry, Douglas P. 2007. *Beyond War: The Human Potential for Peace*. Oxford: Oxford University Press.

Gadamer, Hans. 1989. *Truth and Method*. Translated by Joel Weinsheimer and Donald Marshall. 2nd rev. ed. New York: Crossroads.

Gillis, Wendy. 2013. "Islamic Scholars Experience Diversity of Muslim Practices at U of T Summer Program." *The Star*, August 25. Available at www.thestar .com/news/gta/2013/08/25/islamic_scholars_experience_diversity_of_muslim_ practices_at_u_of_t_summer_program.html.

Goodale, Mark. 2009. *Surrendering to Utopia: An Anthropology of Human Rights*. Stanford, CA: Stanford University Press.

Goodhart, Michael, ed. 2013. *Human Rights: Politics and Practice*. 2nd ed. New York: Oxford University Press.

Gopin, Marc. 2000. *Between Eden and Armageddon: The Future of World Religions, Violence, and Peacemaking*. Oxford: Oxford University Press.

———. 2002. *Holy War, Holy Peace: How Religion Can Bring Peace to the Middle East*. Oxford: Oxford University Press.

Hannah-Jones, Nikole. 2014. "How School Segregation Divides Ferguson—and the United States." *New York Times*, December 21.

Havel, Václav. 1990. *Disturbing the Peace: A Conversation with Karel Hvízdala*. Translated by Paul Wilson. New York: Alfred A. Knopf.

Heft, James L., ed. 2004. *Beyond Violence: Religious Sources of Social Transformation in Judaism, Christianity, and Islam*. New York: Fordham University Press.

Hegel, G. W. F. 1976. *Phenomenology of Spirit*. Translated by A. V. Miller. New York: Oxford University Press.

Heidegger, Martin. 1971. *Poetry, Language, Thought*. New York: Harper & Row.

Hertog, Katrien. 2010. *The Complex Reality of Religious Peacebuilding: Conceptual Contributions and Critical Analysis*. Lanham, MD: Lexington Books.

Hertz, Rosanna, ed. 1997. *Reflexivity and Voice*. Thousand Oaks, CA: Sage Publications.

Heyd, David, ed. 1996. *Toleration: An Elusive Virtue*. Princeton, NJ: Princeton University Press.

High, Steven. 2003. *Industrial Sunset: The Making of North America's Rust Belt, 1969–1984*. Toronto: University of Toronto Press.

Hinton, Alexander Laban, ed. 2002. *Annihilating Difference: The Anthropology of Genocide*. Berkeley: University of California Press.

hooks, bell. 2003. *Teaching Community: A Pedagogy of Hope*. New York: Routledge.

Hunt, Lynn. 2008. *Inventing Human Rights: A History*. New York: Norton.

Ignatieff, Michael. 2001. *Human Rights as Politics and Idolatry*. Princeton, NJ: Princeton University Press.

Ishay, Micheline R. 2008. *The History of Human Rights: From Ancient Times to the Globalization Era*. Berkeley: University of California Press.

Iyengar, B. K. S. 2005. *Light on Life: The Yoga Journey to Wholeness, Inner Peace, and Ultimate Freedom*. Emmaus, PA: Rodale Books.

Jackson, Michael. 2004. *In Sierra Leone*. Durham, NC: Duke University Press.

Johnston, Douglas, and Cynthia Sampson, eds. 1994. *Religion, the Missing Dimension of Statecraft*. New York: Oxford University Press.

Kalson, Sally. 2003. "Cartoonist Draws, Fires a Blank with Pittsburgh Joke." *Pittsburgh Post-Gazette*, November 19. Available at http://old.post-gazette.com/columnists/20031119sally104col2p2.asp.

Kamen, Henry. 1967. *The Rise of Toleration*. New York: McGraw-Hill.

Kang, Jay Caspian. 2014. "Off Target on Toy-Gun Regulation." *New York Times Magazine*, December 16. Available at www.nytimes.com/2014/12/21/magazine/off-target-on-toy-gun-regulation.html.

KDKA. 2014. "Pittsburgh Most Livable City in Continental U.S." *CBS Pittsburgh*, August 26. Available at http://pittsburgh.cbslocal.com/2014/08/26/pittsburgh-most-livable-city-in-continental-u-s/.

Kelsay, John, and Sumner B. Twiss. 1994. *Human Rights and Religion*. New York: Human Rights Watch.

Khaliq, Urfan. 2012. "Freedom of Religion and Belief in International Law: A Comparative Analysis." In *Islamic Law and International Human Rights Law: Searching for Common Ground?*, edited by A. M. Emon, M. S. Ellis, and B. Glahn, 183–225. New York: Oxford University Press.

Kolb, David A. 1984. *Experiential Learning*. New York: Prentice-Hall.

Koneska, Elizabeta. 2009. *Shared Shrines*. Skopje, Macedonia: Macedonian Center for Photography.

Lacey, Marc. 2004. "Since '94 Horror, Rwandans Turn toward Islam." *New York Times*, April 7.

Laursen, John, and Cary Nederman. 1997. *Beyond the Persecuting Society: Religious Toleration before the Enlightenment*. Philadelphia: University of Pennsylvania Press.

Lederach, John Paul. 2005. *The Moral Imagination: The Art and Soul of Building Peace*. Oxford: Oxford University Press.

Lederach, John Paul, and Janice Moomaw Jenner, eds. 2002. *A Handbook of International Peacebuilding: Into the Eye of the Storm*. San Francisco: Jossey-Bass.

Leovy, Jill. 2015. *Ghettoside: A True Story of Murder in America*. New York: Spiegel and Grau.

Lindboe, Anne, Fredrik Malmberg, Maria Kaisa Aula, Per Larsen, Margrét Maria Siguroardóttir, Aaja Chemnitz Larsen, et al. 2013. *Let the Boys Decide on Circumcision: Joint Statement from the Nordic Ombudsmen for Children and Pediatric Experts*. Oslo, September 30. Available at http://barneombudet.no/wp-content/uploads/2013/11/English-statement-.pdf.

Lindholm, Tore, and Kari Vogt. 1993. *Islamic Law Reform and Human Rights*. Copenhagen: Nordic Human Rights Publication.

Lubove, Roy. 1996. *Twentieth Century Pittsburgh*. Vol. 1: *Government, Business, and Environmental Change*. Pittsburgh, PA: University of Pittsburgh Press.

Lynd, Robert S., and Helen Merrell Lynd. 1959. *Middletown: A Study in Modern American Culture*. San Diego: Harcourt Brace Jovanovich.

——. 1982. *Middletown in Transition: A Study in Cultural Conflicts*. San Diego: Harcourt Brace Jovanovich.

Marx, Karl. 1992. "A Contribution to the Critique of Hegel's Philosophy of Right." In *Early Writings*, translated by Rodney Livingstone and Gregor Benton, 243–244. New York: Penguin.

Medina, Jennifer. 2014. "Warning: The Literary Canon Could Make Students Squirm." *New York Times*, May 18.

Meiselas, Susan, and Martin van Bruinessen. 2008. *Kurdistan: In the Shadow of History*. 2nd ed. Chicago: University of Chicago Press.

Mendus, Susan, ed. 1988. *Justifying Toleration: Conceptual and Historical Perspectives*. Cambridge: Cambridge University Press.

Merton, Robert. 1967. *On Theoretical Sociology*. New York: Free Press.

Milner, Marion. 1952. "Acts of Symbolism in Comprehension of the Not-Self." *International Journal of Psychoanalysis* 33 (2): 181–195.

Moyn, Samuel. 2010. *The Last Utopia: Human Rights in History*. Cambridge, MA: Harvard University Press.

Murithi, Tim. 2009. *The Ethics of Peacebuilding*. Edinburgh: Edinburgh University Press.

Nederman, Cary. 2000. *Worlds of Difference: European Discourses of Toleration, c. 1000-1550*. University Park: Pennsylvania State University Press.

Neofotistos, Vasiliki P. 2012. *The Risk of War: Everyday Sociality in the Republic of Macedonia*. Philadelphia: University of Pennsylvania Press.

Nirenberg, David. 1996. *Communities of Violence: Persecution of Minorities in the Middle Ages*. Princeton, NJ: Princeton University Press.

Nordstrom, Carolyn. 2004. *Shadows of War: Violence, Power, and International Profiteering in the Twenty-first Century*. Berkeley: University of California Press.

————. 2007. *Global Outlaws: Crime, Money, and Power in the Contemporary World*. Berkeley: University of California Press.

Nye, Joseph S., Jr. 2000. *Understanding International Conflicts: An Introduction to Theory and History*. 3d ed. New York: Longman.

Oakley, Ann. 1981. "Interviewing Women: A Contradiction in Terms." In *Doing Feminist Research*, edited by H. Roberts, 30–61. London: Routledge.

Ogden, Thomas H. 1986. *The Matrix of the Mind: Object Relations and the Psychoanalytic Dialogue*. Northvale, NJ: Aronson.

Paulson, Michael. 2014. "Colleges and Evangelicals Collide on Bias Policy." *New York Times*, June 10.

Paulson, Michael, and Fernanda Santos. 2014. "Religious Right in Arizona Cheers Bill Allowing Businesses to Refuse to Serve Gays." *New York Times*, February 21. Available at www.nytimes.com/2014/02/22/us/religious-right-in-arizona-cheers-bill-allowing-businesses-to-refuse-to-serve-gays.html.

Perry, Michael. 1998. *The Idea of Human Rights: Four Inquiries*. New York: Oxford University Press.

Philpott, Daniel, and Gerard F. Powers, eds. 2010. *Strategies of Peace: Transforming Conflict in a Violent World*. Oxford: Oxford University Press.

Pittsburgh City Planning. N.d. "Census Data by Neighborhood—Homewood West." Last accessed June 20, 2014. www.city.pittsburgh.pa.us/cp/assets/census/homewoodwest.pdf (site discontinued).

Pittsburgh City Planning. N.d. "Census Data by Neighborhood—Shadyside." Last accessed June 20, 2014. www.city.pittsburgh.pa.us/cp/assets/census/shadyside.pdf (site discontinued).

Pocock, J. G. A. 1973. "Ritual, Language, Power: An Essay on the Apparent Political Meanings of Ancient Chinese Philosophy." In *Politics, Language and Time: Essays on Political Thought and History*, 42–79. New York: Athenaeum.

Putnam, Robert D. 2000. *Bowling Alone: The Collapse and Revival of American Community*. New York: Simon and Schuster.

Rappaport, Roy A. 1999. *Ritual and Religion in the Making of Humanity*. Cambridge: Cambridge University Press.

Rein, Martin, and Donald Schön. 1993. "Reframing Policy Discourse." In *The Argumentative Turn in Policy Analysis and Planning*, edited by Frank Fisher and John Forester (Durham, NC: Duke University Press), 145–166.

Reinharz, Shulamit. 1992. *Feminist Methods in Social Research*. New York: Oxford University Press.

Remer, Gary. 1996. *Humanism and the Rhetoric of Toleration*. Philadelphia: University of Pennsylvania Press.

Richmond, Oliver P., ed. 2010. *Palgrave Advances in Peacebuilding: Critical Developments and Approaches*. London: Palgrave Macmillan.

Riesman, David, Nathan Glazer, and Reuel Denney. 2001. *The Lonely Crowd: A Study of the Changing American Character*. Rev. ed. New Haven, CT: Yale University Press.

Ring, Laura A. 2006. *Zenana: Everyday Peace in a Karachi Apartment Building*. Bloomington: Indiana University Press.

Robertson, Geoffrey. 2013. *Crimes against Humanity: The Struggle for Global Justice*. 4th ed. New York: New Press.

Rossati, Massimo. 2015. *The Making of a Postsecular Society: A Durkheimian Approach to Memory, Pluralism and Religion in Turkey*. Aldershot, U.K.: Ashgate.

Rubin, Alissa J. 2014. "Questions Rebels Use to Tell Sunni from Shiite." *New York Times*, June 25.

Sachedina, Abdulaziz, 2001. *The Islamic Roots of Democratic Pluralism*. Oxford: Oxford University Press.

Sacirbey, Omar. 2006. "Taking a Tough Road to Tolerance: BU Professor Brings People Together by Confronting Differences." *Boston Globe*, October 2.

Sacks, Jonathan. 2002. *The Dignity of Difference: How to Avoid the Clash of Civilizations*. London: Continuum Press.

Saunders, Harold H. 1999. *A Public Peace Process: Sustained Dialogue to Transform Racial and Ethnic Conflicts*. New York: Palgrave.

Scheper-Hughes, Nancy, and Philippe Bourgois, eds. 2004. *Violence in War and Peace: An Anthology*. Malden: Blackwell.

Schön, Donald A. 1983. *The Reflective Practitioner: How Professionals Think in Action*. New York: Basic Books.

———. 1990. *Educating the Reflective Practitioner: Toward a New Design for Teaching and Learning in the Professions*. San Francisco: Jossey-Bass.

———. 1994. *Frame Reflection: Toward the Resolution of Intractable Policy Controversies*. New York: Basic Books.

Schwab, Joseph J. 1969. *College Curriculum and Student Protest*. Chicago: University of Chicago Press.

Seligman, Adam B. 1997. *The Problem of Trust*. Princeton, NJ: Princeton University Press.

———. 2003. "Tolerance, Tradition and Modernity." *Cardozo Law Review* 24 (4): 1645–1656.

———. 2004. *Modest Claims: Dialogues and Essays on Tolerance and Tradition*. Notre Dame, IN: University of Notre Dame Press.

———. 2009. "Living Together Differently." *Cardoza Law Review* 30 (6): 2881–2896.

Seligman, Adam B., and Robert P. Weller. 2012. *Rethinking Pluralism: Ritual, Experience, and Ambiguity*. Oxford: Oxford University Press.

Seligman, Adam B., Robert P. Weller, Michael J. Puett, and Bennett Simon. 2008. *Ritual and Its Consequences: An Essay on the Limits of Sincerity*. Oxford: Oxford University Press.

Shute, Stephen, and Susan Hurley, eds. 1993. *On Human Rights*. New York: Basic Books.

Smith, Wilfred Cantwell. 1991. *The Meaning and End of Religion*. Minneapolis, MN: Fortress Press.

Smock, David R., ed. 2002. *Interfaith Dialogue and Peacebuilding*. Washington, DC: United States Institute of Peace Press.

Soroush, Abdolkarim. 2000. *Reason, Freedom, and Democracy in Islam*. Oxford: Oxford University Press.

Stanton, G., and G. Stroumsa, eds. 1998. *Tolerance and Intolerance in Early Judaism and Christianity*. Cambridge: Cambridge University Press.

Steffens, Lincoln. 1931. *The Autobiography of Lincoln Steffens*. New York: Harcourt Brace.

Stolberg, Sheryl Gay. 2015. "Crowds Scatter as Baltimore Curfew Takes Hold." *New York Times*, April 29.

Tate, Winifred. 2007. *Counting the Dead: The Culture and Politics of Human Rights Activism in Colombia*. Berkeley: University of California Press.

Taylor, Charles. 1985. "What Is Human Agency?" In *Human Agency and Language*. Cambridge: Cambridge University Press.

Tishkov, Valery. 2004. *Chechnya: Life in a War-Torn Society*. Berkeley: University of California Press.

Trotter, Joe W., and Jared N. Day. 2010. *Race and Renaissance: African Americans in Pittsburgh since World War II*. Pittsburgh, PA: University of Pittsburgh Press.

Vargas, João H. Costa. 2006. *Catching Hell in the City of Angels: Life and Meanings of Blackness in South Central Los Angeles*. Minneapolis: University of Minnesota Press.

Walzer, Michael. 1997. *On Toleration*. New Haven, CT: Yale University Press.

Warren, Mark R., and Karen L. Mapp. 2011. *A Match on Dry Grass: Community Organizing as a Catalyst for School Reform*. New York: Oxford University Press.

Wasserfall, Rahel. 1993. "Reflexivity, Feminism and Difference." *Qualitative Sociology* 16 (1): 23–41.

Wasserfall, Rahel, and Shari Goldberg. 2013. "Evaluation Report of the 2013 Connaught Summer Institute of Islamic Studies." CEDAR archives, Newton, MA.

Watkins, D. 2015. "In Baltimore, We're All Freddie Gray: Commentary." *New York Times*, April 29.

Weber, Eugene. 1976. *From Peasants to Frenchmen: The Modernization of Real France, 1870–1914*. Stanford, CA: Stanford University Press.

Weber, Max. 1946. "Politics as a Vocation." In *From Max Weber: Essays in Sociology*, edited by H. H. Gerth and C. Wright Mills, 77–128. New York: Oxford University Press.

Wilkerson, Isabel. 2011. *The Warmth of Other Suns: The Epic Story of America's Great Migration*. New York: Vintage.

Wing, Nick. 2014. "A Grand Jury Did Indict One Person Involved in Eric Garner's Killing—the Man Who Filmed It." *Huffington Post*, December 3. Available at www.huffingtonpost.com/2014/12/03/ramsey-orta-indictment-eric-garner_n_6264746.html.

Winnicott, D. W. 1971. *Playing and Reality*. New York: Routledge.

Winship, Christopher. 1999. "How Can Bitter Enemies Become the Best of Allies?" Unpublished paper, Harvard University, Department of Sociology.

———. 2004. "The End of a Miracle? Crime, Faith, and Partnership in Boston in the 1990's." In *Long March Ahead: African American Churches and Public Policy in Post-Civil Rights America: The Public Influences of African American Churches*, vol. 2, edited by R. D. Smith, 171–192. Durham, NC: Duke University Press.

Winship, Christopher, and Jenny Berrien. 1999. "Boston Cops and Black Churches." *Public Interest* 136 (Summer): 52–68.

Withnall, Adam. 2014. "Denmark Bans Kosher and Halal Slaughter as Minister Says 'Animal Rights Come before Religion.'" *The Independent*, February 18. Available at www.independent.co.uk/news/world/europe/denmark-bans-halal-and-kosher-slaughter-as-minister-says-animal-rights-come-before-religion-9135580.html.

Witte, John, Jr., and M. Christian Green, eds. 2012. *Religion and Human Rights: An Introduction*. New York: Oxford University Press.

Zagorin, Pertz. 2003. *How the Idea of Religious Toleration Came to the West*. Princeton, NJ: Princeton University Press.

Zartman, I. William, ed. 2007. *Peacemaking in International Conflict: Methods and Techniques*. Rev. ed. Washington, DC: United States Institute of Peace Press.

TenPoint Coalition. *See* Boston TenPoint
Coalition
tolerance, 7, 12, 16, 38, 39, 40–44, 56, 58,
140–41, 151, 157
Tönnies, Ferdinand, 146
tradition, 14, 19, 44, 48, 51, 52, 74, 128,
130–32, 138, 139, 149, 157
traditional (African) healing, 13, 92–95,
99, 104, 108
transgender, 13, 38, 83, 95–98, 104,
108. *See also* pesantren
waria
Trembling Before G-d, 32, 100
trust, 12, 14, 21, 36, 45–48, 116–17, 122–23,
142–48, 166
Tudjman, Franjo, 26
Turkey, 4, 10, 56, 68, 71, 77, 133
Bursa, 55, 58, 75–76
Istanbul, 9, 11, 16, 67–71, 77

Uganda, 13, 63, 91–95, 99, 127, 128, 133,
134, 165, 166, 170
Kampala, 11, 92, 93, 128
Mancura, 127, 131
Prometra, 92–95, 99, 104, 108
Unitarian Universalist, 20

United Nations High Commission for
Refugees (UNHCR), 133–34
university, 8, 9, 19, 81, 85, 112, 127–28,
132, 159
Bowdoin College, 112
Harvard, 113, 115
London, 132
Plovdiv, 194
Toronto, 125, 126, 132
Uganda Martyrs, 93, 128
uncertainty, 11, 42, 64, 150
uniqueness, 5, 6, 16, 40, 46, 65, 122, 135,
152

waria *See* pesantren waria
We Are All Neighbours, 23, 110
Weber, Eugene, 3
Weber, Max, 151
Williams, Accelyne, 115
Winnicott, D. W., 166
Winship, Christopher, 115–17

Yugoslavia, former, 26

Zimbabwe, 21, 123–24, 125, 132
Zionist, 15, 23, 72